Inequality, Consumer Credit and the Saving Puzzle

NEW DIRECTIONS IN MODERN ECONOMICS
Series Editor: Malcolm C. Sawyer,
Professor of Economics, University of Leeds, UK

New Directions in Modern Economics presents a challenge to orthodox economic thinking. It focuses on new ideas emanating from radical traditions, including post-Keynesian, Kaleckian, neo-Ricardian and Marxian. The books in the series do not adhere rigidly to any single school of thought but attempt to present a positive alternative to the conventional wisdom.

A list of published titles in this series is printed at the end of this volume.

Inequality, Consumer Credit and the Saving Puzzle

Christopher Brown

Arkansas State University, USA

NEW DIRECTIONS IN MODERN ECONOMICS

Edward Elgar
Cheltenham, UK • Northampton, MA, USA

Published by
Edward Elgar Publishing Limited
The Lypiatts
15 Lansdown Road
Cheltenham
Glos GL50 2JA
UK

Edward Elgar Publishing, Inc.
William Pratt House
9 Dewey Court
Northampton
Massachusetts 01060
USA

A catalogue record for this book
is available from the British Library

Library of Congress Control Number: 2008009890

ISBN 978 1 84720 509 4

Printed and bound in Great Britain by MPG Books Ltd, Bodmin, Cornwall

To Linden Dearing Brown

In appreciation of your steadfast love, humor and support

Contents

Figures

Tables

Acknowledgments

This monograph could not have been written without the support of many individuals. I am especially indebted to Randall Kesselring, who gave training in the use of data editor software and the extraction of public use microdata. Professor Kesselring also assisted on econometric matters and with the Gini ratio estimates that appear in Chapter 7. A number of persons read parts of the manuscript and/or listened to presentations drawn from various chapters and provided valuable comments. These include Eric Tymoigne, Ron Stanfield, Christopher Niggle, John Hall, Anne Mayhew, Fred Lee, Eric Hake, John Watkins, John Henry, Reynold Nesiba, John Wisman, Martha Starr, Robert Prasch and Janet Knoedler. Thanks are due to James Washam for explaining credit derivatives and hedging strategies used by institutional portfolio managers.

I am grateful to the Arkansas State University Faculty Research Committee, which approved my application for research leave in the spring semester 2007. Thanks also to the College of Business Faculty Development Committee and Dean Len Frey for providing summer research grants in 2005, 2006 and 2007. I hope that the present work provides evidence of money well spent.

1. Consumer credit and effective demand

Macroeconomics is the study of the forces that regulate the scale of output and employment (as well as the general price level) in systems featuring private production for market, vast capital goods industries and highly developed securities markets. The main topic of inquiry here is: how does the institution of consumer credit fit in the scheme of macroeconomic causality? Do expansions or contractions in the volume of consumer credit extensions constitute an important independent cause of aggregate-level fluctuations? Does the widespread use of consumer credit tend to increase the amplitude of business cycle expansions and contractions? Have the advanced industrialized economies (and in particular the USA) become more dependent on credit-financed consumption to achieve GDP growth? What is the role of financial innovation in making installment, credit card, home equity and student loans more widely accessible? Can broadened access to credit across income classes countervail the (potentially) depressing effect that rising income inequality exerts on aggregate expenditure? Does advertising, by stimulating the use of consumer credit, have an overlooked macroeconomic dimension? Are standard measures of aggregate household indebtedness adequate in terms of appraising the stress on household budgets from debt service? Is borrowing at the root of the well-publicized collapse of household saving? To what extent does the liberal use of borrowing privileges by households contribute to massive US trade deficits? In light of the importance of credit, is it correct to think in terms of an 'animal-spirited' consumption function? Is a credit-financed surge in consumer spending sustainable? The preceding are among the questions the present work attempts to answer.

1.1 THE PRINCIPLE OF EFFECTIVE DEMAND

I hope that the essays contained in this book will make a contribution to the advancement of post-Keynesian and institutional economics. With respect to the former, a macroeconomic analysis of consumer credit is an attempt at further elaboration and refinement of the principle of effective demand, which is summarized as follows: (1) social reality is transmutable, meaning that 'future economic outcomes may be permanently changed in nature and substance by today's actions of individuals or groups (for example, unions, cartels, or governments), often in ways not perceived by the creators of change' (Davidson 2002, p. 52); (2) the creative or socially reconstitutive aspect of human agency renders the past a statistically unreliable and biased guide to the future – that is, agents face true uncertainty or 'ignorance of future consequences' (Davidson 1991, p. 131) as opposed to probabilistic uncertainty;[1] (3) ignorance of future consequences creates a desire among agents to postpone economic decision-making or, what is the same thing, to accumulate stores of value; and finally (4) liquid or non-producible assets are preferred as stores of value in a transmutable reality.[2] An insufficiency of effective demand is therefore explained by the fact that the demand for stores of value need not result in the employment of real resources because money or securities are not producible things. Unemployment occurs because 'there are in this economy resting places for savings other than reproducible assets' (Hahn 1977, p. 31).

Say's Law ostensibly rules out the possibility of a protracted decline in production activity arising from a deficiency of spending for goods and services, or what is the same thing, a lack of effective demand. Say's Law is informed by the fact that, in an entrepreneurial system, payments disbursed by firms for the use of economic resources (equal to total production costs) are necessarily equivalent to incomes received by resource owners. Thus resource owners receive, as an effect of production, an increase in spending power that is just sufficient to enable them to purchase the newly produced goods at prices that would allow entrepreneurs to cover production costs (inclusive of a normal profit). Hence the familiar textbook pronouncement of Say's Law: 'Supply creates its own demand.'

Davidson (2002) and others have pointed out that Say's Law, and indeed all standard macroeconomic models, are based (implicitly or otherwise) on the assumption of gross substitutability – that is, the view that producible assets (buildings, equipment, etc.) are close substitutes for non-producibles in the assessment of those seeking to defer decision-making. But the inferior liquidity of producibles *vis-à-vis* non-producibles makes the former type ill suited to perform the store-of-value function. Thus unemployment may rise, even if wages and prices are perfectly flexible, when income receipts fail to be recycled for the purchase of things that require the employment of real resources for their manufacture, but rather find a 'resting place' in non-producibles.[3]

1.2 IS SPENDING CONSTRAINED BY INCOME?

The analysis that follows is premised on a particular view of the nature of modern lending agencies or 'financial intermediaries' – that is, financial institutions do not merely transfer spending power from savers to borrowers. Rather, the activities of banks are capable of producing a net increase in the economy's stock of acceptable media for payment.[4] If banks or other lenders were 'pure intermediaries', then spending for new goods and services would, in the global sense, be constrained by income. That is, every act of deficit spending (i.e. borrowing) would necessarily require a corresponding act of saving. But if spending is limited in the aggregate by the flow of current income, how can the economy grow? L. Randall Wray writes:

> [T]he 'real' and 'monetary' sectors and values cannot be dichotomized and separately analyzed. Rising expenditures necessarily require deficits, and deficits require expansion of balance sheets. As balance sheets expand, private sector assets and liabilities are created, some of which are counted as 'money.' Thus, money is privately-created to finance rising expenditures. (Wray 1991a, p. 2)

The reader may object that, in a system where deposit creation is reserve-constrained, the monetization of IOUs by a single bank is severely limited by the probability of an adverse clearing (or reserve drain) *vis-à-vis* other banks. That much is true – if it is assumed the bank is unilaterally expanding its liabilities. Boulding explained that, so long as the banking system is expanding liabilities, adverse clearings in some places must be offset by favorable clearings elsewhere:

> A many-bank system is rather like a number of balloons tied together with a string; if one balloon tries to get away from the others the strings will bring it back, but all the balloons can rise together without difficulty. The 'string' in this case is the loss of cash reserves. One bank expanding loans disproportionately will lose reserves to other banks, but if all banks expand together they will all lose reserves to each other, which means that no bank loses reserves on balance except to the public. (Boulding 1966, p. 107, quoted in Wray 1991b, p. 8)

Keynes noted that, in terms of the effect on the total quantity of bank money, there is no difference between 'income spent' and 'income saved'.[5] The monetization of household IOUs requires no prior act of saving. Thus we arrive at an important first principle: where modern credit facilities exist, spending, whether at the individual or aggregate level, is constrained by liquidity – not income.

1.3 LIQUIDITY-CONSTRAINED SPENDING AND THE 'PASSIVE' CONSUMPTION FUNCTION

A fully articulated principle of effective demand is achieved by piecing together models of the various components of aggregate expenditure. To the extent that consumer credit is consequential for the behavior of macroeconomic time series (the current volume is obviously based on this belief), it must make its influence felt first in the behavior of household spending. That is, if consumer credit does have implications for the scale of output and employment, it must be linked to oscillations in the time paths of consumption expenditure and its subcomponents. Thus we arrive at a necessary condition for a meaningful macroeconomic role for consumer credit: consumption must qualify as a principal independent cause of changes in the scale of economic activity. But does it?

To say that consumption is a 'principal independent cause' is to assert that the parameters of the simple Keynesian consumption function are subject to perturbations that reverberate through the economic system. Taking into account the immensity of the consumer goods sector in comparison to investment goods or export sectors, a small percentage change in exogenous consumption may produce a macroeconomic impact equivalent to that generated by a much larger percentage change in other components of spending. Nevertheless, some in the Keynesian camp have assigned limited importance to 'shifts' of the consumption function in business cycle theory. Hyman Minsky elucidated what might be termed the inchoate Keynesian view:

> In the General Theory the consumption-function construct serves the purpose of identifying the passive, or determined, component of aggregate demand: in no sense is the consumption function the 'heart of macroeconomics,' if modern macroeconomics is identified with Keynes. In Keynes's view it is, if an anatomical analogy is necessary, the passive skeleton of macroeconomics which nevertheless conditions the system's response to stimuli. (Minsky 1975, p. 23)

The passive consumption function makes sense in the context of an economic system wherein households face a 'hard' budget constraint – that is, where spending power is derived from income only. Month-to-month changes in consumption would, on these conditions, be explainable almost entirely by changes in household income. The option to borrow radically alters the situation from the consumer's point of view and opens the way for variables such as household wealth or confidence to assert greater influence on the time path of consumption. Consider, for example, the relationship between housing prices and household spending. Rising housing prices are widely thought to be a key component underpinning the robustness of the consumption sector lately.[6] But note that personal homes are indivisible assets and their sale entails substantial transactions costs. A common effort to realize capital gains from appreciating real-estate values would quickly extinguish the surge of market value that home owners seek to convert to money. Credit furnishes the crucial interstice in the nexus between housing prices and spending inasmuch as the connection between the two is operative only if there is a capacity and a willingness of households to borrow against the increased value of their homes.

Household wealth may, in addition, affect spending through a 'stock price' effect. The majority of those in the USA who own corporate shares do so through participation in tax-deferred pension accounts.[7] As such, they are limited in their ability to realize capital gains through the sale of shares. Does this mean that changes in market valuations of shares are inconsequential for the spending decisions of the 401(k) cohort? Not necessarily. Goods news about the value of pension accounts may dissolve the resistance of many to using credit card privileges for holiday gifts, vacations or other items.

Consider also the role of factors subsumed under the rubric of 'consumer confidence'. Variables that measure confidence (such as the Michigan Mood Index) typically yield strong explanatory power when inserted into econometric specifications for big-ticket durables such as pleasure boats or sports utility vehicles (SUV).[8] But note that the effect of a surge in confidence on spending is obviously limited if consumers are inveterately debt-averse or if borrowing opportunities do not exist. In summary, the 'non-income' determinants of consumption commonly delineated in macro textbooks (e.g. interest rates, wealth or confidence) assume greater power to shape the time path of consumption when credit facilities exist. Consumer credit, by freeing consumption from the restraint exerted by current income or liquid assets held, establishes channels through which the parameters of the consumption function may be perturbed.

1.4   THE RISING IMPORTANCE OF CONSUMPTION

The rising importance of consumption is a striking aspect of recent US economic history. Consumption was equal to approximately 63 percent of total spending for new goods and services during the 1960s. The quarterly average for the 1990s was 67.4 percent. The ratio of consumption to GDP reached a historic peak in 2005 (see Table 1.1). As illustrated by Figure 1.1,

Table 1.1   *Consumption as a percentage of GDP (quarterly average)*

Period	%
1950–1959	62.8
1960–1969	63.1
1970–1979	65.8
1980–1989	66.8
1990–1999	67.4
2000–2006	70.3

Source: Bureau of Economic Analysis.

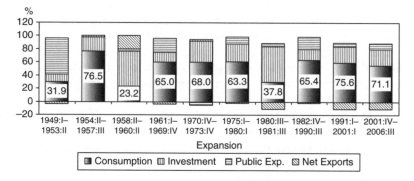

Sources: Bureau of Economic Analysis and National Bureau of Economic Research.

Figure 1.1   *Contribution of consumption to GDP growth in postwar expansions*

consumption has accounted for an unusually large share of GDP growth in the past two expansions.

The strength of consumer spending in the USA over the past decade, and particularly since 2001, has given rise to considerable head-scratching among economists. The consumer spending series seem lately to have become unhinged from fundamentals such as income and employment. The household saving rate moved into negative territory for the first time ever in 2005. Has a new era begun? To shed light on this question, a simple exercise was performed. A consumption model fitted to US monthly data for the period 1972:1 to 1995:12 was used to obtain forecasts of monthly consumption expenditure (in chained 1996 dollars) for 1996:1 through 2006:11.[9] The results are displayed in Figure 1.2. Notice that the forecasting equation consistently underpredicts consumer spending in the post-1996

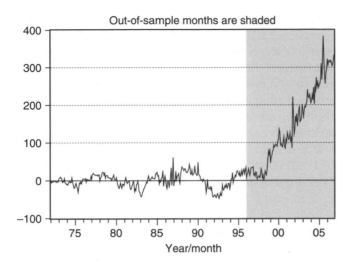

Figure 1.2 *Forecast residuals using consumption specifications fitted to US monthly data, 1972–95 (in billions of chained 1996 dollars)*

period, producing successively larger (positive) forecast errors as the time axis shifts forward. The average monthly forecast error during the recovery from the 2001 recession (2001:11 to 2006:11) is equal to a rather amazing 22 percent of actual consumption (or $277 billion at an annual rate).

What can account for the unexpected robustness of consumer spending *fin de siècle* and deep into the new decade? Product innovation is clearly one factor. The established pattern of development for highly successful durable goods consists of a phase of explosive growth as the product achieves wide market penetration, followed by the 'mature industry' phase in which the main problem for manufacturers is to stimulate 'replacement' demand. The recent past is noteworthy for spectacularly successful product innovations. These include the home computer and internet service, the SUV, cellular phones, the DVD player, serotonin reuptake inhibitors, flat-screen television sets, video-game consoles, MP3 players and iPods. The growth of the home computer segment has few historical precedents. The desire for increased computing power has led to multiple replacement cycles for many households within the past 15 years or so.

Economists and many in the financial press have identified housing prices as the key factor underlying the steroidal behavior of the consumer. Note that home equity is the single largest balance sheet item for most families and is distributed more evenly across households than financial wealth.[10] The median selling price of a home (new and existing) increased by 91 percent between 1996 and 2006.[11] The price spiral ignited, and was ignited by, a recrudescence of speculative activity. 'Get-rich-quick' real-estate strategies were widely proffered, and a popular TV program encouraged viewers to 'flip this house'. A real-estate boom is capable of shifting the consumption function by: (1) increasing the flow of realized capital gains; (2) boosting the borrowing power of home owners; and (3) nourishing consumer hubris and/or quashing resistance to debt-layering among those whose homes have gained in value. Capital gains from real-estate transactions are tightly concentrated and small in comparison with new loans collateralized by personal property – meaning that items (2) and (3) rate higher than item (1) in relative importance for consumer spending. It was stated earlier that '[c]redit furnishes the crucial interstice in the nexus between housing prices and spending'. In other words, appreciating home values are manifest in increased spending to the extent that they provide the basis for additional lending. Thus changing credit conditions may impinge on consumption by altering the spending power inhering in a property with a given market value. As is explained in Chapter 3, the relatively new technique of issuing securities collateralized by home equity, installment and student loans, or credit card receivables is generating powerful macroeconomic effects that economists are just now coming to grips with. Easy access to home equity loans is directly attributable to the development of primary and secondary markets for these derivative securities. The focus on housing prices has tended to obscure the emergence of key financial innovations underlying the growth of consumption.

1.5   THE GROWTH OF CONSUMER BORROWING

The accretion of household debt since the late 1980s is remarkable and without precedent in the USA or elsewhere. Total credit market debt owed by the household sector increased nearly fivefold in nominal terms between 1987 and 2006 (see Figure 1.3). The mean value of debt carried on a family balance sheet in 1995 was $59 900 (2004 dollars). The comparable figure in 2004 was $103 400 – a 73 percent increase in real terms in the span of a decade (see Table 1.2). Income level is a basic indicator of the household capacity to service debt. A debt buildup may not be worrisome if there is a concomitant rise in income. Commentaries on consumer borrowing typically focus on movement over time of the aggregate debt-to-income ratio. Where the USA is concerned, debt has grown at a faster pace than income – as the data in Table 1.3 reveal. See, for example, that the ratio of the mean value of outstanding debts to mean income increased from 0.88 to 1.47 in

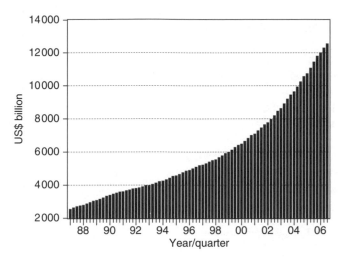

Source: Federal Reserve Board of Governors.

Figure 1.3 *Total credit market debt owed by the household sector*

Table 1.2 *Mean value of outstanding debts by family income percentile (in thousands of chained 2004 dollars)*

Income percentile	Year					
	1989	1992	1995	1998	2001	2004
All families	**52.6**	**56.7**	**59.9**	**73.4**	**77.2**	**103.4**
Less than 20	7.7	13.3	15.3	17.0	17.8	24.6
20–39.9	18.4	20.1	24.0	28.1	29.6	41.7
40–59.9	32.2	35.4	38.4	47.7	50.1	70.0
60–79.9	57.4	57.8	64.8	82.0	80.6	108.9
80–89.9	75.0	81.9	92.7	105.8	117.9	156.3
90–100	150.0	171.8	163.2	199.7	226.1	296.5

Source: *Survey of Consumer Finances.*

the years from 1988 to 2004. Notice also that the ratio jumped sharply after 2001.

In appraising trends in consumer borrowing, it is important to study the distribution of debt across income classes. Consider two families, each with a debt-to-income ratio of 1.0, but the first family has an annual income of $43 000 and the second $200 000. The latter family would, *ceteris paribus*, have more latitude to take on additional debt.[12] Thus a given growth rate

Table 1.3   Ratio of the mean value of outstanding debts to mean family income, by percentile

Income percentile	Year					
	1989	1992	1995	1998	2001	2004
All families	**0.88**	**1.08**	**1.09**	**1.20**	**1.05**	**1.47**
Less than 20	0.89	0.33	1.85	1.84	1.68	2.31
20–39.9	0.86	0.35	1.12	1.23	1.12	1.62
40–59.9	0.85	0.42	1.03	1.19	1.18	1.61
60–79.9	0.96	0.71	1.14	1.32	1.16	1.56
80–89.9	0.84	0.85	1.08	1.14	1.12	1.47
90–100	0.60	0.62	0.76	0.79	0.68	0.99

Source: Survey of Consumer Finances.

of household debt accumulation is more likely to be sustained if high-income families account for most of the new borrowing. The data indicate that high-income individuals have increased their borrowing very significantly since 1989. Table 1.3 shows that, in the period 1989–2004, mean debt owed by a family in the top income decile rose nearly twofold in real terms. However, the growth of borrowing of lower- and middle-income families during the same period was significantly greater relative to income. In 1989 there was virtually no difference between the mean debt-to-income ratio for families in 'less than 20' income percentiles and the ratio for 'all families' (0.89 compared to 0.88). In 1995 the ratio for the bottom 20 percent was 1.85 compared to 1.09 overall, whereas by 2004 the ratio had been pushed up to 2.31. All income groups show a spike in mean debt-to-income ratios since 2001.

Debt is a 'stock' whereas spending is a 'flow'. We can draw inferences about the contribution of credit to spending growth by examining changes in the stock of debt (or net borrowing) over specified time intervals. Moreover, we should be able to say something meaningful about the contribution of credit expansion to the growth of specific categories of spending (consumer durables, mobile homes, education, for example) based on the division of total debt between mortgage loans, installment loans, student loans or other categories. The debt–time profile displayed in Figure 1.3, as well as the data contained in Tables 1.2 and 1.3, include all debt obligations of the household sector. Looking at the problem from a flow-of-funds perspective, mortgage loan extensions made for the purchase of new homes facilitate investment (since new homes are counted as investment for national income accounting purposes) but make a marginal contribution to consumption (e.g., if loan proceeds are used to pay brokers' commissions or other fees classified under the heading of consumer services). Mortgage loans used for the purchase of existing homes have negligible importance for GDP.

One could in principle give a rough estimate of the change in the stock of debt implicated in consumption by separating out debt collateralized by homes from all other household debt obligations. But such an approach would not be indicated if a substantial share of loans collateralized by homes were used for purposes of consumption. The Tax Reform Act of 1986 eliminated the tax deductibility of interest paid on credit cards, bank lines of credit, car and boat loans, and educational loans, a proviso that incentivized the substitution of home equity loans for conventional consumer loans.[13] The growth of home equity lending has been widely publicized. Home equity loans outstanding grew by an average of 18.4 percent per year from 2001 to 2006.[14] Home equity loans are used for a wide variety of purposes: to consolidate consumer debts, to make home improvements, to pay for a child's education, to start a business, pay medical bills and so forth. Monthly data on mortgage debt outstanding typically mix together first mortgages with second and higher mortgages. The Federal Reserve started in 1990 to publish annual data on home equity loans. Thus we may get a better idea of the proportion of new mortgage loan extensions flowing into consumer goods markets. By adding together home equity loans and those loans conventionally categorized under 'consumer credit', we obtain a general picture of the degree to which credit expansion has supported consumption growth.

The data in Table 1.4 bear out the fact that many households have shifted from conventional consumer loans to home equity loans in response to the tax advantages offered by the latter. Home equity loans as a percentage of consumer credit outstanding were equal to 20 percent in 1996 but 39 percent in 2006. Moreover, the net change in home equity borrowing exceeded the net change in consumer borrowing for the first time ever in 2004.

The escalating cost of a college education is commonly cited as a cause of borrowing by university students and their parents.[15] There is an indisputable correlation between rising tuition fees and mushrooming student debt. According to the non-profit Project on Student Debt, average debt levels for graduating seniors (excluding the approximately one-third of graduating seniors with no student debt) increased $9250 to $19 200 between 1995 and 2004 – a 58 percent increase in real terms. Almost two-thirds of graduating seniors at public, four-year institutions had education debt in 2004, and of this group, 10 percent had student debts of $32 994 or more. Meanwhile, average published tuition fees at public,

*Table 1.4   Net change in home equity and consumer credit loans,
            1991–2006 (billions of current dollars)*

Year	(1) Net change in home equity loans (US$ bn)	(2) Net change in consumer credit (US$ bn)	(3) = (1) + (2) (US$ bn)	(4) Change in consumption (US$ bn)	(5) = (3)/(4)
1991	7.3	−8.8	−1.5	167.4	−0.009
1992	−4.9	9.2	4.3	304.8	0.014
1993	−6.7	61.4	54.7	225.2	0.243
1994	11.4	134.8	146.2	267.0	0.548
1995	15.7	147.9	163.6	247.9	0.660
1996	25.1	104.9	130.0	275.7	0.472
1997	34.4	71.1	105.5	301.3	0.350
1998	13.0	97.3	110.3	370.8	0.297
1999	24.4	114.5	138.9	466.5	0.298
2000	73.0	181.0	254.0	377.2	0.673
2001	31.6	151.0	182.6	257.4	0.709
2002	62.2	113.4	175.6	335.4	0.524
2003	92.3	104.0	196.3	384.0	0.511
2004	185.0	116.9	301.9	576.7	0.523
2005	135.3	91.3	226.6	493.5	0.459
2006	130.9	113.7	244.6	508.8	0.481

Sources: Federal Reserve, *Flow of Funds Report*, Tables F.218, F.222, L.218, L.222 and
Bureau of Economic Analysis.

four-year institutions were $2811 in academic year 1995–96 and $5491 for
academic year 2005–06 – a 54 percent increase after adjusting for
inflation.[16]

Clearly an increase in the cost of education will enlarge student borrowing needs. However, we should not conclude that the cause–effect relation
is unidirectional. The cornucopia of student loan money has effectively
insulated institutions of higher learning from sharp losses of enrollment
that higher tuition fees might otherwise provoke. The student loan industry provides state legislators with some cover as they shift the burden of
higher education from the public to the students. The new fad is the construction of 'gold-plated' student unions and other facilities paid for
by 'infrastructure' or other fees. University administrators have enjoyed a
degree of latitude in pursuing ambitious building and athletic programs
that would not exist if the 'customers' lacked supplementary financial
resources.

1.6   CONSUMER CREDIT: THE STANDARD VIEW

A review of the orthodox literature, as well as widely adopted textbooks, might give the impression that consumer credit is of little macroeconomic import. Extended discussions of consumer credit are typically found in papers on the US 'saving puzzle' (the household saving rate – that is, saving as a percentage of disposable income – fell from 15 to near zero percent between 1985 and 2005). The literature also features a recurring argument that debt-financed profligacy of consumers is partly to blame for giant US merchandise trade deficits – an issue discussed in Chapter 7. Otherwise, consumer credit gets scant attention. Certainly there is no recognition that a secular reorientation of social attitudes toward credit-financed consumption, along with growth and increased sophistication among consumer lending institutions, have assumed immense importance in sustaining effective demand.

Standard approaches to macroeconomic theory portray business cycle fluctuations as transitory deviations of output and unemployment from their respective 'natural' levels – meaning values consistent with simultaneous clearing in product and factor markets.[17] In the search for causes of movements of the economy away from its (hypothetical) long-run growth path, the orthodox project has for the most part limited itself to the 'micro sphere'. [18] Fluctuations in aggregate expenditure are thought to produce changes, albeit temporary, in the overall level of economic activity only if product and factor markets are subject to frictions such as wage and price stickiness or informational/forecasting problems related to unpredictable monetary growth. Otherwise, market systems are believed to possess self-correcting mechanisms and quickly adjust to full employment. Note that some have suggested that consumer credit expansion may constitute an element in the 'black box' that connects monetary expansion to aggregate expenditure.[19] The implication is that a monetary initiative may be transmitted to the 'real' economy via expansion of consumer loans by banks and spending by households. However, the money supply (and thus credit expansion under a reserve-constrained regime) is widely thought to be under the control of the monetary authorities. As such, consumer lending, though it may supply a component of monetary transmission apparatus, does not rate as a 'primary' or independent cause of aggregate fluctuations.

Standard economic theory features an 'agent-driven' or 'bottom-up' approach to household saving (and borrowing) behavior.[20] The orthodox technique (sometimes called 'methodological individualism') imposes the requirement that a macroeconomic treatment of consumer credit be grounded in, or derived from, the intertemporal optimization problem of a 'representative' agent.[21] Viewed in the framework of multi-period utility, a demand function for consumer credit materializes because (1) future consumption is less highly valued than present consumption – that is, agents' rate of time preference is greater than 0, so agents by borrowing may equate the marginal utility of consumption across consumption periods;[22] and/or (2) the distribution of income receipts across consumption periods may not match desired spending in each period, so borrowing, offers a technique to smooth consumption expenditure or unhook consumption in any given period from income received in that period – subject to a lifetime budget constraint. The interest rate defines the terms on which future income (or human capital) can be discounted for the purpose of financing current consumption. A surge in household debt (or a decrease in the aggregate saving-to-income ratio) is, according to this view, the cumulative result of intertemporal utility maximization by households, a process that incorporates variables such as the rate of time preference, the ratio of non-human or marketable wealth to human wealth, the dispersion of monthly or annual income around its expected or 'permanent' value, the capacity to borrow against non-marketable assets (such as 'human' capital) and the scheme of relative prices.

Milton Friedman's 'permanent income' hypothesis (see Friedman 1957) should be included under the heading of 'standard' theories of the consumption function.[23] Friedman treats consumer durables as a distinct category of household expenditure because the stream of 'services' provided by cars, washing machines and other durables extends across multiple income periods – unlike non-durables and services, the use-values of which are normally exhausted by the conclusion of the income period in which these items have been purchased. This factor makes consumer durables a nearer cousin to (new) capital goods or housing than to items such as groceries, pharmaceuticals or haircuts. Consumer borrowing can therefore be viewed as an amortization technique that enables the individual to stretch the schedule of payments so that it is coterminous with the useful life of a (durable) good. The application of Friedman's permanent income hypothesis leads to several possible explanations of rising household debt (or reduced saving), including: (1) an increase in share of total expenditure accounted for by durable items – that is, items requiring amortization; (2) an increase in household wealth; (3) a rise in households' (subjective) estimates of their permanent incomes; (4) a decrease in (probabilistic) uncertainty about future labor income that causes a decrease in 'precautionary' saving; and (5) enhanced capacity to borrow against existing wealth.

Among the items mentioned, there is some support in the recent literature for all but that described by point (1) above. The share of consumption accounted for by 'durables' has held fairly steady at around 10 percent for the past two decades. With respect to point (2), most economists agree that, although the market value of assets owned by the household sector has increased very substantially, most of the gains have accrued to the wealthiest families and thus cannot explain the broad-based decline in personal saving in the USA. Recent research based on the permanent income approach interprets the rise in borrowing as a decrease in precautionary saving by households. Hence the issue: what can cause a change in (aggregate) precautionary saving? According to Christopher Carroll (2001), agents may reduce the contribution out of current income to the buffer stock of precautionary liquid assets if degree of (probabilistic) uncertainty about future income is reduced; or the need for a buffer stock of liquid assets is diminished if agents are confident they will be able to borrow at unspecified future dates – that is, 'precautionary saving and liquidity constraints are strongly interconnected' (Carroll 2001, p. 24). Thus the expansion of household indebtedness in the USA might be seen as an optimizing response to a change in the relative price of 'current' consumption (measured in sacrificed future consumption) brought forth by the completion of markets for household IOUs. The emergence of global markets for securities backed by consumer, mortgage or home equity receivables has ostensibly brought the US household sector in contact with a vast pool of financial resources that was previously not within reach, a factor that has reduced the relative price of consumer credit. In practical terms, the completion of markets for consumer credit has meant that a consumer with a given credit score has the option to borrow more than was possible when markets were less complete. Dilip Soman and Amar Cheema (2002) argue that individuals use their credit limits as one way of forecasting incomes: 'If consumers have access to large amounts of credit, they are likely to infer that their lifetime [permanent] income will be high and therefore their willingness to use credit (and their spending) will also be high' (Soman and Cheema 2002, p. 32).

In summary, orthodox theory harbors what we may call a 'neutrality theorem' with respect to household borrowing. If wages and prices are perfectly flexible, and if monetary growth can be accurately forecasted, then expansions or contractions in the scale of household borrowing are thought to have no effect on the scale of output and employment. Household borrowing merely changes the allocation of resources between the production of consumer, investment and public goods. The preceding is a restatement of the well-known 'crowding-out' principle, which is based on the view that the total volume of borrowing is limited by saving, or equivalently, the supply of 'loanable funds'. With a scarce supply of funds available to be borrowed, household borrowing must crowd out borrowing by firms or public sector units (or both). The situation changes somewhat in the open-economy context. To the extent that foreign agents are willing to purchase IOUs of domestic households, consumer credit expansion can proceed without soaking up the domestic supply of finance. External borrowing creates trade imbalances, however. The commonplace remark that 'foreign countries are lending money to US consumers to buy their goods' fits here.[24]

1.7   CONSUMER CREDIT: AN ALTERNATIVE VIEW

There is in the pluralist literature what seems to be an emerging coalescence of thought with respect to the macroeconomics of consumer credit. This collective opinion can be summarized by the following points:

1. Income inequality is, in terms of the collective interests of the elite business and financial organizations that constitute society's dominant power cohort and locus of social control, both good and bad. Rising inequality is good because it means that a larger share of the social dividend goes to profit. At the same time, rising inequality may militate against the growth of the social dividend (and thus the total volume of profits) because of the deleterious impact of mal-distribution on effective demand.
2. Consumer credit expansion, by augmenting the stock of liquid claims to goods, is counteractive to the influence on total expenditure exerted by a hollowed-out income distribution function. Thus consumer credit is a highly important element of an economic equation that permits both rising inequality and growth.
3. The massive uprooting of Protestant antagonisms toward debt is a salient feature of modern social life, a development expedited by the operation of a ubiquitous and relentless institutional machinery that exhorts people to spend and borrow.
4. The behavior of the personal saving rate is one statistical manifestation of the increased dependence on credit expansion to achieve growth.
5. Debt-layering increases the share of current income claimed by debt-servicing, giving rise to doubts about the sustainability of consumer debt-financed growth. Some fear the US economy is nearing a 'turning point' – that is, an episode in which a large segment of households ceases to add debt and allocates an increased share of current income to debt-servicing. Such an event could have devastating macroeconomic consequences.

How is income distribution connected to effective demand, as is suggested by point (1) above? Where incomes are received as generalized claims to goods, income recipients have the option to withhold spending power – that is, to prevent the recycling of their incomes for the purchase of new goods and services. By accumulating liquid claims to goods, agents contribute to a deficiency of spending relative to productive capacity. Thus, in a monetary system, the manner in which liquid claims to goods are distributed across income groups has implications for effective demand.[25] Think of a world in which spending power is derived from income only. A redistribution of liquid claims to goods in favor of groups with comparatively lower propensities to spend out of income will, *ceteris paribus*, widen the gap between actual and potential output.

Michael Kalecki formalized the distribution–effective demand argument in a pair of articles (see Kalecki 1943, 1954). For Kalecki, the wage share in national income (w) is determined by the controversial 'degree of monopoly' and the ratio of the materials bill to the wage bill (j). The degree of monopoly is measured by the markup of price over unit prime costs (k). Hence the wage share is expressed by:

$$w = \frac{1}{1 - (k - 1)(j + 1)} \tag{1.1}$$

The wage share is inversely related to the degree of monopoly (k) and the ratio of the materials bill to the wage bill (j).[26] To incorporate the micro-level distribution relationship distilled by equation (1.1) into a theory of the determination of total output, Kalecki (1954, p. 236) posited total wage and salary income (V) as a function of total (private) income (or output) (Y):

$$V = \alpha Y + B \tag{1.2}$$

The term B is a constant and α, which denotes share of wages in national income (Y) that is determined independently of Y, assumes a value between zero and 1. The value of α is perfectly correlated with w and hence is determined by k and j. Assuming no taxes, V is simply the difference between gross income (Y) and profits (P).

$$\frac{Y - P}{Y} = \alpha + \frac{B}{Y} \tag{1.3}$$

Now rearrange equation (1.3) to obtain:

$$Y = \frac{P + B}{1 - \alpha} \tag{1.4}$$

Profits in absolute terms (P) are determined by investment and the propensity to consume out of profits, consistent with the familiar summarization of Kalecki's theory – that is 'workers spend what they get; capitalists get what they spend'. It can be seen from equation (1.4) that an increase in the degree of monopoly, to the extent that it diminishes the wage share in national income (α), will reduce output (Y). The profit share in national income will increase, but not real profits expressed in absolute terms.

To summarize: total income is divided between profit (income of capitalists) and wages and salaries (income of workers). As a rule, the propensity to spend out of wage and salary income is greater than the propensity to spend out of profits. Therefore an increase in the degree of monopoly, by shifting the distribution of income in favor of profits at the expense of wages and salaries, would tend to reduce the ratio of spending to total income.

Kalecki's model has its shortcomings. The myriad of factors that govern the division of national income into functional shares are subsumed under the 'degree of monopoly'. Moreover, a change in the distribution of wages or profits among income classes (as measured by, say, the Gini ratio) should impinge on aggregate spending – even if functional shares remain constant. Even so, Kalecki uncovered an important fallacy of composition. That is, a single business unit gains from reducing the wage bill or otherwise 'taking cost out' since market conditions in its own industry are likely to be unaffected as a consequence of a decrease in wage or salary income (or benefits) that the firm itself has initiated. A drive on the part of all business units to reduce the wage bill is likely, on the other hand, to shift a greater share of national income to groups with comparatively smaller propensities to consume and thus depress overall economic conditions.

In the era of shareholder capitalism (see Brown 1998), when top corporate officials are evaluated and compensated almost exclusively on the basis of stock price performance, the pressure to meet or exceed earnings expectations is intense. Any strategy effective in taking cost out – for example, outsourcing, downsizing, reengineering or offshoring – recommends itself to corporate decision-makers. The wholesale embrace of cost-cutting business policies, taken against a pro-business, free-trade political backdrop, and meeting minimal resistance from blue- and white-collar workers, did over a period of years contribute to a substantial 'hollowing out' of the income distribution function. The popular term for this phenomenon is 'disappearing middle class'.

The record of US economic performance would seem to give a resounding disconfirmation of the hypothesis that income distribution matters for effective demand. Figure 1.4 illustrates the time path of the Gini ratio and the growth rate of real consumption during the period 1980–2005. A cursory examination of the numbers would appear to suggest that, if anything, rising inequality (as measured by the Gini ratio) has provided a

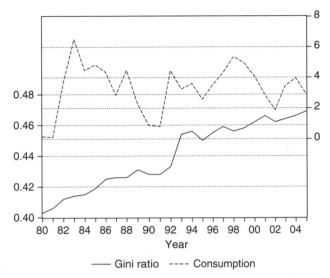

Sources: Bureau of the Census, Historical Income Table H-4; Bureau of Economic Analysis.

Figure 1.4   The Gini ratio for families, annualized growth rate of real consumption (%)

stimulus to growth – at least after 1992. Appearances can be deceiving, however. I will argue that the surge in debt-financed spending has placed the inequality–spending link in abeyance – but not indefinitely. Two statistical facts point to the importance of consumer credit in overcoming the effects of income inequality. For one thing, compared to a different era when income was distributed more evenly, achieving a specified rate of growth of consumption takes more borrowing relative to consumption than it once did (all other factors held constant). A second factor pertains to the household saving rate – which is obviously related to borrowing. The increased dependence on borrowing to sustain growth has its statistical manifestation in the behavior of the household saving rate, which fell sharply after 1993 (see Figure 1.5). Widened credit access enables people to maintain a habitual standard of living when their (real) incomes decline. It also allows individuals or groups on the losing side of the redistributive equation to limit the size of 'lifestyle gap' that separates them from higher income groups. A key aspect of the present book (addressed in Chapter 2) is to develop a plausible explanation of why income disparities give rise to expanded credit use.

Warren S. Gramm was the first economist to establish a connection between what we may term 'Kalecki's Paradox' and consumer credit. In a neglected 1978 paper, Gramm wrote:

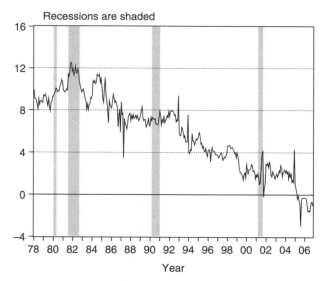

Recessions are shaded

Year

Source: Bureau of Economic Analysis.

Figure 1.5   The personal saving rate (%)

For the individual employer, low wages mean low costs and higher profits. The aggregative problem of product demand is submerged, perhaps mystified, in the extension of consumer credit. It might be preferable for all *others* to pay high wages as the more sound base for keeping demand for one's own product high. But there is a second, more subtle, socioideological base for capitalist preference for generally low wages reinforced by credit-based demand: Low wages are necessary to 'keep workers in their place,' which is at work. High incomes lead to worker 'independence,' to intermittent choice of leisure over work, and at the extreme to buying one's way out of worker status altogether. Thus installment credit . . . became consolidated naturally, perhaps unconsciously, on the ideological–economic grounds of meeting the capitalists' desire for a low-paid labor force, at the same time that purchasing power is reinforced. (Gramm 1978, p. 309)

Like orthodox or 'mainstream' economics, institutionalism seeks to explain human behavior. For institutionalists, however, the outstanding fact about human behavior is its tendency, within a given society or institutional milieu, to be correlated, repetitive and predictable. Behavior is, for the most part, habit-driven – such as stopping for red lights, using debit cards, or turning down the thermostat at bedtime. Regular patterns of behavior result from the influence of culture or institutions on individuals. Hodgson (2006, p. 163) writes that '[I]nstitutions are durable systems of established and embedded social rules and conventions that structure social interaction'. Another way to look at household borrowing is to view individual behavior in the context of an economic and social system that maintains its functionality by the unremitting influence of a unique or regime-specific social habit structure. A 'top-down' approach seeks to identify the institutional factors at work in the establishment and modification of a social habit structure. The existence of such a structure may be inferred from two observations: (1) most human behavior is produced by a habitual response to external stimuli; and (2) when presented with a large class of stimuli, individuals within a given social/institutional matrix behave in a roughly parallel manner. A society can be defined as an amalgam of correlated patterns of thought and behavior. Societies depend on a complex institutional infrastructure to bring the thoughts and actions of individuals into agreement with larger, often elite, imperatives.

Institutionalists, as apostles of the 'top-down' methodology, simply argue that in so far as so many aspects of human thought and behavior are influenced by culture (as evidenced by the consonance of thought and behavior), it is highly likely that consumption and saving behavior are also shaped by influences from above. Hodgson writes:

> [S]ocio-economic systems do not simply create new products and perceptions. *They also create and recreate individuals.* The individual not only changes his/her skill purposes and preferences, but also revises his/her skills and his/her perceptions of his/her needs. (Hodgson 2006, p. 162)

Douglas and Isherwood (1996) argue that much of what we call 'consumption' is the purchase and use of items necessary for participation in established social rituals and/or the maintenance of group or class affiliation. Goods provide marking services 'in the sense of classifying objects' (Douglas and Isherwood 1996, p. 50). Specific items (gold, silver, designer gowns or California wines) would be ineffective for marking purposes unless those goods were 'endowed with value by the agreement of fellow consumers' (ibid., p. 51). Thus many goods have value to us in direct proportion to their value to others. As Douglas and Isherwood explain:

> Each person is a source of judgments and a subject of judgments; each individual is in the classification scheme whose discriminations he is helping to establish. By the presence of his fellows at his family funerals and weddings, by their regard for his birthdays, in their visits to his sickbed, they render marking services to him. The kind of world they create together is constructed from commodities that are chosen for their fitness to mark events in an appropriately graded scale. (Ibid.)

This volume invites the reader to think of household spending, saving and borrowing behavior in the context of a socio-economic system that maintains its functionality by the unremitting influence of a unique or regime-specific social habit structure. An issue of paramount importance concerns the role of power elites in the construction and maintenance of a cultural/institutional infrastructure that shapes the contours of thought and action.[27]

1.8   AN OUTLINE OF THE BOOK

The purpose of Appendix 1A is to give a brief and concise summary of the post-Keynesian position on the meaning and economic significance of saving. Veteran readers of the post-Keynesian literature will find nothing new here, and these readers should proceed directly to Chapter 2. Others are advised to read this appendix carefully, as it articulates points of view at variance with the common understanding of saving. For example, post-Keynesians assert that investment, as well as the expansion of bank credit, requires no prior (voluntary) act of abstinence or saving. Moreover, post-Keynesians argue that interest rates are determined (mainly) by the 'state of liquidity preference' – not household thriftiness or the marginal product of capital.

Chapter 2 contains a theoretical explanation of the household debt surge and the decline of saving. It starts from the premise that most of what people do (including spending, saving and borrowing) is regulated by habit. Thus a satisfactory account of consumer behavior must be built from a theory of habit selection. Such a theory must be capable of explaining how habits come to be established and displaced by new habits, as well as the social or correlated character of the matrix of human routines.

The astronomic growth in the scale of consumer borrowing, and the increasing diversity of items bought on credit, are principal themes of the present work. The emergence of a social habit structure amenable to credit use is obviously conditioned on the spread of borrowing opportunities. Chapter 3 surveys key innovations in the consumer credit field dating to the 1919 – key in the sense of achieving a secular improvement in the availability of various types of consumer lending arrangements for individuals at nearly all income/wealth levels.

The aim of Chapter 4 is twofold: first, to review and critically appraise current (dominant) theories about the 'saving puzzle' – that is, the mystery pertaining to the stunning decline in household and personal saving rates; and second, to assess the importance of changes in the distribution of income in explaining the decline of personal saving in the USA. Mainstream approaches to the saving puzzle focus on unrealized capital gains (which are not included in measured saving), home ownership and housing prices, shifts over time in the desired level of precautionary saving, and lifecycle effects. With respect to the second aim, a miscellany of statistical tools (including Granger causality testing and regression analysis) is deployed to shed light on the post-1960 empirical link of income distribution to household saving.

A main argument contained in this volume is that the US economy has become dangerously reliant on household debt expansion for continued growth. The purpose of Chapter 5 is to identify and discuss the macroeconomic risks arising from consumer credit dependence.

The 'Minsky effect' is the term used in Chapter 5 to describe an episode wherein a substantial share of households attempt to improve balance sheet quality by ceasing to borrow and sharply reducing or liquidating existing debts. Chapter 6 uncovers evidence of Minsky-type events in the US economic record. The chapter also appraises the present risk of Minsky-effect-induced collapse of consumer spending.

Chapter 7 begins with an analysis of the relationship between consumerism, the debt surge and the mushrooming US trade deficit. The present work claims that the surge in economic inequality is an important factor in the decline of household saving. The growing trade deficit is to a large degree an outgrowth of the new pattern of vertical organization by US-based corporations. The relocation of production activity to *maquiladoras*, to Southern India or to China's Guandong Province is implicated in the hollowing out of the US income distribution function and thus constitutes an indirect cause of the saving collapse. The argument that the USA needs foreign saving to offset the shortage of domestic saving is critiqued.

Final remarks are contained in Chapter 8.

NOTES

1. By uncertainty, J.M. Keynes did not meant to distinguish 'merely what is known from what is probable. The game of roulette is not subject, in this sense, to uncertainty . . . The sense in which I am using the term is that . . . there is no scientific basis on which to form any calculable probability whatever. We simply do not know' (Keynes 1937, p. 113).
2. Davidson explains that 'If nonproducibility is an essential aspect of the characteristic of liquidity, then when agents fear an uncertain future they will refrain from exercising some of their income claims on current resources by buying liquid assets to hold as a store of value. This holding of nonproducible liquid assets can provide a long-run security blanket against uncertainty by postponing the need to spend one's claims on real resources, thereby providing utility in a way that producibles cannot' (Davidson 2001, p. 396).
3. The importance of nominal wage or price rigidities in explaining unemployment is a key point of demarcation between the new Keynesian and post-Keynesian economics. Standard Walrasian macroeconomics depends on the Pigou or 'real balance' effect to prove the tendency of market systems to full employment under conditions of wage and price flexibility. See Pigou (1943), Modigliani (1944), Haberler (1960, pp. 240–44) and

Patinkin (1965). Michael Kalecki explained that the Pigou effect is of dubious reliability as a macroeconomic stabilizer in a credit money system – that is, where money is both asset and liability: 'The increase in the real value of the stock of money generated by a price decline does not mean a rise in the real value of possessions if all the money (cash and deposits) is "backed" by credits to persons and firms; i.e., if all assets of the banking system consist of such credits. For in this case, to the gain of money holders there corresponds an equal loss of the bank debtors. The total real value of possessions increases only to the extent to which money is backed by gold' (Kalecki 1944, pp. 131–2). See also Basil Moore (1988) and Brown (1992).

4. Depository institutions expand the means of payment by the creation of what Von Mises (1953, p. 177) termed 'derivative deposits', which come into existence when a bank sells its deposits in exchange for a borrowers promise to pay.

5. Keynes (1937, p. 233) wrote that saving 'has no special efficacy, when compared with consumption in releasing cash and restoring liquidity . . . [T]here is, therefore, just as much reason for adding current consumption to the rate of increase of new bank money in reckoning the flow of cash available to provide new "finance," as for added saving.'

6. For example, Case et al. (2005) recently completed a 14-country, 25-year time series analysis and reported that housing wealth is statistically more important than financial wealth in explaining changes in consumer spending. See also Tang (2006).

7. According to the 2004 *Survey of Consumer Finances*, more than half (50.2 percent) of all households in the USA owned some corporate stock. But for the majority of these, stock ownership is 'indirect', through participation in retirement plans.

8. There has been a recent flurry of papers that argue that consumer confidence is a strong predictor of household spending. See, for example, Gelper et al. (2007) and Kwan and Cotsomitis (2006a, 2006b). For a dissenting view, see Ludvigson (2004).

9. The dependent variable is consumption in billions of chained 1996 dollars (C). The explanatory variables are disposable income in chained 1996 dollars (YD); the Standard & Poor Index of 500 Stocks ($SP500$); and the rate of interest charged by finance companies on 48-month car loans (r). C, YD and r are seasonally adjusted. The equation was estimated using least squares. The results are as follows (t-statistics in parentheses):

$$C = -22.8 + 0.98\,YD + 0.01\,SP500 - 6.64r \qquad R^2\text{-}adj. = 0.97$$
$$(-1.82) \quad (31.92) \quad (3.91) \qquad (-9.20)$$

10. Non-financial assets (of which the primary residence is the largest component) accounted for 64.3 percent of total household assets in 2004, according to the *Survey of Consumer Finances*.

11. This figure comes from the Bureau of the Census.

12. This conclusion follows from the fact that the income left after debt service is much greater for the high income household, even allowing for considerable differences in the hire-purchase terms of credit between the two families.

13. The provisions of the Act pertaining to interest on consumer loans became effective in 1991. Congress believed deductibility of interest 'provided an incentive to invest in consumer durables rather than assets which produce taxable income and, therefore, an incentive to consume rather than save . . . By phasing out the present deductibility of personal interest, Congress intended to eliminate from the prior tax law a significant disincentive to saving' (Joint Committee on Taxation [JCT] 1987, p. 263). But Maki (2001) reports that the new tax had virtually no effect on saving, but rather resulted in a change in the composition of debt between mortgage and consumer debt.

14. These data come from the Federal Reserve, *Flow of Funds Report*, Table L.218.

15. For example, a recent *Knight Ridder Tribune Business News* editorial ('Tuition-Setting Regents Should Consider Future Student Debt Load', 2 December 2006, p. 1) criticized a decision by Arizona State University in Tempe to raise tuition by 9.1 percent: 'The escalating costs have a dramatic impact. As the *Tribune*'s Ryan Gabrielson reported Wednesday,

more than half of current ASU graduates are borrowing more for their education than they can afford to pay back while still in school. That's up from 39 percent just five years earlier, and is among the highest increases among comparable universities across the nation.'

16. These figures are taken from the *Trends in College Pricing 2005*, a publication of the College Board.

17. Macroeconomics instructors can vouch for the fact that the concept of a 'natural' unemployment rate is particularly difficult to explain to students. A widely used macroeconomics textbook by Olivier Blanchard defines it as follows: 'The equilibrium unemployment rate . . . is such that the real wage chosen in wage setting . . . is equal to the real wage implied by price setting . . . The equilibrium unemployment rate . . . is called the natural rate of unemployment . . . [A]ssociated with the natural level of employment is the natural level of output' (Blanchard 2000, pp. 117–18).

18. The term 'standard macroeconomic theory' covers all models (including rational expectations, the new quantity theory approaches associated with Milton Friedman, and the new Keynesian economics) that rely on wage and price rigidities or informational problems to explain aggregate fluctuations. R.J. Gordon notes that '[t]he task of new-Keynesian economics is to explain why changes in the aggregate price level are sticky' (Gordon 1990, p. 1116).

19. Ben Bernanke and Mark Gertler, who posit a 'bank lending' or credit channel of the monetary transmission mechanism, write that 'research that has established that changes in monetary policy are eventually followed by changes in output is largely silent about what happens in the interim. To a great extent, empirical analysis of the effects of monetary policy has treated the transmission mechanism itself as a "black box" ' (Bernanke and Gertler 1995, p. 27).

20. Christopher Carroll (2000, p. 110) writes that '[m]acroeconomists pursuing microfoundations for aggregate consumption have generally adopted one of two approaches: either to model microeconomic consumption behavior carefully and then to aggregate, or to understand thoroughly the behavior of a "representative consumer" in general equilibrium and then to introduce microeconomic risk and heterogeneity. The broad conclusion from the "bottom-up" approach has been that precautionary saving and microeconomic heterogeneity can profoundly change behavior.'

21. Nobel laureate Robert Lucas (1983) dismissed the simple Keynesian theory of consumption as 'bad science' because the 'fundamental psychological law' upon which it is based lacks a sound microtheoretic foundation – that is, it applies only at the aggregate level.

22. The multi-period utility function is described by:

$$U = U\beta(C_t) + U\beta^2(C_{t+1}) + \ldots + U\beta^n(C_{t+n})$$

where $\beta = \dfrac{1}{1-\sigma}$ and σ is the time preference parameter.

23. Though, as Carroll notes, Friedman's hypothesis 'never actually specified a formal mathematical model derived explicitly from utility maximization' (Carroll 2001, p. 23).

24. A recent comment by Reagan Administration top economist Martin Feldstein is representative of the standard view: 'The relatively rapid increase in consumer spending in the past decade and a half, and the resulting decline in the savings rate, is the primary reason for the large trade deficit and the associated capital inflows. But capital inflows have been possible only because foreign countries are willing suppliers of those funds. Low U.S. savings relative to U.S. business investment is necessarily mirrored by high savings relative to business investment in other countries. Their savings end up as investment in the United States rather than in other countries because of the United States' large consumer-driven trade deficit' (Feldstein 2006, p. 87).

25. David Hamilton has written that '[o]ne of the difficulties in the industrial economy is the failure of its ceremonial system of distribution, based on imputed productivities, to redistribute sufficiently to keep the reciprocal flow goods and money at a constant or

increasing rate. It was precisely this aspect of the industrial system to which J.M. Keynes addressed himself' (Hamilton 1991, pp. 944–5).

26. Kalecki derived this equation as follows: let W denote the wage bill and M the materials bill. $(k-1)(W+M)$ is equal to the share of national income claimed by overhead and profits. Thus the wage share (w) is given by:

$$w = \frac{W}{W + (k-1)(W+M)}$$

Dividing this equation through by W and letting $j = M/W$ yields equation (1.1). See Kalecki (1943, pp. 204–38).

27. John Watkins writes: 'The evolution of consumer credit involves the use of corporate power to remove liquidity constraints that historically have limited consumer spending. Lack of liquidity constrains consumer spending, hindering the ability of corporations to turn consumer assets into corporate profits. Power stems from the size of financial resources that corporations command, the willingness to use those resources to remove institutions that constrain consumer spending, and the willingness to create new institutions that encourage spending' (Watkins 2000, p. 909).

REFERENCES

Bernanke, B. and M. Gertler (1995), 'Inside the black box: the credit channel of monetary policy', *Journal of Economic Perspectives*, **9** (4), 27–49.

Blanchard, Olivier (2000), *Macroeconomics*, 2nd edition, Upper Saddle River, NJ: Prentice Hall.

Boulding, Kenneth R. (1966), *Economic Analysis: Volume II*, 4th edition, New York: Harper & Row.

Brown, C. (1992), 'Commodity money, credit money, and the real balance effect', *Journal of Post Keynesian Economics*, **15** (1), 99–107.

Brown, C. (1998), 'Rise of the institutional equity funds: implications for managerialism', *Journal of Economic Issues*, **32** (3), 803–21.

Carroll, C. (2000), 'Requiem for the representative consumer? Aggregate implications of microeconomic consumption behavior', *American Economic Review*, **90** (2), 110–16.

Carroll, C. (2001), 'A theory of the consumption function, with and without liquidity constraints', *Journal of Economic Perspectives*, **15** (3), 23–46.

Case, K.E., J.M. Quigley and R.J. Shiller (2005), 'Comparing wealth effects: the stock market versus the housing market', *Advances in Macroeconomics*, **5** (1), 1–21.

Davidson, P. (1991), 'Is probability theory relevant for uncertainty? A Post Keynesian perspective', *Journal of Economic Perspectives*, **5** (1), 129–43.

Davidson, P. (2001), 'The principle of effective demand: another view', *Journal of Post Keynesian Economics*, **23** (3), 391–410.

Davidson, Paul (2002), *Financial Markets, Money, and the Real World*, Northampton, MA: Edward Elgar Publishing.

Douglas, Mary and Baron Isherwood (1996), *The World of Goods: Towards an Anthropology of Consumption*, revised edition, New York: Routledge.

Feldstein, M. (2006), 'The return of saving', *Foreign Affairs*, **85** (3), 87.

Gelper, S., A. Lemmens and C. Croux (2007), 'Consumer sentiment and consumer spending: decomposing the Granger causal relationship in the time domain', *Applied Economics*, **39** (1), 1–24.

Gordon, R.J. (1990), 'What is New-Keynesian economics?', *Journal of Economic Literature*, **28** (3), 1115–71.

Gramm, W. (1978), 'Credit saturation, secular redistribution, and long run stability', *Journal of Economic Issues*, **12** (2), 307–27.

Haberler, Gottfried (1960), *Prosperity and Depression*, Cambridge, MA: Harvard University Press.

Hahn, Frank H. (1977), 'Keynesian economics and general equilibrium theory', in G.C. Harcourt (ed.), *The Microfoundations of Macroeconomics*, London: Macmillan, pp. 29–47.

Hamilton, D. (1991), 'The meaning of anthropology in economics', *Journal of Economic Issues*, **25** (4), 937–49.

Hodgson, G. (2006), 'What are institutions?', *Journal of Economic Issues*, **40** (1), 1–25.

Joint Committee on Taxation (1987), *General Explanation of the Tax Reform Act of 1986*, Washington, DC: US Government Printing Office.

Kalecki, Michael (1943), 'Studies in economic dynamics', in J. Osiatynski (ed.), *Collected Works of Michael Kalecki*, vol. 2, Oxford: Clarendon Press, 1991, pp. 117–90.

Kalecki, M. (1944), 'Professor Pigou and the classical stationary state: a comment', *Economic Journal*, **54**, 131–2.

Kalecki, Michael (1954), 'The theory of economic dynamics', in J. Osiatynski (ed.), *Collected Works of Michael Kalecki*, vol. 2, Oxford: Clarendon Press, 1991, pp. 207–338.

Keynes, John M. (1937), 'The General Theory', *Quarterly Journal of Economics*, reprinted in D. Moggridge (ed.) (1973), *The Collected Writings of John Maynard Keynes*, vol. XIV, London: Macmillan.

Kwan, A.C. and J.A. Cotsomitis (2006), 'The usefulness of consumer confidence in forecasting household spending in Canada: a national and regional analysis', *Economic Inquiry*, **44** (1), 185–98.

Kwan, A.C. and J.A. Cotsomitis (2006), 'Can consumer confidence forecast household spending? Evidence from the European Commission Business and Consumer Surveys', *Southern Economic Journal*, **72** (3), 136–44.

Lucas, Robert E. (1981), *Studies in Business-Cycle Theory*, Cambridge, MA: MIT Press.

Ludvigson, S. (2004), 'Consumer confidence and consumer spending', *Journal of Economic Perspectives*, **18** (2), 29–44.

Maki, D. (2001), 'Household debt and the Tax Reform Act of 1986', *American Economic Review*, **91** (3), 305–20.

Minsky, Hyman (1975), *John Maynard Keynes*, New York: Columbia University Press.

Modigliani, F. (1944), 'Liquidity preference and the theory of interest and money', *Econometrica*, **14** (1), 45–88.

Moore, B. (1988), 'The endogenous money supply', *Journal of Post Keynesian Economics*, **10** (3), 373–85.

Patinkin, Don (1965), *Money, Interest, and Prices*, second edition, New York: Harper & Row.

Pigou, A. (1943), 'The classical stationary state', *Economic Journal*, **53**, 434–351.

Soman, D. and A. Cheema (2002), 'The effect of credit on spending decisions: the role of credit limit and credibility', *Marketing Science*, **21** (1), 32–54.

Tang, K. (2006), 'The wealth effect of housing on aggregate consumption', *Applied Economics Letters*, **13** (3), 189–211.

Von Mises, Ludwig (1953), *The Theory of Money and Credit*, New Haven, CT: Yale University Press.
Watkins, J. (2000), 'Corporate power and the evolution of consumer credit', *Journal of Economic Issues*, **34** (4), 909–33.
Wray, L.R. (1991a), 'Boulding's balloons: a contribution to monetary theory', *Journal of Economic Issues*, **25** (1), 1–20.
Wray, L.R. (1991b), 'Savings, profits, and speculation in capitalist economies', *Journal of Economic Issues*, **25** (4), 951–75.

APPENDIX 1A   WHY DOES SAVING MATTER?

Saving . . . is a mere residual. Assuming decisions to invest become effective, they must in doing so either curtail consumption or expand income. Thus the act of investment cannot help but causing the residual or margin, which we call saving, to increase by a corresponding amount.

J.M. Keynes (1936, p. 64)

The analysis or modeling of household saving behavior obviously springs from the belief that saving (as a macroeconomic magnitude) is something meaningful or consequential. The statement that saving is important is not especially controversial. Certainly the majority of professional economists will not need convincing on this point. So why bother developing a rather extended argument on the question of 'why saving matters'? The reasons are twofold. First, the issue of the nature and economic significance of saving constitutes a main area of rupture separating post-Keynesianism from the dominant strains of macroeconomic analysis. Second, the arguments contained in the chapters that follow are predicated upon, and informed by, a particular view of saving, and it is therefore necessary to make the reader familiar with this point of view.

Saving and Production Possibilities

The pace of capital accumulation is indisputably related to the division of resources between consumer goods and capital goods (including public overhead capital or infrastructure). In the 'special' case of full employment, an increase in consumption must involve a sacrifice or opportunity cost which is measurable (in theory) by foregone production of capital goods. Understood in the full employment (classical) context, saving (in the verb sense) means the act of freeing up resources for alternative use by refraining from the purchase of items with positive elasticities of production.[1] Less spending for consumer goods and services, or equivalently, more saving, ostensibly increases the relative return to employment of resources in the production of capital goods and thus catalyzes a shift in that direction. Neale has noted that, according to this logic, 'the biggest non-consumers, and therefore the biggest savers, must be paupers, for they consume less than even the most miserly middle-income and rich people' (Neale 1991, p. 1161).

A more realistic view holds that many, if not most, consumer goods industries possess – even at cyclical peaks – reserve capacity that could be put into use with fairly minimal (diminishing returns) impact on unit cost. Excess capacity in investment goods industries also tends to be the norm – with occasional bottlenecks developing here and there.[2] The implications of 'not-consuming' with respect to capital goods production are obviously much different in the 'general case' as compared with the special, full-employment case. Where reserve capacity exists, no sacrifice in terms of reduced consumption is required.

What is Saving?

The term 'saving' describes a thing as well as an action – that is, saving is both noun and verb. The 'entity' aspect of saving can be clarified by use of John Adams's subtractivist principle (Adams 1991). Specifically, let A denote 'assets after' and B 'assets before'. Let $A - B = C$, where C is 'saving during'. Thus the term in its noun sense signifies a net increase in the stock of assets occurring between two points in time. The question is: what assets? Furthermore, does it matter for analytical purposes whether saving is constituted of concrete things (e.g. buildings, machinery) as opposed to non-producibles (such as bank deposits)?

Note that the term 'saving' is also used to designate what many think of as a highly consequential activity – that is, the voluntary act of freeing up 'resources' for alternative uses. Saving is conceived as the substance produced by the activity of saving – that is, the action of refraining from the use/consumption/destruction of resources at one's disposal. But this raises another conundrum. Specifically, is the saver abstaining from the use of economic resources (land, labor and capital) or from the use of monetary claims to goods? And does it matter? Or, is the exhaustion of monetary resources equivalent to, or impossible without, the use of real resources?

Primitive versus Modern Concept of Saving

Saving is a slippery concept, largely because its meaning has evolved. We need to be careful to distinguish between the primitive and modern (Keynesian) concepts of saving. Saving (in the noun sense) is, whether in its primitive or modern incarnation, the difference between two flows, and is itself a flow – that is, a variable measured per unit of time. In the primitive case, saving is the difference between the flow of physical output produced and consumption during an accounting period, where 'consumption' takes on its primitive connotation – meaning the destruction of use-values intrinsic to commodities.[3] What we call today 'depreciation' is simply a measure of a specific type of primitive consumption – the destruction in one (accounting) period of the stock of manmade instruments of production due to normal wear and tear, accidents, fires or acts of nature. By contrast, modern saving is the difference between two intangible, monetary flows – income and spending. Keynes defined saving as 'equal to the excess of income over consumption' (Keynes 1936, p. 63). Thus saving is on the one hand defined as the net addition to the stock of producible, useful things, or alternatively, as the net increase in unexercised liquid (intangible) claims to goods. While the use of the term 'saving' by contemporary economists is invariably meant to designate the latter, the dominant point of view attests to the lingering influence of the primitive concept.

Why Does Saving Matter? The Standard View

There exists a yawning gap between standard and post-Keynesian/institutional views with respect to the nature and significance of saving. A thoroughgoing treatment of alternative views would require a full-length article, if not a book. Nevertheless, we shall attempt to explain the main points of controversy here. The standard and post-Keynesian literature also feature divergent views as to the economic implications of the decline of personal savings rates (as highlighted in Figure 1.5 above). We begin with a sequence of postulates intended to convey the essence of the orthodox (classical) view:

1. Saving materializes as an effect of acts of volitional abstinence by income recipients.
2. Saving is a necessary precondition for investment.
3. Saving is the source of finance or 'loanable funds'.

Postulates (2) and (3), if valid, establish a powerful logic for making saving an object of public policy. It stands to reason that, if the growth rate of the economy's productive apparatus is limited by saving, the community has an interest in regulating its level.[4]

Moreover, postulate (1) suggests that policies that reward (incentivize) abstinence and punish (disincentivize) consumption are indicated to get more a good thing – saving.

The loanable funds (or time preference) theory of interest will be familiar to most readers. The (real) rate of interest depends, according to this theory, on the supply of, and demand for, saving which, as was indicated by postulate (3) above, is conceived to be the fount of monies which could be borrowed to finance investment. The theory predicts that, *ceteris paribus*, a decline in household saving (a shift of the saving curve) in combination with a surge in public sector borrowing (such as we have seen during the Bush II Administration) would cause real interest rates to rise and thus have an adverse effect on domestic investment. Evidence from the post-2001 era shows no such effects, however. In fact, real interest rates fell quite

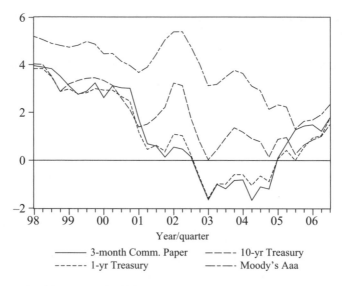

Sources: Federal Reserve Bank of New York and Bureau of Labor Statistics.

Figure 1A.1   Inflation-adjusted interest rates (%)

substantially between 2001 and 2005 (see Figure 1A.1). Defenders of loanable funds claim that the recent course of real interest rates exposes no
defect in their theory. Rather, the thought-experiment suggested above
failed to take account of two key factors, namely (1) business saving (or
retained earnings); and (2) massive flows of foreign portfolio capital into
dollar-denominated financial assets. According to figures compiled by the
OECD, corporate saving as a percentage of GDP has remained fairly stable
at 3 to 4 percent since 1990, though there has been a slight increase since
2001.[5] But the rise of corporate saving has fallen well short of what would
have been required to offset the decrease in household saving (as described
in Table 4.1 in Chapter 4), not to mention the disappearance of federal government saving and ballooning federal deficits after 2000. That leaves a
decisive role for the influx of foreign portfolio capital, or what is evidently
considered by some to be the same thing – foreign saving – in explaining (in
the loanable funds context) the recent course of real interest rates. As the
story is told, a salient aspect of global economic integration is the development of institutions and the proliferation of technologies that enable the
cross-national mobility of saving. Thus there is a tendency for the deepen-
ing of channels through which saving can flow to its highest value use – irre-
spective of national boundaries. The cross-national mobility of saving is
equivalent to the repeal of Walras's Law at the country level – that is, aggre-

gate (domestic) spending is no longer constrained by aggregate (domestic) income.

Seed-corn Analogy

Saving in the primitive sense is simply the proportion of output produced in a given period that is not (in the primordial sense) consumed. Economic theory treats saving as volitional – that is, whatever the value of saving turns out to be is at least partly a cumulative effect of a great number of individual decisions to defer consumption. Which raises the question – if saving *is* volitional, precisely *when* do decisions to save occur? That is, is the question of the share of output left over at the end of the production period effectively settled before production starts, or can saving decisions be taken *ex post* – meaning after current period production plans have been finalized? The answer depends on whether output produced is divided between consumables and non-consumables. The character of non-consumables is such that their use-value cannot be (excepting catastrophic events) completely exhausted at the end of the period in which they are produced. If the production of non-consumables is possible, then (1) saving decisions are made *ex ante*; and (2) whatever agencies holding the power to control the division of resources employed between the production of consumables and non-consumables also control society's saving. Viewed in this context, saving is fundamentally a decision about *what* to produce.

By contrast, the seed-corn story abstracts from the consumables–non-consumables dichotomy. If goods produced are not equally suited to the satisfaction of immediate needs or for roundabout production, production and saving decisions are disjoined – that is, decisions to produce and to save not coeval, executed by separate agencies, and conditioned by disparate factors.

Finance and Funding

Loanable funds is an abstinence theory for a monetary economy. The idea that the pace of investment (or capital goods production) is limited by contemporaneous, volitional acts of abstinence among income recipients is deeply ingrained. Indeed, the common understanding of saving and investment goes a long way toward explaining social tolerance of gross disparities in the distribution of income and wealth. However, we shall attempt to explain why the price and availability of finance – defined as the liquidity necessary to bridge the interval between the disbursement of factor costs and the receipt of income within a production period (see Davidson 1986) – have nothing to do with *how much* people save, but are related to *how* they save or the strength of their preferences for liquid stores of value.

Production takes time, disbursements and receipts are not coordinated, and therefore firms (including capital goods producers) experience cash-flow problems. Enlargement of the scale of output depends on the readiness of the banking system to expand its deposit liabilities in accommodation of the financing needs of firms. But can banks expand their liabilities with no prior increase in saving? That is, does the proportion of income spent impinge on the price and or/availability of bank-intermediated finance?[6] Keynes's answer was unambiguous:

> Saving has no special efficacy, as compared with consumption in releasing cash and restoring liquidity . . . [T]here is, therefore, just as much reason for adding current consumption to the rate of increase of new bank money in reckoning the flow of cash available to provide new 'finance,' as there is for added saving. (Keynes 1973, p. 233)

A bank that unilaterally expands its deposit liabilities increases its exposure to adverse clearings. Applying this principle at the aggregate level involves a fallacy of composition. When the banks expand in concert, an adverse clearing for the system as a whole can only develop if: (1) there is tightening by the central bank; or (2) there is an increased preference for currency holdings by the public. The preceding is a restatement of the 'Boulding's balloons' principle discussed earlier.

Capital goods manufactures need finance. Capital goods buyers need funding, or 'an "investment fund" for the buyer to make payment to the seller on the delivery date' (Davidson 1986, p. 103). Investment may be funded internally (by use of retained earnings or, equivalently, business saving) or externally, in which case underwriters will be required to float securities in primary issue markets. The successful funding of investment requires first of all a stock of liquid assets that can be disbursed for the purchase of newly issued securities. But this much is assured. Why? Because, once the production of capital goods is complete, such goods represent a share of output that is not available for purchase or use by households. At the same time, the production of capital goods requires the employment of real resources and the distribution of factor income. Thus the flow of capital goods production within a given time interval must generate an equivalent flow of real saving which takes the shape of unexercised liquid claims to goods. This is what Keynes meant in defining saving as a residual.[7] It can be demonstrated that the net increase in liquid assets during an accounting period is invariant with respect to consumption expenditure, *ceteris paribus*. A greater or lesser propensity to consume merely alters the distribution of liquid assets across the balance sheets of households, firms, government units and foreigners – but it does not change the absolute amount available for the purchase of new issues. The task of underwriters is to 'capture' saving (which is widely scattered across domestic and foreign balance sheets) through the marketing of new securities. Of course primary security issues may be undersubscribed – but this is not owing to any lack of saving.

Role of Liquidity Preference

The liquidity preference theory originates from a key insight: in mature industrialized economies the flow of new security issues in any relatively short time interval is rather miniscule in proportion to the enormous stock of previously issued securities. G.L.S. Shackle explained the implications of Keynes's insight:

> Against these pre-existing masses, always poised for release onto the market by any sufficient movement of the interest rate, little influence can be exerted by the quantities of new bonds issued, or of savings newly accumulated, within a brief past interval, in the hands of those waiting to return them, via purchase, of new bond issues, to the business community. It is thus the interest rate . . . can be too high to allow for full employment. (Shackle 1967, p. 207)

Yields of securities dealt in organized secondary markets are not determined by the rate of time preference (in interaction with the marginal productivity of capital), but rather by the preferences of the wealth-holding public as between money, near monies, longer-dated bonds and shares, and other stores of value. Given the powerful influence of central banks at the short end of the term structure, the 'state of liquidity preference' is of greater import for the price (and availability) of funding as compared with finance.

Most agree that the price of finance (the rate of interest on short-term bank loans) is established by a markup over the cost of attracting liabilities – most notably large-denomination certificates of deposit held mainly by yield-sensitive institutional depositors. Yields of non-transactions deposit must be competitive with those offered by near monies (Treasury bills or commercial paper, for example) – otherwise, banks face the danger of disintermediation. The power of central banks to influence banks' cost of funds derives largely from their holdings of a strategic asset – short-dated, gilt-edged securities, the yields of which form the rock bottom of the complex of (domestic) interest rates.

Old securities are substitutable with new issues. Undulating prices in secondary markets (produced by shifts of market sentiment for bearish to bullish or vice versa) must impinge on the prices at which comparable securities are placed in primary issue markets. Rising liquidity preference – interpreted as a general flight of portfolio controllers from securities characterized by low capital uncertainty (e.g. uncertainty of future value due to market revaluation) to low capital uncertainty assets like Treasury bills or bank deposits – can frustrate plans to fund investment via new security offerings.[9] For example, the collapse in the volume of initial public offerings in 1999 was all about the broad-based plunge in prices of (previously issued) small capitalization stocks and had nothing whatsoever to do with household thrift.

Why Does Saving Matter? An Alternative View

Chapter 2 presents the argument that the decline of the personal saving rate should be (partly) interpreted as an effect of sharply rising inequalities in income and wealth, in combination with widened credit availability. Post-Keynesians are mainly concerned with saving rates because they provide (at a disaggregated level) a valuable index of the economic health and psychological wellbeing of households. A household with positive saving enjoys a surplus of income flows relative to those which are just sufficient to maintain a lifestyle that is 'culturally adequate' (as defined in Chapter 2). The capacity of individuals to plan for the future, to survive misfortune, and generally to enjoy some degree of control over their lives, is laid bare in the statistical sense by the fraction of income receipts not spent. The satisfactoriness of the saving rate as a social welfare measure improves as we move to successively lower income levels. That the average saving rate of households in the bottom two income quintiles has decreased sharply since the 1980s tells us that, on balance, income growth for these families has failed to keep pace with the rising cost of culturally adequate consumption regimens. The personal and social costs of this development, in terms of stress and anxiety, frustrated hopes, family strife, divorce, bankruptcy and so on, are likely to have been enormous. In summary, saving matters (at the micro level) because it provides a simple measure of changes over time in the toll levied on individuals by consumerism.

NOTES

1. A good is producible – that is, has a positive elasticity of production – if its production entails the employment of real resources. By contrast, the demand for money or bonds requires a zero or negligible employment of real resources.
2. A contemporary example is the shortage of construction cranes attributable largely to the colossal Chinese construction boom. Reports of crane shortages and stalled construc-

tion projects proliferated in the summer of 2007. Crane manufacturers such as Hitachi–Sumitomo currently have a major backlog of orders.
3. Keynesian economics brought forth an analytically important redefinition of consumption. That is, before Keynes consumption was not understood to be the same thing as 'consumers' expenditure'. As Kenneth Boulding explained, 'Up to the time of Marshall, the meaning of the word "consumption" was fairly clear. It meant, what it literally means, the destruction of commodities – i.e., of valuable things – in the way they were intended to be destroyed' (Boulding 1945, pp. 155–6).
4. On a related note, the fact that the maximum marginal rate on capital gains income (most of which accrue to very-high-income individuals) in the USA is currently set at 15 percent (as compared with 35 percent on wage and salary income) is typically defended on the grounds that, because it creates incentives for saving, it will also stimulate investment. Feldstein (1989, 2005) is a well-known expositor of this view.
5. See Figure 4.1, page 86.
6. Terzi (1986–87) used flow-of-funds analysis to illustrate the independence of bank-intermediated finance from saving.
7. Wray writes that 'neither the savers not the saving can be identified until *after the fact*, which is to say that neither the savers nor the saving can exist until nonconsumption spending has occurred. While it is true that nonconsumption spending must create income-flow savings simultaneously, the direction of causation is clear . . . [C]redit for . . . savings lies with the spender and not with the saver' (Wray 1992, p. 257, italics in the original). See also Brown (1993).
8. Davidson writes: 'Normally, the capital goods producer has an established customer–client relationship with his commercial banker. Consequently, the signed purchase order contract is usually more than sufficient collateral for the commercial banker to be willing to commit the bank to finance the producer's production costs via a short-term (working capital) loan for the duration of the production period' (Davidson 1986, p. 104).
9. I have argued elsewhere that rising liquidity preference should be understood as an increase preference for assets which offer low capital uncertainty, of which money proper is merely one category. Rising liquidity preference, or a 'flight to safety' by portfolio controllers, typically results in a *decrease* in the yields of near monies. See Brown (2003–04).

REFERENCES

Adams, J. (1991), 'Surplus, surplus, who's got the surplus? The subtractivist fallacy in orthodox economics', *Journal of Economic Issues*, **25** (1), 187–97.
Boulding, K. (1945), 'The consumption concept in economic theory', *American Economic Review*, **35** (2), 1–14.
Brown, C. (1993), 'The abstinence theory, liquidity preference, and the saving–investment nexus', *Journal of Economics*, **19** (2), 31–9.
Brown, C. (2003–04), 'Toward a reconcilement of liquidity preference and endogenous money', *Journal of Post Keynesian Economics*, **26** (2), 323–37.
Davidson, P. (1986), 'Finance, funding, saving, and investment', *Journal of Post Keynesian Economics*, **9** (1), 101–10.
Feldstein, M. (2005), 'Raise taxes on saving? Tell Joe it ain't so', *Wall Street Journal* (Eastern edition), 8 December, A16.
Feldstein, M. (1989), 'Tax policy for the 1990s: personal saving, business investment', *American Economic Review*, **79** (2), 108–13.
Keynes, John M. (1936), *The General Theory of Employment, Interest, and Money*, New York: Harcourt Brace Jovanovich.

Keynes, John M. (1973), *The Collected Writings of John Maynard Keynes*, vol. XIV, ed. Donald Moggridge, London: Macmillan.

Neale, W.C. (1991), 'Who saves? The rich, the penniless, and everyone else', *Journal of Economic Issues*, **25** (4), 1160–66.

Shackle, G.L.S. (1967), *The Years of High Theory*, Cambridge: Cambridge University Press.

Terzi, A. (1987–88), 'The independence of finance from saving: a flow-of-funds interpretation', *Journal of Post Keynesian Economics*, **9** (2), 188–97.

Wray, L.R. (1992), 'What is saving and who gets the credit (blame)?', *Journal of Economic Issues*, **26** (1), 256–62.

2. The household debt surge and the theory of habit selection

A principal thesis of this book is that increasing income inequality gives rise to a greater dependence on credit for the maintenance of consumption expenditure. A corollary to this thesis is that the (negative) effects of widening income disparities (with respect to output and employment) are likely to be more consequential if consumers are antipathetic to debt. The broad-based consumerism of modern life has therefore been enabled by a gradual leveling of social and psychological barriers to credit-financed spending. Indeed, many consumers today exhibit a willingness to borrow that nearly all among the previous generation would have found appalling. The purpose of this chapter is to give a theoretical explanation of this crucial development.

The thesis is advanced that, in general, people borrow because their incomes are not adequate to afford a culturally sufficient market basket of goods and services, where cultural sufficiency signifies the individual capacity to 'match goods to classes of social occasions [the aim of which is to] help create the social universe and find a creditable place in it' (Douglas 1982, pp. 25–6). Soaring income inequality is associated with expanding consumer credit use and decreased saving for two (main) reasons: (1) it increases the disparity for many between actual income and the income required to purchase a culturally sufficient basket of goods and services; and (2) by actuating ever more public opulence by social elites, rising income skewness may diminish the cultural sufficiency inhering in a given array of consumer items. The eradication of lingering Protestant antagonisms to credit-financed consumption was, however, a necessary condition for the full-scale emergence of consumerism (Watkins 2000). The household debt surge is the balance sheet manifestation of a reordered social habit structure. Making sense of the household debt bubble therefore requires an understanding of the process by which parallel habit systems come to be established and reconfigured. The phenomenon under examination here provides an opportunity for the application of the institutional theory of habit formation, which has lately been upgraded with new knowledge from neuroscience, anthropology, evolutionary biology and evolutionary psychology.

Consumer credit is the inevitable counterpart of consumerism. We seek to develop the theme that the consumer ethos is best understood as a cultural adjustment to a new system of economic organization – one that requires for its survival the absorption of vast quantities of output. Thrift and the satiability of wants militate against the requisite recycling of incomes for consumer expenditure. Cultural change is necessary to put thrift in abeyance. We explore the role of the modern incarnation of Veblen's 'leisure class' (Veblen 1899) in catalyzing broad shifts in consumption behavior. The maintenance of output and employment depends also on the establishment of new (or hitherto unknown) types of wants, an activity that employs some of society's most able individuals.

2.1   THE THEORY OF HUMAN NATURE AND 'CONCEPTUAL INTEGRATION'

The model of consumption developed here is an attempt at *conceptual integration* or 'the principle that the various disciplines within the behavioral and social sciences should make themselves mutually consistent, and consistent with what is known in the natural sciences as well' (Cosmides et al. 1992, p. 4). The project starts from the premise that the Keynesian and institutional approaches to consumption are in need of update or rearticulation in light of the new knowledge in fields such as anthropology, evolutionary psychology and neuroscience. Most human behavior (including spending behavior) is, according to the institutional view, habit-driven and culturally regulated. Consumer preference is not immutable, but is changeable by the reaction of instincts to external stimuli or conditioning. In fact, the use of the term 'consumer preference' is misleading in that we are claiming that most of what people do, and most of what they think about what they do, is a function of habit. The emergent catholic amenability to the sale of IOUs is accordingly understood as a shift in the structure of personal habits. Thus we are endeavoring to explain: (1) how habits come to be established, and in particular the role of instincts and culture in the formation of habits; (2) the process by which entrenched habits of behavior and thought are displaced by new ones; and (3) the high degree of correlation observed in the personal habits of those belonging to, or residing within, a given culture, social class, occupation, age group or other relevant category.

Hans Jensen has asserted that 'all socioeconomic theories contain, either implicitly or explicitly, a theory of human nature' (Jensen 1987, p. 1039). The institutional concept of human nature, which we may refer to as the 'instinct–habit–culture' (I–H–C) theorem, is far removed from the maximizing, choice-consistent, informed 'representative agent' that comprises the elementary particle of classical economic thought. Though many non-economists view *homo economicus* as a quaint relic, his elite status within the field of economics endures.[1] This phenomenon is explained partly by the importance of 'economic man' as supplier of appropriate 'initial conditions' to practitioners of the axiomatic approach to economic theory. As mathematical proofs of existence, uniqueness and stability (and the social optimality of market resource allocation) cannot be deduced from functions lacking the necessary curvature and continuity properties, axiomatic analysis is partly the search for assumptions (or axioms) about producer or consumer behavior that give the profit or utility functions the requisite qualities. Gerard Debreu made this plain in his seminal *Theory of Value*:

> [G]iven a set completely pre-ordered by preferences, does there exist an increasing real-valued function on that set [a utility function]? The answer to the existence question is: not necessarily so. The main object of this section will therefore be to give an assumption on preferences . . . from which the existence of a utility function can be proved. In fact, this function would be of little interest if it were not continuous; the assumption on preferences should therefore enable one to prove that there is a *continuous* utility function. (Debreu 1959, pp. 55–6)

Debreu's writing implies that the concept of human nature embedded in the 'best developed theory' (the Arrow–Debreu version of Walrasian general equilibrium) has been selected on the criterion of mathematical tractability and not correspondence to empirical observation or conceptual integration as defined above. Similarly, the application of utility theory to problems such as addiction or racial discrimination depends on preferences that are stable and 'exogenous' (see Stigler and Becker 1977). The theorem that consumer tastes are mutable and subject to cultural influences is not, or at least should not be, controversial. At the same time, fidelity to an obsolescent, Benthamite view of man is a necessary condition for the deployment of techniques that, for many, define the essence of economic 'science'. Although the I–H–C theorem stands in much closer relation to our present state of knowledge about man and society, it furnishes a poor platform for the use of traditional economic methods. If Robert E. Lucas (1980, p. 700) is correct in claiming that 'progress in economic thinking means getting better and better abstract, analogue models, not better verbal descriptions about the world', then the present analysis may contribute little. Let the reader be the judge.[2]

2.2   THE INSTINCT–HABIT–CULTURE THEOREM

Our objective is to achieve a better understanding of spending and saving behavior. The analysis starts from the position that '[a] real understanding of the problem of consumer behavior must begin with a full recognition of the social character of consumption patterns' (Duesenberry 1967, p. 19). The main outlines of our theory can be summarized as follows:

1.   'Human nature' is a term used to describe the cluster of *instincts* which, as a consequence of the process of natural selection, have achieved primacy and denote the essence of the species.
2.   Human behavior is *instinct-driven* – that is, human action is motivated (consciously or unconsciously) by instinct-based needs.
3.   There is a strong tendency for the repetition of behaviors that produce satisfactory results, where 'satisfactory results' connotes the assuagement of instinctual desires by canonical means.
4.   Man's 'habitual bent' ripens repeated actions into 'habits'. Thus man's 'makeup' consists of a complex structure of habits that give rise to predictable behavioral routines.
5.   Institutions, by prescribing or reinforcing some behaviors and proscribing others, shape the structure of habits and give them a social character.
6.   A shift in the social structure of habits (including spending and saving habits) is (in the normal case) effectuated by institutional (or cultural) change. A theory of institutional change is therefore necessary to explain changing patterns of household behavior.

The institutional theory of human behavior is firmly based on Charles Darwin's theory of evolution, which contains three ideas: natural selection, heredity and variation. Israel Rosenfield and Edward Ziff (2006, p. 12) summarize the modern version of the theory:

> Small random changes – variations – occur in organisms through the mutations of genes, and when these changes give an organism a greater chance of survival, they persist from one generation to the next through natural selection. That is, organisms with traits better adapted to the environment they inhabit will have better reproductive success than other members of the same species that do not possess the advantageous traits. In each successive generation, then, an ever larger proportion of the species in question will possess the mutation that produces the advantageous traits.[3]

Instinct is the hereditary tendency toward particular types of behavior in response to certain stimuli. The psychologist Jacob Kantor wrote that 'an instinct being a primary act and therefore entirely "undebauched by learning," must be looked upon as one of the primary functional elements in the embryological development of the human organism' (Kantor 1920, p. 51). Veblen viewed instincts as 'the prime movers in human behavior . . . [that] make anything worth while, and out of their working emerge not only the purpose and efficiency of life, but its substantial pleasures and pains as well' (Veblen 1964, p. 1). The gears of natural selection turn very slowly, such that the aggregate of instincts that sum to 'human nature' are those that proved most useful in solving problems affecting reproduction faced by Pleistocene hunter-gatherers. Cosmides et al. (1992, p. 5) write:

> The few thousand years since the scattered appearance of agriculture is only a small stretch in evolutionary terms, less than 1% of the two million years our ancestors spent as Pleistocene hunter-gatherers . . . Therefore, it is improbable that our species evolved complex adaptations to agriculture, let alone to post industrial society. Moreover, the available evidence strongly supports [the] view of a single, universal pan-human design, stemming from our long existence as hunter-gatherers.

According to this view, the social instinct – manifest in a desire for acceptance and recognition, a capacity for shame, and a fear of criticism or ostracism – became a salient aspect of the human psychological makeup because those individuals or groups possessed of a strong social proclivity gained advantages *vis-à-vis* those not so well endowed, and thus achieved greater reproductive success. Instinct motivates action toward a definite goal, and we may differentiate among instincts on the basis of the aims to which action is purposefully directed.

> [W]hat distinguishes one instinct from another is that each sets up a characteristic purpose, aim, or object to be attained, different from the objective end of any other instinct. Instinctive action is teleological, *consciously* so, and the teleological scope and aim of each instinctive propensity differs characteristically from all the rest. (Veblen 1964, p. 3, italics added)

Instinct-based actions may be referred to as 'behavioral expressions', which are successful or unsuccessful depending on the results achieved. A given instinct may have numerous behavioral expressions, some of which may entail the purchase of goods or services. For example, the security instinct may cause the individual to fasten her seat belt, to purchase a home security system, to use a sunscreen or to avoid passive cigarette smoke. The social instinct is capable of producing a myriad of behaviors, from dieting to taking up yoga. Emulation has multiple representations, from the copying of better fishing or agricultural methods to the imitation of dress or sporting activities.

Institutional economics starts from the premise that '*most* of what people do is *governed* by the institutions of their society' (Neale 1987, p. 1178). Institutions are 'systems of established and prevalent social rules that structure social interactions. Language, money, law, systems of weights and measures, table manners, and firms (and other organizations) are thus all institutions' (Hodgson 2006, p. 2). Institutions are identifiable by three characteristics: (1) people doing; (2) the rules 'giving the activities repetition, stability, predictable order'; and (3) folkviews, which '*justify* the activities or *explain* why they are going on, how they are related, what is thought important and what unimportant in the patterns of regularity' (Neale 1987, pp. 1182–3). Institutions are social technologies that rein in anti-social human impulses and facilitate the 'extended order of human cooperation' (Hayek 1988, p. 119).

We now develop the following arguments: (1) discovery of successful behavioral expressions necessitates learning; (2) there is a tendency toward the repetition of successful behavioral expressions – a process that leads to habit; and (3) the range of successful behavioral expressions is defined/circumscribed by institutional factors. It follows from points (1) to (3) that institutions intervene in the process of habit formation by delimiting the set of successful and permissible behavioral expressions. It also stands to reason that individuals functioning within a given institutional nexus will display congruent habit structures. The term 'congruent habit structures' is equivalent to 'custom'.[4] Custom, manifest in both parallel behavior and thought, requires education.

The process of adjustment to life in a community is a long and arduous one. Social life imposes the unremitting requirement of conformity with codes of behavior, the miscellany of what one 'may do, may not do, must do, and must not do' in manifold forums (e.g. school, city council, the grocery store, the workplace, the neighborhood organization, the sports arena). But society's rules are not programmed into the genes. They must be learned. An infant making loud noises at church does not draw reproach, whereas a six-year-old is deemed mature enough to have learned the standards of decorum during worship. For the six and older crowd, boisterous public displays are an inappropriate behavioral expression of an instinctive need. Note also that a 45-year-old, having had the opportunity to perform a much larger number of repetitions at church services, is more likely than a six-year-old to maintain good behavior without conscious thought – that is, as a matter of habit.

The capacity of an individual to function effectively within society depends crucially on the emergence of a beneficent habit structure.[5] Dewey has defined habit as 'an *acquired* [italics added] predisposition to *ways* or modes of response' (Dewey 1922, p. 42). Research in neuroscience has established that habit formation is quite literally an aspect of brain development. There is evidence that the striatum of basal ganglia deep within the brain is implicated in learning and the establishment of routines that enable humans to operate on 'automatic pilot' in many aspects of life – for example, one may think about a paper when washing the dishes (Graybiel and Kubota 2003; Yin and Knowlton 2006). Repeated behaviors do not occur without a neurological 'green light' or reward furnished by neurotransmitters such as dopamine. Dopamine, serotonin and other neurotransmitters are chemicals that provide positive reinforcement for behavioral expressions. Although the neuroscience is complex, we can nevertheless say that, as a rule, behaviors that are chemically rewarded will be repeated, and those not receiving a reward will not. The crucial thing to understand for our purposes is the importance of external cues in producing the neurological reaction necessary for habit selection. Evidence from animal studies supports the view that approval or reward has a powerful effect on learning because it stimulates the production of neurotransmitters (De Waal 1996).

If behavior is habit-driven, and if most of what people do is governed by institutions, then institutions must be the mechanism for the selection of habits. An obvious example of an institution that shapes the habits of nearly all individuals within its purview, and thus gives rise to correlated patterns of behavior, is the 40-hour work-week. Hodgson and Knudsen write:

> [H]abits cannot exist apart from the human organisms in which they reside. They exist on a psycho-neural substrate; they are formed and stored in the individual human nervous system. This in turn depends on the development of each individual, involving both genetic and environmental influences. Habits depend crucially upon stimuli from the social environment . . . In social evolution there are additional mechanisms to supplement habit replication, which often weed out or alter aberrant habits. Mechanisms of social conformity are particularly important. For example, if people have incentives to conform and disincentives to rebel, then these mechanisms can partially overcome the copying infidelities of habit replication. In general, social institutions help to stabilise and channel behaviour and habits. (Hodgson and Knudsen 2004, p. 289)

The names 'Anasazi' or 'Maori' designate peoples with idiosyncratic habits, social practices, values and belief systems produced by distinctive institutional schemes. The new learning in neuroscience suggests that culture wires the brains of its subjects in a unique pattern, making people think and act cognately.

Consumption, like other human behaviors, is largely a matter of routine. Habit plays the determinative role with respect to the mix of goods and services selected, as well as the timing of their purchase. The influence of habit and routine gives rise to stable, predictable patterns of consumer behavior. For example, many can accurately guess the items (and brands) their spouses will bring home from the grocery store. Demand forecasts prepared by consumer goods manufacturers and retailers owe much of their reliability to the force of consumer habit. An institutional theory must explain how habits emerge from the (repeated) performance of acts, or the adoption of belief systems, that have cultural sanction.

2.3   CONSUMPTION AND SOCIAL EMBEDDEDNESS

There are very good reasons for individuals to pay attention to their social standing. The *Wall Street Journal* editorial page mythology posits class as the outcome of an economic race in which the competitors start from more or less the same place. That is, class affiliation is a function of economic success – but not vice versa. The Horatio Alger myth derives its (putative) legitimacy from the handful of spectacular success stories in business, entertainment or athletics that can always be pointed to. For those not endowed with exceptional talent or luck (the vast majority), class affiliation is, to an important extent, prior to, and determinative of, economic success. Class membership confers advantages – it makes for a 'staggered start' in the race for prep school or university admissions, job placements, marital partners, business loans, political appointments or social invitations. Access to valuable information and the opportunity to interface with persons of influence are often denied to those who lack adequate social proximity.

It was stated earlier that the idea that preference has an ethnocentric, cultural dimension should not be controversial. Indeed, Adam Smith, J.S. Mill, F.A. Hayek and other leading lights have observed that individual tastes are molded by culture.[6] A reasonably extensive research has developed on the problem of interdependent or 'endogenous' preferences (for a review, see Bowles 1998; see also Zizzo 2003). There is plenty of evidence to show that spending behavior is correlated, especially among households within a given socio-economic class. The association of class and spending behavior is so pronounced in contemporary society that one can ordinarily establish the former based on the latter (and vice versa).

Keynes delineated two classes of human needs, namely 'those needs which are absolute in the sense that we feel them whatever the situation of our fellow humans may be, and those which are relative in the sense that we feel them only if their satisfaction lifts us above, makes us feel superior to, our fellows' (Keynes 1930, p. 365). The distinction is important because the former class of needs is satiable and therefore cannot be relied upon to generate a sufficiently robust growth of demand. A high proportion of expenditure earmarked for 'needs of the second class' is a salient feature of the affluent nations. But the change in the composition of consumer budgets between the two categories does not come about automatically – it needs culture to effectuate it.

The importance of institutions in the formation of consumer habits is revealed by a tendency toward the selection of buying routines that are generally viewed as appropriate to one's social group. As Mary Douglas puts it, 'the real moment of choosing is the choice of comrades and their way of life' (Douglas 1982, p. 455). 'Good' spending habits bring the individual into conformity with 'a set of socially prescribed patterns of *correlated* behavior' (Bush 1987, p. 1076). Institutions are systems of shared values and expectations. Membership in a particular social milieu (or 'class') means adherence to standards of education, career, income, and perhaps political outlook.[7] Class also connotes a wide array of standards of material consumption. These standards apply not only to the quantity of goods consumed but, more importantly, to their quality. People situated at disparate social strata own homes, drive cars, watch TV, drink alcoholic beverages and take vacations. Consumer 'choice' is often reducible to gradations in the quality of items that nearly everyone buys.[8] The quality of clothing, food and alcohol, automobiles, watches, consumer electronics, university degrees, leisure pursuits, vacation destinations and other consumptive items is the chief source of invidious distinction. Of course, there will be intra-class variations in the specific brands purchased, but these will often amount to the difference between Coke and Pepsi or between a Ford and Dodge pickup. The maintenance of social position compels an expenditure regimen that must be repeated and is, to a substantial degree, predetermined.

People buy things to satisfy an assortment of physiological, social and psychological needs, and the purchase of a specific item is often not connected to a single instinctual desire. Serving *foie gras* at a cocktail party sends a signal about class. But it also may cater to an acquired taste of the host. The desire for status is a powerful motive to action, and 'honorific consumption' is a culturally warranted behavioral expression of this instinctive need – at least within the present-day context.[9] The qualitative dimension of consumption is strongly conditioned by social class. An item is of high quality largely to the extent that its possession broadcasts the economic prowess of its owner. For instance, for what other conceivable purpose would people desire conspicuously placed clothing labels? The possibility of 'status goods' depends on the concordance of beliefs about quality.

The social character of 'taste' is uncovered by congruent opinions with respect to the quality and/or serviceability of goods and services. How many are prepared to doubt Duesenberry's (1967, p. 21) claim that '[i]f a large number of people were asked to rank, in order of preference, a number of different types of automobiles, houses, or cuts of meat, the rank correlation would be high'? Although few are willing to admit they are seeking prestige by the acquisition of a certain type of car, purse or watch, the enjoyment of owning these items would undoubtedly be lessened if there were no one to acknowledge or praise their quality. To be sure, the quality of merchandise and services is often appraised by objective criteria (such as price, clarity, thread count, megapixels, graduation rate, gigabytes of memory, or percentage of virgin wool). But far from confuting our basic point, it actually reinforces it. The use of objective systems of appraisal is learned, parallel, and thus institutional in nature. Informed people agree that 5.2 megapixels is better than 4.0 megapixels or that 24-carat is better than 18-carat. Qualitative standards provide a socially valid proof of the statement 'my camera is better than your camera'.

2.4   EMERGENCE OF CONSUMERISM

Veblen wrote that '[t]o a greater extent than any other known phase of culture, modern Christendom takes its complexion from its economic organization' (Veblen 1975, p. 1). Veblen's statement implies that it is possible to establish a causal link between the exigencies of modern, publicly owned corporations and an assortment of behaviors subsumed under the heading of 'consumer culture'. We are accustomed to thinking of the firm as an agency that must adjust itself to the desires of the consumer or face extinction. That is, the direction of causation runs from consumer preference to the behavior of firms – and not vice versa. Defenders of this view can point to (plausible) real-world examples to make their case. However, that 'consumer sovereignty' occasionally holds sway in the marketplace does not negate the fact that the shaping of consumer preferences and routines is a cardinal function of the modern firm. Moreover, the prevalence of consumer culture is advantageous to virtually all firms. The present problem is to explain the natural and social mechanisms that bring consumer spending habits and belief systems into coalescence with the imperatives of business.

The institution of public (or absentee) ownership was crucial in achieving the implementation of large-scale, cost-efficient production and distribution systems. Public ownership had manifold economic and social consequences that have been written about extensively. These include: (1) the transfer of economic decision-making power to the managerial elite (resulting from the separation of ownership and control); (2) a shift in distribution of society's wealth in favor of a passive share and bondholding class; and (3) the accretion of a vast stock of corporate bonds and shares. Sustaining production and employment within corporate enterprises requires perpetual validation of 'liability structures' (Minsky 1975). Under the new regime, the welfare of the community was inextricably linked to the sufficiency of corporate cash flows. Mass consumerism was a collective behavioral adaptation to the desiderata of mature capitalism. New institutional utensils were necessary to uproot the lingering 'cultural influences of Protestantism toward debt and spending' (Watkins 2000, p. 909).

The institutional transition to modern consumerism is addressed by Veblen in *The Theory of the Leisure Class*. The emulative instinct is a genetically programmed predisposition to replicate the behavior of other, usually more successful, individuals or groups. Hayek (1948) has stressed the importance of emulation in the diffusion among peoples of the species' accumulated know-how.[10] Pecuniary emulation is a particular behavioral expression of an instinctive drive – one that assumes critical importance in the era of large-scale merchandising. Pecuniary emulation comes into its own once the quality of goods possessed becomes a primary focus of invidious comparison. The leisure class, an institution that traces its genesis to the distinction between 'noble and ignoble employments', evolved to serve as the model of meritorious consumption:

> [O]ur standard of decency in expenditure, as in other ends of emulation, is set by the usage of those next above us in reputability; until, in this way, especially in any community where class distinctions are somewhat vague, all canons of reputability and decency, and all standards of consumption, are traced back by insensible gradations to the usages and habits of thought of the highest social and pecuniary class – the wealthy leisure class . . . It is evident that these canons of expenditure have much to say in determining the standard of living for any community and for any class. It is no less evident that the standard of living which prevails at any time or at any given social altitude will in its turn have much to say as to the forms which honorific expenditure will take, and as to the degree to which this 'higher' need will dominate a people's consumption. In this respect the control exerted by the accepted standard of living is chiefly of a negative character; *it acts almost solely to prevent recession from a scale of conspicuous expenditure that has once become habitual.* (Veblen 1899, pp. 105–6, italics added)

The aim of marketers is not to establish a social habit structure conducive to the survival of corporatism. Advertisers seek to sell particular brands, products or services, and often this must be accomplished by redirecting consumer expenditure away from rival brands, products or services. Nevertheless, modern marketing agencies are a decisive element in the vortex of 'reconstitutive downward causation' or scheme of institutions that 'give rise to new perceptions and dispositions of individuals' (Hodgson 2003, p. 166). Corporatism as a system is not viable without immense, continuous and predictable expenditure flows. The plastic dimension of the species – that is, the cluster of behavioral tendencies manifested by the hard core of evolved adaptive mechanisms – can be remodeled to generate behavior that, when cumulated across individuals, keeps the system thriving. Institutions, as opposed to individual preference, are the remodeling mechanism. Effective marketing consists of creating favorable or commercially advantageous behavioral expressions of instinctive needs or specialized adaptive mechanisms. Specialized adaptive mechanisms for mate selection can explain a wide range of feminine wiles, from seductive facial expressions to subtle changes in posture, gait or voice inflection. It is likely that, of the entire class of habits or behaviors related to mate selection, those involving the purchases of goods and services constitute only a small subset. Nevertheless, a vast amount of talent and resources goes toward the construction and maintenance of pathways linking specialized adaptive mechanisms for mate selection to expenditures for facial cleansers, hosiery, spas, shoes, abdominal exercisers, diet books and so forth.

The possibility of invidious comparison depends on the emergence of public forms of consumption, or what Veblen coined 'conspicuous consumption' (Veblen 1899, p. 19). Ownership of a sports car may invite invidious comparison by an anonymous passing motorist. Knowledge of differential equations will not. Public displays of goods by elites are helpful because they stimulate invidious comparison. The public character of consumption is aided by several factors, including: (1) a lack of 'strong barriers against the association among individuals of different status' (Duesenberry 1967, p. 30); (2) population mobility; and (3) the diffusion of communications technology.[11]

Veblen's work pre-dates modern advertising. The advertising industry has from its beginning been a source of controversy. Economic studies have examined the relationship between advertising and market structure, profits, costs and product prices, as well as the 'informative' or 'persuasive' nature of advertising.[12] Marketers seek to increase sales of particular goods and services. An ad campaign is successful if it redirects spending in favor of a particular good (say Duracell batteries) at the expense of substitute goods (Eveready batteries). Thus the question arises: 'Is marketing neutral with respect to aggregate consumption expenditure?' The preceding analysis suggests reasons why the answer may be 'no', that marketing may have a constructive macroeconomic effect. A chief function of modern marketing is, by the use of communications media, to facilitate invidious comparison. By the arousal of envy and covetousness, marketers assist individuals in discovering needs of which they were hitherto unaware. A less charitable view holds that the advertising industry takes on a role in the creation of new needs through shrewd manipulation of the public. Whatever the case, the women's clothing and cosmetic industries offer a fine example of this phenomenon. The beautiful female forms on the billboards, in the TV commercials, or on the magazine covers at the grocery checkout provide ample opportunity for critical self-appraisal. The aggressive selling of moisturizers, primers, lipsticks, eyeliners, polishes, waxes, dyes, fragrances and cosmetic surgery is illustrative of Galbraith's theorem that

[t]he fact that wants can be synthesized by advertising, catalyzed by salesmanship, and shaped by the discreet manipulations of the persuaders shows that they are not very urgent. A man who is hungry need never be told of his need for food. If he is inspired by his appetite, he is immune to the influence [of advertising]. (Galbraith 1958, p. 151)

Modern marketing is not strictly a matter of inciting the emulative impulse. Salesmanship targets many instinctive needs. A woman may have breast implants for fear that her spouse will lose interest. A man may have a hair transplant for similar reasons. Michelin had considerable success with a campaign emphasizing the safety of its tires. It is transparent that many beer commercials seek to arouse the sexual urges of their customer base – young men. The machinery of natural selection has not delivered the species to a state of perfect adaptation to its physical, social and technological environment. But this fact presents an opportunity for the creation of advantageous habits – advantageous to firms, that is. Writes Jason Epstein:

The vestigial adaptations to primordial rigors that have shaped human nature become troublesome, even deadly, as environments change. Take for example the human addiction to sugar and fat, the physiological basis for the worldwide success of America's fast food diet, with its beckoning aroma of sizzling meat, its sweet shakes and sodas and now the source of widespread pathology, complaint, and controversy. The evolutionary function of these ancient appetites – fat stored as a hedge against famine and sugar for quick energy to flee predators or seize prey – is now in today's much different environment morbidly maladaptive, even fatal, yet irresistibly attuned to our evolved nature, even among the abstemious Japanese whose oily salmon, tuna, and eel over sweetened rice are also an international favorite and, except for the important substitution of fish oil for animal fat, nutritionally analogous to a Big Mac and a shake. (Epstein 2004, p. 4)

People tend to establish spending routines characteristic of their peer group. The resulting lifestyle comes to be regarded as normal. Maintaining the style that one has grown accustomed to entails recurring monthly outlays for housing (or mortgage), cell phone service, cable TV, club dues, car payments and so forth. Paying bills is a repeated behavior, and thus is guided by habit. Habit matters with respect to the timing as well as the method of payment. Why do so many continue to forsake the convenience of online bill paying (or debit cards) for the old method of writing checks? Answer: habit.

Note that spending can be effected by reducing credits or increasing debits. This is equivalent to stating that we may finance our expenditures with spending power derived from income or from borrowing. Household purchases can be subdivided into two categories: (1) those purchases that should be financed out of current income (or accumulated savings); and (2) those for which it is permissible to use debt-finance. Once again, we have reasonably uniform views as to which purchases belong in categories (1) and (2), respectively. For example, nearly everyone would agree that one should not purchase grocery items on credit. On the other hand, most people place the purchase of a home, a car or a college education in category (2).

2.5   ORIGINS OF HABITUAL CREDIT USE

Borrowing becomes a habit through borrowing. The arguments developed above suggest that the emergence of a social habit structure conducive to debt-financing would have been impossible without an enlargement of socially approved borrowing opportunities. Several factors have contributed to a secular improvement of borrowing power for families located at virtually every economic station. These include: the captive finance company (see Banner 1958), changes in Federal Reserve policy regarding the rediscount of consumer receivables (see Brown 2005), credit scoring and the securitization of consumer receivables (see Brown 2007).

The arrival of the 'overspent American' (Schor 1998) as a representative type was preceded by a series of steps, with each step corresponding to the removal of a social taboo on a specific category of borrowing. The initial, crucial step was the normalization, in the 1920s, of installment financing of automobiles. The new mode of transport presented a difficult dilemma for many. To be without a car was to risk economic and social marginalization. At the same time, 'honest people did not go into debt to buy nonessentials' (Gramm 1978, p. 310). Grimes (1926, p. 8) commented that outright purchase 'involved a great inroad upon savings, upon which the thrifty man is loath to draw'. Thus a stigma was overcome because first-time car buyers determined they would rather be in debt than deplete precious liquid assets – a vital hedge against unpredictable future financial troubles.

The lesson of autos, and later furniture, household appliances and personal computers, appears to be that social attitudes are sufficiently elastic to accommodate borrowing for items once they have achieved the status of quasi-necessities. On the other hand, the aggressive marketing of credit has surely played a role shifting items such as consumer electronics up the hierarchy from 'wants' toward 'needs'. Whatever the case, taboos on specific uses of credit have evaporated one after another, the cumulative effect of which was to introduce a profound change in the psychology of household finance.

We noted above that habits are formed as an effect of repetition. Most adults, certainly those over the age of 30, have borrowed to purchase a car more than once. Even though the act of signing an installment agreement (usually) happens infrequently, the earmarking of a sum of money each month for the car payment becomes so regularized that many come to think of it as just another inconvenient fact of life – like the electric bill. Thus, while installment borrowing itself can scarcely be viewed as a habit (since the repetition required for the formation of such a habit would be lacking for any moderately sane individual), debt-servicing is an entrenched habit for the vast majority. The habit of debt repayment militates in favor of adding new debt as existing, previously issued IOUs are retired. For those accustomed to carrying debt on their balance sheets, the thought of adding more debt elicits a lesser degree of apprehension. The reason is that veteran borrowers tend to think in terms of flows – meaning the change in periodic monetary outlays claimed by debt-service – rather than stocks. We may assert, as a general principle, that the more experience a given population has with borrowing, the greater the likelihood it will increase its borrowing in reaction to a change in real income, value of real-estate holdings or pensions, or, as is discussed in the next section, the distribution of income or wealth.

A credit card holder has a pre-established line of credit that may be used at any time for the purchase of virtually any good or service. As many can attest, the opportunity for repetitive use – to buy gasoline, clothing, airline tickets, groceries and many other items – makes credit cards habit-forming. Beyond the dimension of frequent usage, the credit card habit is reinforced by the sometimes, if not often, ambiguous line between 'convenience' and 'revolving' use. That is, the person using a credit card for routine grocery purchases may feel strongly that such items ought not to be bought on credit. The decision to borrow actually comes later, when the person discovers they are not able to pay off their credit card balance in full. A countless number of credit card purchases are convenience *ex ante* and revolving *ex post*.

2.6   INEQUALITY, CULTURAL SUFFICIENCY AND SAVING

The individual preoccupation with status or relative social position is not, from the perspective of evolutionary psychology, a character defect. It is, rather, an evolved adaptive mechanism to the ancestral reality that 'falling behind one's local rivals can be lethal' (Frank 2005, p. 138). When food supplies are intermittent because of wars or acts of nature, class affiliation is frequently the difference between survival and starvation. The law of natural selection is to blame for why people do not suffer the loss of status well, and will sometimes (if not frequently) resort to extreme measures to avoid it. The key point for our purposes is that effective behavioral expressions of instinctive drives are culture- or context-specific. The proximate source of status could be hunting prowess, age, number of wives or children, college admission scores, the make of a pickup truck or the label on a woman's handbag. The purchase, use and display of goods is, for the reasons detailed above, the predominant means by which people seek to communicate their position to others in mature capitalist systems. Consumption behavior is for the same reasons a primary object of emulation.

To be culturally sufficient, a consumption regimen must comprise those items the individual requires as a matter of personal dignity. It must also provide a safeguard against social demotion. The monetary outlays entailed by the purchase of a culturally sufficient market basket of goods and services will vary according to time, place and class status. As a heuristic device, we may posit the existence of a state of socio-economic equilibrium characterized by the following properties: (1) the consumption expenditures of every person or family are just sufficient to enable each individual or family to maintain their social position relative to all other individuals or families; (2) there is a given level and distribution of (real) spending power; and (3) the market baskets of goods corresponding to cultural sufficiency reflect the cumulative effects of product innovation and marketing enterprises up to a given point and also include 'whatever the custom of the country renders it indecent for creditable people to be without' (Smith 1937). Let C_i denote the culturally sufficient level of expenditure of agent i, as defined above. In socio-economic equilibrium, the following condition would hold:

$$C = \sum_{i=1}^{n} C_i \qquad (2.1)$$

where C is total consumption expenditure and n is the number of individuals. Thus, in equilibrium, aggregate saving is given by:

$$S = Y - \sum_{i=1}^{n} C_i \tag{2.2}$$

where Y is aggregate income. The equilibrium saving ratio is given by:

$$\frac{S}{Y} = \frac{Y - \sum_{i=1}^{n} C_i}{Y} \tag{2.3}$$

Now we are prepared to ask what factors might cause a change in the equilibrium saving ratio. These fall into three categories, two of which are not mutually exclusive: (1) a change in real income or wealth; (2) a change in the distribution of purchasing power (from whatever source); and/or (3) a change in the real cost/composition of culturally sufficient market baskets.

The reader will recall that Veblen's insights were recast in Duesenberry's relative income hypothesis, which sought to reconcile the apparent contradiction (presented by time series data) between the short-run and long-run behavior of the average propensity to consume. The habitual standard of living gives a microtheoretic basis to Keynes's 'fundamental law' of consumption, particularly as it applies to a decrease of incomes that afflicts a substantial part of the community. Note also that agents enjoy greater power to resist a lifestyle retrenchment in the face of an economic downturn when the option to borrow is present. If consumer behavior conforms to Keynes's fundamental law, then a change in real income should, *ceteris paribus*, cause a change in the average propensity to consume (APC), or the ratio expressed by equation (2.3) above. Duesenberry (1949) hypothesized a normal or habitual level of consumption for each family, which is established on the basis of family income history as well as invidious comparison with families situated on the next rung of the social ladder. The force of habit prevents a full retreat of households from the lifestyles they have grown accustomed to – even in hard times. The behavior of the APC during business cycle contractions is therefore consistent with the naïve Keynesian story. Duesenberry's principal contribution lay in explaining the factors underpinning the long-run constancy of the APC, which he portrayed analytically as an 'upward drift' of the short-run (naïve) consumption in reaction to secular increases in real income. Specifically, Duesenberry argued that growth prompts a reordering of consumption habits among elites, a development that is transmitted to other segments of society by the mechanism of invidious comparison and emulation. To recast the idea with the terminology used here, the real prices of culturally sufficient market baskets are sensitive to (peak) levels of aggregate or average real income.

Duesenberry's 'ratchet hypothesis' fits the US postwar data very well until we reach the 1980s, when the distribution of income begins to change quite substantially. A counterfactual analysis of the behavior of the APC (and APS) in the USA since 1980, conditioned on knowledge of cross-sectional differences in the APC between income groups at the end of the 1970s, would most likely predict a decrease, or at least no change, in the (long-run) APC. One would have thought that, in so far as the bulk of new income growth since 1980 was concentrated among the top income percentiles – that is, those groups with the highest propensity to save – the overall ratio of saving to income would rise. However, as was described in Chapter 1, the record shows that the APS has fallen dramatically in the past quarter-century. We now endeavor to explain the falling APS on the basis of two factors: (1) the degrading effect of inequality with respect to the cultural sufficiency attached to established or habitual consumption regimens; and (2) widened credit availability which assists individuals in maintaining their consumption status when the real cost of doing so rises.

A major change in the division of liquid claims to goods cannot occur without profoundly upsetting society's delicate class structure. Rising status always comes at the expense of others. In analyzing the behavioral implications of surging inequality, we should perhaps differentiate between the fabulously wealthy, the cohort of those who are merely rich and the *nouveau riche*. Improved economic fortunes may in each case be followed by a change in the mix or quality of items of public display, or what Fred Hirsch (1976) termed 'positional goods', though it may be more evident in the latter group.[13] Frank (2005, p. 137) uses the term 'positional externalities' to describe a consumer 'arms race' ignited by a shift in 'relative consumption' which is in turn produced by increased income inequality. For the multitude, the established consumption regimen is no longer satisfactory in preventing social demotion. Frank argues that the struggle by people to restore their relative position does, in the context of the consumer society, occasion an unfortunate shift in emphasis to positional goods (such as housing and SUVs). For example, the average size of a home occupied by a middle-income family has grown by more than 50 percent since 1975. But, as Frank explains, it is not strictly a case of mansion envy:

> Increased spending at the top of the income distribution has not only imposed psychological costs on families in the middle, it has also raised the cost of achieving many basic goals. Few middle-income parents, for example, would be comfortable knowing that their children were attending below-average schools. Yet the amount that any given family must spend to avoid that outcome depends strongly on the amounts that others spend. In particular, the quality of public schools in America is closely linked to local property taxes, which in turn depend on local real estate prices. The upshot is that people cannot send their children to a public school of even average quality if they buy a home in a school district in which house prices are well below average. (Frank 2000, p. 258)

The SUV and light pickup segment provide other examples of positional externalities. Many have justified their purchase of expensive, heavy and gas-guzzling pickups or SUVs by the risk of sharing the road with pickup and SUV drivers. The evolution of the SUV segment illustrates how an intricate system of social terracing may grow out of qualitative changes in a positional or status good that many people own. It was perhaps inevitable that as the SUV industry reached maturity, the market leaders – the Chevy Blazer and Ford Explorer – would lose cachet. Ford responded with a special 'Eddie Bauer' edition of its Explorer. At about that time, the makers of luxury sedans – Acura, Infiniti, Lexus, BMW, Mercedes – entered the high-margin SUV bonanza. The SUV is today the most visible status-marker in contemporary American life. It also is a major contributor to the growth of consumer debt.

Positional externalities levy a brutal emotional toll on youth – even on those whom some among the older generation would view as spoiled rotten. Inundated with TV, web and magazine images of young people living the good life, and in many cases surrounded by peers who flash expensive clothing, electronics, cars, athletic equipment or other positional goods, the contemporary American youth needs a lot of stuff to elude social oblivion.[14] Inspection of university parking lots reveals that, even at modestly priced state schools, many students drive expensive vehicles. The spiraling price of a suitable consumption basket has many students working long hours and running up big debts.

To restate the argument: rising income inequality gives 'winners' the monetary wherewithal to consolidate and aggrandize their status by way of conspicuous consumption, a circumstance that perforce abates the cultural sufficiency derived from old buying routines. The post-1995 debt surge is (partly) a cumulative effect of individual efforts to preserve relative position by the expedient of borrowing.

2.7 CONCLUDING REMARKS

The principal thesis advanced here was that the recent expansion of household debt liabilities in the USA should be understood as the balance sheet efflux of a reordered social habit structure. The chapter sought to make the debt surge comprehensible by the application of an upgraded or modern version of the institutional theory of habit selection.

A fundamental theorem of institutional thought is that new (or modified) social habit structures, as manifest in rearranged (but parallel) behavioral patterns, are not possible without institutional change. Thus the question arises: what causes institutions to change? The solution to the problem proposed above is perhaps more derivative of Marx than of institutionalism. That is, we may think of household spending, saving and borrowing habits as components of a Marxian 'superstructure' unique to the contemporary economy. Particular emphasis was given to the role of institutions in reshaping habit structures and belief systems to fit the collective interests of society's dominant power cohort (in Marxian terms, the 'base'). Thus it is not inaccurate to state that the culture of borrowing flourishes because it serves the objectives of those at the locus of social control (elite financial and business organizations) for people to borrow.[15] After all, who can dispute the fact that these units are responsible for the allocation of vast resources for the development of a relentless, ubiquitous institutional machinery that exhorts people to borrow and spend?

NOTES

1. Veblen criticized classical theory largely on the basis that it harbored an outdated concept of human nature:

    > In all the received formulations of economic theory, whether at the hands of English economists or those of the Continent, the human material with which the inquiry is concerned is conceived in hedonistic terms; that is to say, in terms of a passive and substantially inert and immutably given human nature. The psychological and anthropological preconceptions of the economists have been those which were accepted by the psychological and social sciences some generations ago. The hedonistic conception of man is that of a lightning calculator of pleasures and pains who oscillates like a homogeneous globule of desire of happiness under the impulse of stimuli that shift him about the area, but leave him intact. He has neither antecedent nor consequent. He is an isolated definitive human datum, in stable equilibrium except for the buffets of the impinging forces that displace him in one direction or another. Self-imposed in elemental space, he spins symmetrically about his own spiritual axis until the parallelogram of forces bears down upon him, whereupon he follows the line of the resultant. When the force of the impact is spent, he comes to rest, a self-contained globule of desire as before. Spiritually, the hedonistic man is not a prime mover. He is not the seat of a process of living, except in the sense that he is subject to a series of permutations enforced upon him by circumstances external and lien to him. (Veblen 1898, p. 391)

2. Samuel Bowles notes that the primitive Hobbesian conception of man

    > neatly elides the influence of social arrangements on the process of human development and thus greatly simplifies the task of economic theory. But the scope of economic inquiry is thereby truncated in ways which restrict its explanatory power, policy relevance, and ethical coherence. If preferences are affected by policies or institutional arrangements we study, we can neither accurately predict nor coherently evaluate the consequences of new policies or institutions without taking account of preference endogeneity. (Bowles 1998, p. 75)

3. The main source of controversy today in evolutionary biology does not concern the issue of whether species actually evolve (or change), but rather focuses on the precise nature of the mechanisms that produce changes over time in various species. Specifically, the

debate centers on the question of *transformational* (Lamarckian) versus *variational* evolution. Consider the case of houseflies that have become resistant to DDT. A transformational explanation would claim that houseflies *as a group* developed a resistance or adapted to a new environment in which DDT was present. The variational view is different:

> Because of *random* mutations of genes that affect the sensitivity of flies to insecticide, some flies were more resistant and some less. When DDT was widely applied, the sensitive flies were killed and their genes were lost, while the resistant forms survived and reproduced, so that their genes were passed on to future generations. Thus the species as a whole became resistant to DDT. (Lewontin 2000, pp. 54–5, italics added)

4. 'Habit is repetition by one person. Custom is repetition by the continuing group of changing persons. It has a coercive effect on the individual' (Commons 1959, p. 155).
5. A well-known quotation from Aristotle's *Nichomachean Ethics*: 'excellence is . . . won by training and habituation . . . We are what we repeatedly do. Excellence, then, is not an act but a habit.'
6. Adam Smith noted that 'few men . . . are willing to allow that custom or fashion have much influence upon their judgments concerning what is beautiful. . . . [They] imagine that all the rules which they think ought to be observed in each of them are founded upon reason and nature, not habit or prejudice' (Smith 1759, V, *i*). See Albert Hirschman (1977) for a summary of views by these economists and others on the subject of interdependent preferences.
7. For a theoretical treatment of the importance of culture in the formation of political views, see Aaron Wildavsky (1987).
8. Paul Sweezy argued that consumer choice is limited by the (sometimes planned) restriction of alternatives. For example, the purchase and maintenance of a car is a major budget item for most families. The need for cars does not emanate 'from human nature' but rather is 'created by living in a certain kind of society' wherein cars are not merely the 'only mode of transportation' but there is a 'locational pattern that implies universal separation of work and residence' (Sweezy 1972, p. 662).
9. The term originated with Veblen (1899, pp. 27–8), who explained the origin of the present-day link between status and the ownership of goods of high quality:

> The initial phase of ownership, the phase of acquisition by naive seizure and conversion, begins to pass into the subsequent stage of an incipient organization of industry on the basis of private property (in slaves); the horde develops into a more or less self-sufficing industrial community; possessions then come to be valued not so much as evidence of successful foray, but rather as evidence of the prepotence of the possessor of these goods over other individuals within the community. The invidious comparison now becomes primarily a comparison of the owner with the other members of the group. Property is still of the nature of trophy, but, with the cultural advance, it becomes more and more a trophy of successes scored in the game of ownership carried on between the members of the group under the quasi-peaceable methods of nomadic life. And it is even more to the point that property now becomes the most easily recognized evidence of a reputable degree of success as distinguished from heroic or signal achievement. It therefore becomes the conventional basis of esteem. Its possession in some amount becomes necessary in order to any reputable standing in the community.

10. Hayek (1948, p. 57) writes that 'The competitive market process acts as an *inter-subjective* discovery procedure in which contradictory ideas are constantly tested against one another and where successful methods are disseminated via the process of emulation.'
11. Wilfred Dolfsma provides an example of how innovations in communication (specifically radio) led to the spread of the pop music culture from the USA to the UK after World War II. See Dolfsma (2002).

12. See, for example, Dixit and Norman (1978), Leffler (1981), and Becker and Murphy (1993).
13. Frank writes: 'I use the term *positional good* to denote goods for which the link between context and evaluation is the strongest and the term *nonpositional good* to denote those for which this link is weakest. In terms of two thought experiments, housing is thus a positional good, vacation time is a nonpositional good' (Frank 2005, p. 137).
14. For example, the MTV *Sweet Sixteen* program highlights extreme ostentation among teenagers and leads one to wonder how many parents, worried their teens may feel cheated by comparison, have added to credit card balances to pay for lavish birthday parties.
15. This is essentially the argument previously made by Gramm (1978) and Watkins (2000).

REFERENCES

Banner, P. (1958), 'Competition, credit policy, and the captive finance company', *Quarterly Journal of Economics*, **43** (2), 251–8.
Becker, G. and K. Murphy (1993), 'A simple theory of advertising as a good or bad', *Quarterly Journal of Economics*, **108** (4), 941–65.
Bowles, S. (1998), 'Endogenous preferences: the cultural consequences of markets and other institutions', *Journal of Economic Literature*, **31** (1), 75–111.
Brown, C. (2005), 'Is there an institutional theory of distribution', *Journal of Economic Issues*, **39** (4), 915–31.
Brown, C. (2007), 'Financial engineering, consumer credit, and the stability of effective demand', *Journal of Post Keynesian Economics*, **29** (3), 429–55.
Bush, P.D. (1987), 'Theory of institutional change', *Journal of Economic Issues*, **22** (3), 1075–116.
Commons, John (1959), *Institutional Economics*, Madison, WI: University of Wisconsin Press (1934).
Cosmides, Leda, John Tooby and Jerome Barkow (1992), 'Evolutionary psychology and conceptual integration', in J. Barkow, L. Cosmides and J. Tooby (eds), *The Adapted Mind*, New York: Oxford University Press, pp. 3–18.
Debreu, Gerard (1959), *Theory of Value*, New Haven: Cowles Commission.
Dewey, John (1922), *Human Nature and Conduct: An Introduction to Social Psychology*, New York: Holt.
Dixit, A. and V. Norman (1978), 'Advertising and welfare', *Bell Journal of Economics*, **9** (1), 1–17.
Dolfsma, W. (2002), 'Mediated preferences – how institutions affect consumption', *Journal of Economic Issues*, **36** (2), 449–57.
Douglas, Mary (1982), *In the Active Voice*, Boston, MA: Routledge and Kegan Paul.
Duesenberry, James S. (1949), *Income, Saving, and the Theory of Consumer Behavior*, Cambridge, MA: Harvard University Press.
Duesenberry, James S. (1967), *Income, Saving, and the Theory of Consumer Behavior*, Cambridge, MA: Harvard University Press.
Epstein, J. (2004), 'Mystery in the heartland', *The New York Review*, **51** (15), 5–9.
Frank, R.H. (2000), 'Does growing inequality harm the middle class?', *Eastern Economic Journal*, **26** (3), 253–64.
Frank, R.H. (2005), 'Positional externalities cause large and preventable welfare losses', *American Economic Review*, **95** (2), 137–41.

Galbraith, John K. (1958), *The Affluent Society*, Boston: Houghton Mifflin.
Gramm, W.S. (1978), 'Credit saturation, secular redistribution, and long-run stability', *Journal of Economic Issues*, **12** (2), 307–27.
Graybiel, Ann and Yasua Kubota (2003), 'Understanding corticobasal ganglia networks as part of a habit formation system', in M.A. Bédard, Y. Agid, S. Chouinard, S. Fahn, A.D. Korczyn and P. Lesperance (eds), *Mental and Behavioral Dysfunction in Movement Disorders*, Totowa, NJ: Humana.
Grimes, William (1926), *Financing Automobile Sales*, New York: A.W. Shaw.
Hayek, Friedrich A. (1948), *Individualism and Economic Order*, Chicago, IL: University of Chicago Press.
Hayek, Friedrich A. (1988), *The Fatal Conceit*, Chicago, IL: University of Chicago Press.
Hirsch, Fred (1976), *Social Limits to Growth*, Cambridge, MA: Harvard University Press.
Hirschman, Albert O. (1977), *The Passions and the Interests: Political Arguments for Capitalism Before it Triumphed*, Princeton, NJ: Princeton University Press.
Hodgson, G. (2003), 'The hidden persuaders: institutions and individuals in economic theory', *Cambridge Journal of Economics*, **27** (2), 159–75.
Hodgson, G. (2006), 'What are institutions?', *Journal of Economic Issues*, **40** (1), 1–25.
Hodgson, G. and T. Knudsen (2004), 'The firm as an interactor: firms as vehicles for habits and routines', *Journal of Evolutionary Economics*, **14**, 281–307.
Jensen, H. (1987), 'The theory of human nature', *Journal of Economic Issues*, **21** (3), 1039–73.
Kantor, J.R. (1920), 'A functional interpretation of human instincts', *Psychological Review*, **27**, 50–72.
Keynes, John M. (1930), *Treatise on Money*, Volume II, London: Macmillan.
Leffler, K. (1981), 'Persuasion or information? The economics of drug prescription advertising', *Journal of Law and Economics*, **24** (1), 45–74.
Lewontin, Richard (2000), *It Ain't Necessarily So. The Dream of the Human Genome and Other Delusions*, New York: New York Review of Books.
Lucas, R.E. (1980), 'Methods and problems in business cycle theory', *Journal of Money, Credit, and Banking*, **12** (4), 696–715.
Minsky, Hyman (1975), *John Maynard Keynes*, New York: Columbia University Press.
Neale, W.C. (1987), 'Institutions', *Journal of Economic Issues*, **21** (3), 1177–206.
Rosenfield, I. and E. Ziff (2006), 'Evolving evolution', *The New York Review*, **53** (8), 12–17.
Schor, Juliet (1998), *The Overspent American*, New York: Basic Books.
Smith, Adam (1937 [1776]), *The Wealth of Nations*, New York: The Modern Library.
Smith, Adam (1981 [1759]), *Theory of Moral Sentiments* eds, D.D. Raphael and A.L. Macfie, Indianapolis: Liberty Fund.
Stigler, G. and G. Becker (1977), 'De gustibus non est disputandum', *American Economic Review*, **67** (2), 76–90.
Sweezy, P. (1972), 'Comment', *Quarterly Journal of Economics*, **86** (4), 658–64.
Veblen, T. (1898), 'Why is economics not an evolutionary science?', *Quarterly Journal of Economics*, **12**, 373–97.
Veblen, Thorstein B. (1899), *The Theory of the Leisure Class: An Economic Study in the Evolution of Institutions*, New York: Macmillan.

Veblen, Thorstein (1964), *The Instinct of Workmanship and the State of Industrial Arts*, New York: W.W. Norton.
Veblen, Thorstein (1964 [1914]), *The Instinct of Workmanship and the Industrial Arts*, New York: Augustus Kelley.
Veblen, Thorstein (1975 [1904]), *Theory of Business Enterprise*, Clifton, NJ: Augustus Kelley.
Watkins, J.P. (2000), 'Corporate power and the evolution of consumer credit', *Journal of Economic Issues*, **34** (4), 909–32.
Wildavsky, A. (1987), 'Choosing preferences by constructing institutions: a cultural theory of preference formation', *American Political Science Review*, **81** (1), 3–21.
Yin, H.H. and B. Knowlton (2006), 'The role of basal ganglia in habit formation', *Nature Reviews Neuroscience*, **7**, 464–76.
Zizzo, J. (2003), 'Empirical evidence on interdependent preferences: nature or nurture?', *Cambridge Journal of Economics*, **27** (6), 867–80.

3. A brief history of innovation in the consumer credit industry

In Chapter 2, the decline of the personal saving rate was explained as the manifestation of an effort by a broad swath of households to maintain their relative consumption (or lifestyle) standards under pressure of sharply rising disparities of income and wealth. It was argued that an expansion of credit-financed expenditure can limit the degree to which 'consumption inequality' rises in the aftermath of an increase in income or wealth inequality, but this necessarily requires, *ceteris paribus*, a decrease in the average propensity to save among borrowing units. We now turn to the role of innovation in achieving a long-run relaxation of the household liquidity constraint. This chapter offers a description and appraisal of organizational, technical and financial innovations deemed important to the growth of the consumer credit industry beginning in the 1920s. These innovations are: the 'captive' finance company; lengthening loan maturities; credit scoring; and the securitization of consumer loan receivables. The chapter also contains a section that examines the growth of payday lending, asset-based lending, and other types of lending arrangements targeted to households with low incomes and/or poor credit histories.

3.1 THE CAPTIVE FINANCE COMPANY

The forward integration into previously non-integrated activities such as wholesale and retail distribution was a defining feature of the post-bellum business revolution. Alfred Chandler (1988) explained the new pattern of downstream integration by the inadequacy of pre-existing systems of marketing and distribution to the requirements of modern mass production.[1] The development of a wide-ranging dealer network was a necessary, but not sufficient, condition for the mass merchandising of big-ticket items such as autos, appliances and pianos. Dealers also required the wherewithal to finance inventories – that is, to obtain 'wholesale' finance – since manufacturers ordinarily required payment upon delivery. The successful marketing of durables also required the capacity to offer installment or 'retail' credit to the buyer at the point of sale. The historical evidence indicates, however, that markets for wholesale and retail credit were notoriously unreliable during the interwar period.[2]

It may surprise some to learn that the consumer durable goods revolution of the 1920s was nearly stillborn because of credit problems. The commercial banking sector did not initially respond to the new demands for credit brought forth by the explosive growth of consumer goods industries – at least not directly. The direct participation of banks in markets for wholesale and consumer finance was marginal – especially before 1935.[3] The void was filled by specialized sales finance companies, of which there were approximately 1500 by the year 1925.[4] Although their direct participation in markets for wholesale and installment financing was limited, banks nevertheless held the key to the system. Sales finance companies were highly leveraged, as measured by the ratio of assets to capitalization. Lacking access to non-bank or disintermediated sources for credit, the viability of these units was based on securing lines of credit at banks as well as the regularized discounting of consumer receivables by the commercial banking sector.[5] Thus some of the nation's most important industries were vulnerable to a sudden change in policy of banks toward the discounting of finance company paper. As is discussed in Chapter 4, beginning in 1930 banks began to shun finance company paper in favor of high-grade securities and paper eligible for rediscount under the Federal Reserve's Regulation A. The result was major congestion in markets for wholesale and retail finance – a factor that hindered the recovery of the consumer durable goods sector during the Depression.

The 'captive' finance company is a wholly owned subsidiary of a non-financial corporation. Its primary function is to provide wholesale and retail financing in accommodation of the marketing requirements of its parent corporation. Daimler Chrysler, Nissan, Honda, Toyota, Izusu, Ford, Yamaha, General Electric – all have captive financing arms.[6] Historical accounts reveal that the integration of durable goods manufacturers into the finance industry was motivated by a realization of the strategic importance of credit as well as dissatisfaction with the performance of the banking sector in this sphere. A letter dated 15 March 1919 (the date of the public announcement of the formation of General Motors Acceptance Corporation or GMAC) from GM President William Durant to J. Amory Haskell, GMAC's first president, makes the point:

> The magnitude of the business has presented new problems in financing which the present banking facilities seem not elastic enough to overcome . . . Hence the creation of General Motors Acceptance Corporation; and the function of that Company will be to supplement the local sources of accommodation to such extent as may be necessary to permit the fullest development of our dealers' business. (Quoted in Sloan 1964, p. 303)

We are obliged to ask: how does the merger of giant industrial concerns and hitherto independent finance companies serve to enhance the general availability of wholesale and installment credit? As noted above, capitalization is unimportant in the consumer finance business. To finance positions in wholesale and retail receivables, finance companies must borrow on a massive scale. Perpetual access to markets for short-dated commercial paper and longer-dated bonds is essential. Captive finance units typically experienced a quantum improvement in their ability to raise funds as a result of their acquisition by a dominant firm.[7] The creditworthiness (as reflected by bond ratings) and borrowing power of the major durable goods manufacturers is transferable to their finance units. Bond issues of captive finance arms are often explicitly underwritten by their parent corporation.

The captive finance company has sometimes been called upon to exercise a 'lender' of last resort' function on behalf of its parent under conditions of monetary restraint. 'Lock-in' effects arising from the maturity imbalance between their consumer receivables and liabilities make profit margins on consumer loans sensitive to the terms on which banks can rollover their short-term liabilities. Thus banks may seek to reduce their exposure to consumer debt in an environment of rising short-term interest rates. As discussed in Chapter 7, there is ample evidence that GMAC and other captive finance units moved to stabilize the market for consumer finance in 1980 and 1981 – a period when banks withdrew from the market en masse.[8]

3.2   LENGTHENING OF LOAN MATURITIES

The capacity of a household to carry a given amount of debt on its balance sheet depends partly on the hire purchase terms (the interest rate or average percentage rate, application fees, or maturity measured in months) affixed to installment debt contracts to which it is party. Table 3.1 is based on the following assumptions: (1) $20 000 has been borrowed to finance the purchase of a car or other item; (2) the interest rate is 9 percent per year; and (3) annual income is equal to US family median in 2005 ($46 326). The lone variable is term to maturity. We see from this table that lengthening the maturity of the debt contract reduces the monthly payment, both in absolute terms and as a percentage of monthly income.

To see the situation more clearly, consider the following hypothetical situation. A median-income family has determined that it can allocate *no more* than 25 percent of its gross monthly income to servicing installment debt obligations. If the interest rate is 9 percent, what is the family's 'debt ceiling' – that is, the maximum amount it can owe without violating the 25 percent maximum? Clearly, the answer depends on the average maturity

Table 3.1   *Monthly payment and debt ceiling for a median-income family*
($46 326)

Maturity (months)	Monthly payment ($)[a]	Monthly payment/ monthly income[a]	Debt ceiling ($)[b]
12	1794.03	0.453	11 362.93
24	913.69	0.237	20 640.25
36	635.99	0.165	29 917.57
48	497.70	0.129	39 194.89
60	415.17	0.108	48 472.21

Notes:
[a]   Assuming a $20 000 installment loan at 9 percent interest.
[b]   Based on the assumption that debt service claims 25 percent of gross monthly income for a median-income household and a 9 percent interest rate.

of installment loans outstanding. Assuming a 9 percent interest rate, a one-year increase in average maturity raises the debt ceiling by about $773. Table 3.1 (last column) presents calculations for a median-income family based on the debt ceiling for different assumptions about maturity. Notice that by increasing the maturity of installment debt from 24 to 48 months, the maximum debt that can be carried while remaining the 25 percent limit nearly doubles ($20 640.25 to $39 194.89).

The 1950s offer a laboratory to monitor the behavioral effects of a sudden, significant change in maturities offered on installment loans. Direct controls on hire purchase terms, in effect from 1948 to 1952, limited the maximum maturity of an installment contract to 12 months. The 24-month auto loan was introduced with great success in 1953. Installment debt outstanding surged thereafter, rising by more than 23 percent in 1955 alone. The post-1953 debt build-up provoked concern on the Council of Economic Advisors and among Federal Reserve officials.[9] In an oft-cited article, Enthoven (1957) argued that fears about a debt bubble were overblown. The 1950s debt spiral was to be expected given the abnormally low debt-to-income ratios at the end of World War II. Using a lifecycle model, Enthoven predicted that, in the long run, the growth rate of debt outstanding would converge to the growth rate of income. Surprisingly, Enthoven's paper completely ignored the effect of lengthening maturities on the capacity to carry debt. Moreover, it fails to account for the fact that the psychology of household finance is modified once credit is an established aspect of culture. Specifically, there is a developing tendency to take action (or to justify it after the fact) on the basis of cash flow, as opposed to balance sheet, calculations. The relevant factor is *not* the amortized value

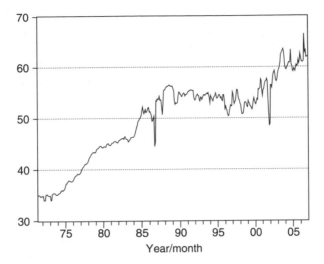

Source: Federal Reserve Board.

Figure 3.1   *Average maturity of new auto loans at finance companies (in months)*

of the stock of household durables in relation to existing installment liabilities, but rather the fraction of current income absorbed by debt servicing. Assuming households were at or near their respective 'debt ceilings' (as established by subjective appraisals as to the maximum allowable allocation of monthly income for debt service), a shift from 12- to 24-month maturities on installment debt contracts would have created a lot of room for new debt – as the calculations in Table 3.1, Column 4 attest.

Figure 3.1 illustrates changes in the average maturity of new auto loans issued by finance companies since 1971. The average maturity of a new car loan was 62 months in December 2006, up from 49 months in January 2002. There is a strong statistical correlation between average maturity and growth of installment debt.[10] It is difficult to believe that lengthening maturities on consumer debt contracts is not an important factor in explaining the growth of borrowing – and the decline of saving.

3.3   CREDIT SCORING

Credit scoring – the practice of constructing a quantitative measure or 'score' to serve as an estimator of a borrower's future repayment performance – has varied social and economic implications. We restrict ourselves here to a narrow set of questions. Specifically, is it accurate to say that the political sanctioning and subsequent normalization of credit score-based lending contributed to a long-run easing of the household liquidity constraint? And if so, how? We answer in the affirmative to the former question and list three primary reasons to regard credit scoring as an important financial technology: (1) it is a source of economies of information; (2) it permits the application of actuarial techniques in the construction of loan portfolios; and (3) it enables lenders to segment borrowers and engage in price discrimination or 'risk-based' pricing.

Although it is now an ensconced aspect of everyday life, the regular use of credit scores in consumer and mortgage lending decisions is fairly recent. The Equal Credit Opportunity Act (Title VII of the Consumer Credit Protection Act) of 1974 made it unlawful for creditors to discriminate on the basis of race, color, religion, national origin, sex, marital status or age, but at the same time legalized the use of 'an empirically derived, demonstrably and statistically sound, credit scoring system'.[11] The search for improved credit-scoring algorithms has matriculated through increasingly sophisticated statistical methods, from logit analysis to neural networks and fuzzy systems.[12] By the 1990s, virtually all consumer and mortgage lending agencies were reliant on credit reports and scores supplied by the big three credit bureau – Experian, Equifax and TransUnion.

Computing a credit score that serves as sound predictor of future creditworthiness is not possible without marshalling a great deal of information – and not only about the prospective borrower. Assessing the future loan performance of a borrower is accomplished by way of reference to the average repayment history of a large group of individuals with similar financial characteristics.[13] Assembling and processing the vast stores of data required for constructing useful credit-scoring systems is prohibitively costly for all save the largest consumer lending institutions (e.g. Citigroup or Wachovia). The credit bureau is an entity that enables the allocation of the colossal informational costs of credit scoring across a large number of users – that is, lenders. Thus economies of information are achieved in credit scoring by the diffusion of informational costs.

Credit scoring is a form of actuarial analysis. A lender cannot, on the basis of a credit score, know with accuracy the likelihood of delinquency or default for any *specific* loan. However, prior knowledge of credit scores can provide answers to questions such as the following: if 1000 loans were made to borrowers with the same credit score, what is the probability that 10, 35, 118, or any other number of borrowers will eventually default? Thus credit scoring provides a basis for building diversified or 'granular' portfolios of auto, credit card, or other consumer receivables where loan losses can be forecasted with reasonably small errors.

For better or for worse, the project of making more profitable use of credit bureau data employs some big brains (see Avery et al. 2000). It was common during the industry's embryonic phase for consumer lenders to establish a 'cutoff' score for successful loan applications. As a rule, credit was extended to all with qualifying credit scores *on the same hire purchase terms*. A change in lending policy sometimes simply meant a change in the cutoff score. Lenders were reluctant to raise interest rates (or fees) to accommodate riskier borrowers for fear of adverse selection – that is, higher rates may push better credit risks out of the market.[14] The situation facing consumers is different today. A credit card holder may be paying a much higher rate of interest (or average percentage rate) on outstanding balances than another card holder with a better credit score – even if the credit cards have been issued by the same bank. In fact, a recent paper by Wendy Edelberg (2006) finds that, whereas credit card interest rate spreads between low- and high-risk borrowers were virtually nil before 1995, rates paid by high-risk card holders are substantially higher on average today.[15] Credit scores are a tool of market segmentation. Credit applicants are segregated into risk groups according to their credit scores. Note also that the fine print of credit card contracts typically permits the issuer to change the terms of existing accounts (or reassign accounts to different risk groups) if card holders' credit status should change. Credit terms are set with the aim of maximizing net cash flow from loans within a given risk category. This practice is known as 'risk-based' pricing.

How does risk-based pricing lead to expanded availability of credit? Before the new regime, consumer credit markets were more prone to the type of non-price rationing described by Stiglitz and Weiss (1983). As Edelberg explains:

> If lenders declined to charge very high-risk households sufficiently high interest rates before the mid 1990s, lending to this group may have proved significantly unprofitable, and households may have been rationed ... With risk-based pricing, lenders should offer those households debt with higher interest rates rather than reject them. If at least some of these borrowers have sufficiently high reservation rates, debt among very high-risk households should rise. (Edelberg 2006, p. 2292)

We saw in Chapter 1 (Table 1.3) that debt-to-income ratios of low-income families have increased sharply since 1995. Although credit ratings are by no means perfectly correlated with income, this information gives a fair approximation of the overall effect.

Taking into account the linkage of the collection and storage of financial information to credit scoring and expanded credit availability, it does not overstate things to assert that the existence of vast stores of accurate personal financial data is a key factor underlying the robustness of the US consumption sector. We may also predict that prospects for consumption growth in China, Russia, India and other emerging economies will be improved by the maturation of consumer databases in those nations.[16]

3.4   SECURITIZATION OF CONSUMER RECEIVABLES

Securitization is the process of restructuring non-marketable loans into standardized, marketable assets. This section contains a description and analysis of a recent financial innovation – the 'asset-backed security' or ABS. The ABS is a security collateralized or 'backed' by a pool of credit card receivables, installment loans or student loans. We shall attempt to explain why the ABS is a critically important innovation in terms of expanding household borrowing opportunities. Evidence is provided in support of the assertion that, as a result of the proliferation of the ABS, a vast number of households have experienced an augmentation of their borrowing power for reasons unrelated to their credit scores.

How does the asset securitization technique work? As was noted above, finance companies traditionally financed positions in consumer receivables through bank loans or the issue of commercial paper. Under the new regime, consumer receivables are sold to a 'special purpose vehicle' (SPV) – that is, a company created for the purpose of reorganizing these pools of consumer receivables into homogeneous lots that can be placed with large pension funds, insurance companies and other institutional portfolios. Thus the role of the finance company is largely transformed from lender to loan originator.[17] A trust agreement is created at the point of issue, which requires the transfer of hire purchase agreements (or credit card or student loans receivables, as the case may be) to a trust not controlled by the loan originator (the finance company) or the SPV. The newly issued securities are collateralized by the assets of the trust. The trust assets have been screened by the originator, a rating agency, and, in some cases, by an independent guarantor. The new notes issued by the SPV typically carry an investment grade, making them substitutable with short-dated Treasury issues or commercial paper.[18]

The placement of asset-backed securities proceeds in the same manner as the primary issue of corporate equities or bonds. A prospectus is circulated. Investment banks take the securities to market (and as might be expected, competition for the lucrative fees that can be realized through ABS placement is fierce). Recent issuers of asset-backed securities include Honda Finance, Nissan Motor Acceptance Corporation, Toyota Motor Credit, Mitsubishi Finance, the Credit Store, Chase Manhattan Bank, Circuit City,

Nieman Marcus, Dillards, J.C. Penney, Sears, Dayton-Hudson, Federated Department Stores, Banc One, Capital One, Citicorp, Ford Motor Credit Corporation, General Motors Acceptance Corporation and MBNA. Ian Giddy notes that

> [t]he asset securitization process, while complex, has won a secure place in corporate financing and investment portfolios because it can, paradoxically, offer originators a cheaper source of financing and investors a superior return. Not only does securitization transform illiquid assets into tradable securities, but it also manages to transform risk by means of the separation of sound financial instruments from a company with little or no loss. (Giddy 2005)

Demand for asset-backed securities has been robust lately – indeed, new issues have been regularly oversubscribed. In addition to their liquidity and attractive return, ABSs appeal to banks, insurance companies, pension funds, and other institutions because the risks attached to them can be hedged with the use of other structured financial products – that is, derivatives. An institution seeking to hedge positions in stocks, commodities, currencies or other assets may purchase an option to sell a market basket of stocks, commodities and so on at a specified price at a specified future date. The value of the option is therefore 'derived' from the value of the underlying assets. The explosive growth of derivatives trading since their introduction in the 1980s is explained by two factors: (1) the growing concentration of financial assets in professionally managed portfolios; and (2) developments in theory of finance – most importantly the Black–Scholes model of options pricing.[19]

The most widely used device is the over-the-counter credit default swap.[20] This is an arrangement whereby the hedging party makes periodic 'coupon' payments to a counterparty that is obligated to make a payment to the first party in the event of a 'credit event' (e.g., default or a downgrade by rating agencies), the size of the payment being dependent on the market value of the 'reference assets' following the credit event.[21] Total return swaps, or agreements between two parties to exchange the total returns from financial assets, is another means by which agents may insure against prepayment, interest rate or default risk.[22]

Figures 3.2 and 3.3 illustrate the growth of securities outstanding collateralized by credit card (revolving) and consumer installment (non-revolving) receivables. Securities of this type have increased more than 20-fold since 1989. Forty-two percent of the growth of consumer credit outstanding between 1989 and 2005 was accounted for by the growth of asset-backed securities. Sixty-two percent of the growth of revolving credit outstanding since 1989 was accounted for by the issue of securities backed by non-revolving (installment) receivables.

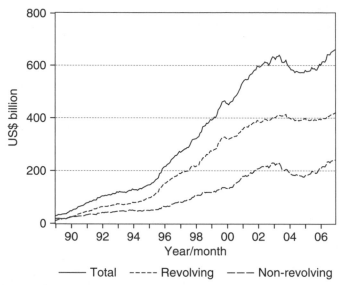

Source: Federal Reserve Board.

Figure 3.2   Asset-backed securities outstanding from US issuers (in billions of dollars)

Figure 3.4 describes asset-backed securities outstanding by type. The Bond Market Association reported that, in December 2006, the value of asset-backed securities outstanding was $2.13 trillion. Bonds backed by mortgage and consumer receivables collectively accounted for 32 percent of the bond market in 2004, compared to 27 percent for US government and agency debt and 20 percent for corporate debt.[23]

When mortgage or consumer receivables are illiquid, the general availability or 'supply' of credit (or finance) is limited by the tolerance of wealth holders (or controllers) for illiquidity. The securitization of consumer receivables removes the constraint on the expansion of mortgage or consumer lending arising from the allergic reaction of wealth controllers to non-tradable assets. By morphing into securities, consumer debts gain entrance to a vast new market which at present is roughly co-extensive with the aggregate of professionally managed pools of financial assets worldwide.[24] Assuming asset-backed securities accounted for an unchanging fraction of holdings for these units, growth of institutional portfolios would bring forth a shifting demand for these instruments, *ceteris paribus*. The prodigious growth of financial asset pools under professional management is a striking development of the past quarter-century. Financial

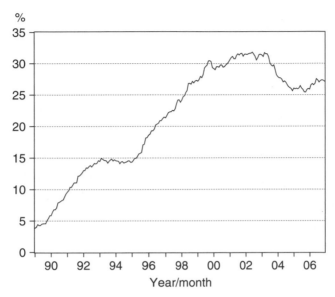

%

Source: Federal Reserve Board.

Figure 3.3 *Asset-backed securities as a percentage of total consumer credit outstanding in the USA*

assets of 'institutional investors' in OECD countries nearly doubled in money terms between 1993 and 2001. The market value of assets held in US institutional portfolios increased by a staggering $102 trillion, or 112 percent, in the same period.[25] It should also be pointed out that the size of institutional portfolios has increased in relative as well as absolute terms. That is, the proportion of total intangible assets under professional management has increased markedly. Institutions account for the lion's share of daily volume on exchanges worldwide.

What factors can explain the tremendous growth of portfolio assets under professional management? Demographics are one factor. The USA, Europe and Japan have recently seen bulging huddles of postwar cohorts advance through the peak years of the earning lifecycle. Monthly flows into pension and mutual funds have been proportionately high. The Employment Retirement Security Act (ERISA) of 1974 gave favorable tax treatment to funds committed to pension plans (ERISA established the 'defined contribution' pension plan known as the 401(k)). The abolition of fixed brokerage commissions (i.e. brokers' fees set at a fixed industry percentage of the value of transactions) by the Securities and Exchange

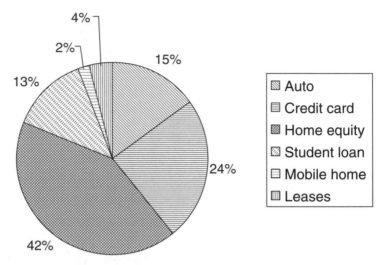

Note: ᵃ As of 31 December 2006.

Source: The Bond Market Association.

*Figure 3.4   Asset-backed securities outstanding by type*ᵃ

Commission in 1975 sharply reduced transactions costs for institutions and created economies of scale in purchase and sale of securities.

Post-Keynesians distinguish between finance and funding.[26] Finance refers to short-term loans to production units (farmers, retailers, contractors, for example) required to bridge the gap between the disbursement of factor costs and the receipt of income from the sale of commodities, services, etc. Finance is provided mainly by the banking system. Funding is the term used to describe liquidity required to purchase long-lived durable assets (factories, hotels, for example) and is acquired via the issue of securities. Our purpose here is to give evidence that the explosive growth of primary and secondary markets for securities backed by household receivables has produced powerful funding effects. The term 'funding' is used to denote the mechanics involved in making liquidity available – not its ultimate disposition. To be sure, a significant share of the spending power created by the issue of ABSs has been allocated for the purchase of non-durable items or services such as restaurant meals or airline tickets.

The ability of individuals to qualify for credit may vary according to income, length of employment or any number of factors weighed in credit-scoring algorithms. As was mentioned above, the term 'expanded credit availability' refers to enlarged borrowing opportunities of a person with a

Table 3.2   Average number of credit cards, average total credit limit by income level, selected years (2004 dollars)[a]

Income range ($)	Year							
	1989		1995		2001		2004	
	Ave. # credit cards	Ave. credit limit ($)	Ave. # credit cards	Ave. credit limit ($)	Ave. # credit cards	Ave. credit limit ($)	Ave. # credit cards	Ave. credit limit ($)
$6750–$11 750	0.078	854	0.488	1 876	0.538	2 575	0.564	3 590
$23 492–$28 492	0.565	2 835	1.194	5 861	1.244	7 296	1.405	7 857
$41 727–$46 727	0.967	5 175	1.667	10 757	1.810	12 210	1.833	14 000
$68 160–$73 160	1.133	9 936	2.270	15 368	2.056	18 993	2.200	18 667
$120 107–$125 107	1.561	14 644	2.732	23 190	2.030	32 524	2.748	28 160

Note: [a] Average number of credit cards is the average number of Visa, Mastercard, Discovery and Optima card accounts open. Average credit limit is the combined total credit lines on aforementioned accounts.

Source: Author's calculations from the *Survey of Consumer Finances*. Adapted from *Journal of Post Keynsian Economics*, vol. 29, no. 3 (Spring 2007), 445. Copyright © by M.E. Sharpe, Inc. Used by permission.

given credit score. Financial innovation has the potential to stimulate effective demand (and reduce aggregate saving) because it raises the maximum amount that can be borrowed by households located at virtually all levels of the creditworthiness scale.

The tri-annual *Survey of Consumer Finances* (*SCF*) includes financial information for a sample of approximately 22 000 US households. By using sample weights, it is possible to draw inferences about important financial variables for the population. With regard to the issue of credit availability, two questions contained in the survey are particularly relevant. One asks respondents to report the number of Visa, Mastercard, Discovery and Optima card accounts they have open. Another asks respondents to report the combined credit limit they have been extended on the aforementioned cards. A secular improvement in credit availability can be uncovered by examining changes over time in the average number of credit cards, and average credit limits, for households within the same income ranges.

The data reported in Table 3.2 were extracted from *SCF* public-use micro-data for survey years 1989, 1995, 2001 and 2004. The income ranges selected are $5000 intervals at the midpoint of income quintiles, based on US Bureau of the Census income data. So, for example, the range $68 160 to $73 160 (2004 dollars) is at the center of the second-highest fifth of households. The data are consistent with the hypothesis that the post-1987 era featured very substantial ABS-related funding effects, a theme we return to in Chapter 6.

3.5   FINANCIAL ENGINEERING AND SUBPRIME LENDING

This section will argue that the maturation of markets for MBSs (mortgage-backed securities) and ABSs established conditions favorable for an increase in the scale of high-risk or 'subprime' lending. Subprime loans are those which collateralize mortgage or asset-backed securities rated 'A −' or lower by Standard & Poors.[27] Subprime borrowers have FICO (Fair Isaac Corporation) credit scores below 620 on a 350–850 scale (about 25 percent of US individuals have credit scores below 620).

There are two principal categories of subprime activity: mortgage lending and credit cards. There are differences in market structure between the two. Subprime mortgage lending features a large number of brokers or loan originators, many of whose operations are local in scope. By contrast, a handful of big players such as Providian and HSBC account for a large share of subprime credit card issuances. At the 2006 peak, subprime mortgages accounted for roughly 25 percent of mortgage originations, or about $600 billion. Subprime credit card lending is also huge business. It is estimated that approximately 70 million subprime credit card accounts were active in the summer of 2007. Both segments advanced on a similar track: take-off in the 1990s (early 1990s for credit cards, late 1990s for mortgages), explosive growth during 2003–05, then contraction in 2006–07 amid a flood of defaults. Exposure to subprime mortgages pinched profits at many institutions and contributed to the failure of two Bear Stearns-affiliated hedge funds in late spring of 2007 (see Ng and Simon 2007). Those with low incomes or poor credit histories found credit harder to come by as underwriting standards were tightened.

Agents are liable to engage in riskier behavior if they can shift risk to other agents. This is the principle of 'moral hazard' (Arrow 1971). Derivative instruments serve no other purpose than to facilitate the pooling, slicing, spreading and redistribution of many types of risk. We previously explained how ABS holders use derivatives to hedge credit, prepayment and interest-rate risk. Portfolio insurance has greatly affected the behavior of financial market participants. The evidence is consistent with the view that derivatives have powered the quest for yield to a higher pitch. The option to hedge has fortified the demand for high-yield tranches of consumer or mortgage debt – securities that, *sans* hedging, might be classified as too risky. The performance of the financial system (in terms of converting poorer-quality IOUs into liquid purchasing power) is enhanced (at least in the near term) by the risk-spreading innovations.

High yields are, from the collective point of view, durably proportional to risk. The quest for yield must therefore work its way down the credit-scoring hierarchy to high-risk borrowers – that is, those willing to pay very high interest rates and fees because they lack borrowing alternatives. The eye-popping returns posted by some major holders of collateralized debt obligations (such as hedge funds) are typically explained by the use of leverage and complex trading strategies (as is discussed in Chapter 5; accounting *legerdemain* also plays a role). The high-brow character of financial engineering should not divert attention from its seamier side, however. The derivatives-powered quest for yield has drawn some 'respectable' financial institutions into the market space once controlled by the loan shark, the pawn shop and the rent-to-own business, prompting some to label subprime lenders as 'banksters'. A report prepared by an HUD–Treasury Task Force in 2000 reached the following conclusion: 'By providing a source of funding, those who purchase or securitize high cost or subprime loans may, knowingly or unknowingly, support the activities of predatory loan originators' (p. 10).

The option to move receivables off balance sheet alters the incentive structure facing mortgage loan originators. Delinquencies and charge-offs play a lesser role in the profit calculus.[28] The new regime creates a profit incentive to monetize all IOUs that can be passed through the securitization pipeline. Much of the fury over the subprime mortgage crisis has been directed at unscrupulous, fly-by-night mortgage brokers, and rightly so. At the same time, the survival of these units depends on an elaborate apparatus that facilitates the purchase, pooling, slicing, re-issuing and hedging of loan receivables originated by them.

3.6   PAYDAY LENDING

The economic exploitation of the poor, the ignorant, the desperate, the aged, or the infirm is nothing new. What is new is the stunning multiplication of business units that target low-income and minority consumers. Once relegated to the fringe or the underground, these units have moved nearer to the center of economic life. The reader may wonder: are the financial innovations described above in any way responsible for the recent, proliferating growth of predatory lending? In the case of subprime mortgage and consumer lending, the answer is clearly yes. The connection between financial engineering and predatory businesses such as payday lending is more difficult to pin down.

What types of lending practices might be fairly labeled as predatory? The collection of interest (or fees) that 'reasonable' people deem usurious or unconscionable is an obvious example. In addition, there is lender (or originator) indifference with respect to the borrower's capacity to repay. Asset-based lending – that is, lending strictly on the basis of the value of property used as collateral (such as a house, car or boat) without regard to the borrower's income or credit score – falls into this category. Another instance is given by mortgage, home equity, or debt consolidation loans structured with 'balloon' payments that predictably create a need for the borrower to refinance (to avoid default or foreclosure). And this list is by no means exhaustive.[29]

If the rampancy of predatory lending practices is an accurate gauge of economic hardship, then the degree of financial distress experienced by many households in the USA must be rising. How else to explain the explosive growth of the roundly disparaged payday loan industry? Payday lending is now a $25 billion-a-year business.[30] There are about 22 000 payday loan offices nationwide, and the industry lately has moved online.[31] The *Toledo Blade* recently reported, 'the number of payday lending offices [in Ohio] rose nearly 15-fold between 1996 and 2006 to 1,562. That is more than the combined total of restaurants operated by the McDonalds, Burger King, and Wendy's chains' (Pakulski 2007, p. 1). The big players include Advance America (2600 locations in 36 states) Check Into Cash (1200 locations in 30 states), ACE Cash Express (1557 stores in 36 states and the District of Columbia) and Check 'n' Go (1322 outlets in Ohio). Several of the largest payday lenders (such as ACE Cash Express) are publicly traded companies.

A payday loan would seem a rational choice only for persons in desperate financial straits. The borrower is, in effect, selling his or her receivables (a forthcoming paycheck) at a discount that nearly all would think usurious. Nevertheless, it is estimated that about 5 percent of US households have taken out at least one payday loan.[32] Payday lenders do not perform credit checks on prospective borrowers. Qualifying for a payday loan normally requires that one have a home address, a driver's license, a checking account, and earnings of at least $1000 per month. According to Stegman (2007, p. 169), 'a typical example would be that in exchange for a $300 advance until the next payday, the borrower writes a postdated check for $300 and receives $255 in cash – the lender takes a $45 fee off the top'. Interest rates on payday loans range as high as 400 percent in Washington State (Stark 2006, p. 1). Missouri State Attorney General Jay Nixon recently claimed the average annual interest rate on a payday loan in his state was 422 percent (reported in Wenske 2007).[33] Stegman notes that 'it is fairly common for payday loans to be rolled over into the next time period for an additional fee, and thus the fees are often paid several times a year' (Stegman 2007, p. 170). The propensity to roll over payday loans partly explains why '[a] typical Virginia borrower repays $776 on a $355 payday loan' (Edwards 2007, p. 1).

Payday lending itself cannot be termed innovative. The Consumer Federation of America reports that the practice of extending credit against postdated checks was common during the Depression (Fox 2004). Payday lenders have developed novel ways of evading state usury laws, however. The most important tactic is known as 'rent-a-charter'. The Depository Institutions and Monetary Control Act of 1980 (DIDMA) permits state-chartered, FDIC-insured banks to export 'home' interest rates and thus pre-empt some consumer protection statutes. Fox reports:

> [B]anks are alleged to be 'renting their charters' to payday lenders to front for loans that would be in violation of state law if made directly by the payday lender . . . In a typical . . . arrangement, the payday lender markets loans, solicits borrowers, disburses loan proceeds, services and collects the loan . . . Loans are usually sold back to the payday lender within the day, with the bank retaining five to fifteen percent of the face value of the transaction. (Fox 2004, pp. 11–12)

Former New York Attorney General Eliot Spitzer described the practice as 'nothing more than loan sharking that has been legitimized by a loophole in a federal statute' (quoted in Louis 2003, p. 3).

Financial innovation is an appropriate subject for this volume because it has relevance for the household liquidity (or spending) constraint (and thus effective demand). That is, we have been concerned with innovations that contribute to the augmentation of household spending power. Such an augmentation generally occurs when financial institutions sell their (newly created) deposits in exchange for household IOUs. Consumer loan transactions produce at least two effects. First, there is the funding or liquidity effect. Deposits created as a result of new loans are an addition to the economy's stock of generally acceptable payment media. The second is the income distribution effect, which arises from the payment of interest (or fees) on loans. Predatory lending is repugnant because (besides pushing people nearer to financial ruin) it has deleterious distributional consequences.[34]

Although payday lenders are not banks (and thus do not create deposits), their activities may nevertheless stimulate total credit expansion. That is because payday lenders rely on bank financing. Thus bank credits are likely to expand in some proportion to the stock of payday receivables outstanding, *ceteris paribus*. Even so, the funding effects of payday lending are likely to be rather anemic in comparison with other types of lending. 'Funding' refers to the efficacy of debt (or equity, in the case of firms) in terms of stretching payment schedules to match the useful life of tangible consumer (or producer) goods. The short maturity of payday loans means that the spending of loan recipients can never stray far from income receipts within the same period. Payday lending cannot be considered effective in loosening the liquidity constraint on household spending – except in the very short term.

Like all loan transactions, payday loans constitute the purchase of money today in exchange for a promise to pay money at a future date. However, the income redistribution effects associated with payday lending are far more severe on a per-dollar-lent basis as compared to more respectable forms of consumer lending. Payday borrowers earmark a preposterous share of income for payment of interest. Viewed over a multi-paycheck horizon, a payday loan liability can severely reduce spending power available for the purchase of goods and services.

NOTES

1. Alfred Chandler (1988, p. 230) writes: '[V]olume producers of durable goods . . . discovered that the wholesaler was unable to handle the initial product demonstrations to customers, unable to provide the necessary consumer credit, and unable to provide continuing repair and service of goods sold'.
2. The inadequacy of financing arrangements was a regular complaint in the auto industry. Martha Olney writes: 'Until about 1915 dealers financed small inventories internally. But after 1915 the size of inventory increased and most dealers needed some form of external financing to carry inventories. Existing avenues for financing were inadequate. Manufacturers could not afford to offer direct factory credit and banks refused to offer adequate inventory financing because of the cancellation clause in the dealers' franchise agreement' (Olney 1988, pp. 385–6). Rolf Nugent reported that 'the shortage of instalment facilities had put greater restraints upon the sales of automobiles than upon the sales of most other types of consumers' durable goods' (Nugent 1939, p. 93).
3. Juster (1966) attributed the 'huge expansion of commercial bank participation in the consumer installment credit market after 1935' to '[l]egislation passed . . . to facilitate the financing of home improvements permitted the Federal government to guarantee up to 20 percent of the face value of home improvement loans; such loans were defined broadly enough to permit the inclusion of household durable goods' (ibid., p. 56).
4. This figure is taken from Kuhn (1986, p. 80). Nugent writes that '[t]he remarkable growth of instalment finance companies after the World War solved the problem of retail financing . . . From the beginning of 1922 to the Fall of 1929 the growth of passenger car sales was paralleled by an even more rapid growth in the number of instalment finance companies and in the net amount of retail automobile instalment contracts . . . held by these companies' (Nugent 1939, p. 93).
5. Nugent (1939) writes: 'The very earliest instalment finance companies relied heavily upon the use of bank credit to supplement their working capital. Later, the principal instalment finance companies began to sell their short-term notes to banks, either directly or through commercial paper brokers . . . The instalment finance company,

therefore, was an intermediary agency . . . in the sense that it served to bridge the gap between the consumer and the commercial banks' (ibid., pp. 95–6).

6. Ford formed its first finance unit (Universal Credit Corporation) in 1928 and then sold it in 1933. Kuhn (1986) claims that Henry Ford's aversion to credit had damaging consequences: '[W]hile Ford extensively integrated his firm, he kept the vital activity of credit provisioning outside his controlled sphere. He refused then to admit that the mass production and mass distribution of consumer durables – no matter how cheap – demanded mass finance to clear the market pipeline' (ibid., p. 275).

7. See Banner (1958).

8. See Brown and Viar (1990).

9. Enthoven (1957) writes that '[t]he Council of Economic Advisors urged the enactment of legislation re-establishing standby controls . . . At the request of the Council, the Board of Governors of the Federal Reserve System undertook a study and, in March 1957, produced five volumes on various aspects of consumer installment credit' (Enthoven 1957, p. 919).

10. A partial correlation coefficient between average maturity of new loans issued by finance companies and inflation-adjusted auto loans outstanding from finance companies, calculated using monthly data for 1971:6 to 2006:11, has a value of 0.67.

11. This language is taken from the Federal Reserve's Regulation B, which can be accessed at www.federalreserve.gov/boarddocs/press/bcreg/2003/20030305/attachment.pdf. The Board of Governors issues regulations pursuant to the Equal Credit Opportunity Act.

12. For a description of recent advances in credit-scoring techniques, see Thomas et al. (2005).

13. Credit-scoring algorithms are proprietary, but among the variables thought to influence credit scores are: length of employment, home ownership, the gap between credit card balances and credit limits, and promptness in payment of bills.

14. Insurance companies such has Allstate have lately used credit scores to set insurance rates, but have been subject to legal challenges from states. See Marron (2007).

15. Edelberg (2006) also reports that risk-based pricing is mainly confined to the credit card segment. Interest rate differentials on auto or student loans continue to be minimal.

16. There is evidence this process is well under way. The *American Bankers' Association Journal* recently reported that 'Russian banks have had to build up their own databases through trial and error because they can't rely on a national credit bureau. Experian did set up a credit bureau in April 2005 with around 20 banks including International Moscow Bank, Raiffeisen Bank, Baltiyskiy Bank, Bank Vozrozhdeniye, and International Industrial Bank. However, Experian's credit bureau has yet to reach a level of usage or customer volume that one would expect in a U.S. or Western European context' (S10). The article also commented that 'a national credit bureau would be a tremendous asset for the Russian consumer finance sector' (S10).

17. The reader will notice the great similarity between mortgage-backed securities (MBSs) and ABSs. The MBS is a tradable instrument collateralized by mortgage loans held in special-purpose vehicles. The largest issuers are Freddie Mac (Federal Home Loan Mortgage Association) and Fannie Mae (Federal National Mortgage Association), government-created entities which are now privately owned. The growth of the secondary market for MBSs is widely credited for improving access to mortgage loans and increasing the rate of home ownership. MBS holders use derivatives to hedge prepayment risk. Since mortgage debt instruments typically give borrowers the option to pay off their notes at any time, mortgage-backed securities have 'embedded call options' (Lee 2003, p. A14). Profit margins of leveraged MBS holders (particularly those with substantial long-term debt) are interest-sensitive since a decline in rates will cause a surge in prepayments as home owners refinance on more favorable terms. Freddie Mac, which had 'retained' MBS holdings exceeding $1.5 trillion in 2006, is the single largest user of prepayment derivatives. The MBS has transformed the structure of the mortgage lending industry. Data obtained from the *Federal Reserve Bulletin* indicate that whereas in 1976 traditional mortgage lenders (commercial banks and savings & loans) held a combined 62.5 percent of mortgage debt outstanding on their books, by 2004 their share had fallen to 34.8 percent. The proportion of mortgage debt held by 'mortgage pools or trusts' rose from 5.6 percent in 1976 to 47.9 percent in 2004.

18. Steven Schwartz (1994, p. 137) explains the advantages of securitization from the point of view of the issuer: 'A securitization transaction can provide obvious cost savings by permitting an originator whose debt securities are rated less than investment grade . . . to obtain funding through a special purpose vehicle where debt securities have an investment grade.'

19. See Black and Scholes (1973). For a discussion of the importance of the Black–Scholes theorem in the development of the derivatives trading, see Rubinstein (1987).

20. Choudhry (2004) is a good source to consult for an explanation of different types of structured finance.

21. The *Wall Street Journal* reported that hedge funds were counterparties to derivative contracts insuring positions in GM and Ford Motor debt, and suffered large losses when the rating agencies downgraded these issues in May 2005. See Whitehouse (2005).

22. For a description, see Fabozzi (2003).

23. These figures come from the Bond Market Association and were reported in Luchetti (2004).

24. Giddy explains that 'securitization issues are still difficult for retail investors to understand. Hence most securitizations have been privately placed with professional investors' (giddy.org/abs; 1 July 2005).

25. These figures are taken from the OECD database.

26. See Davidson (1986).

27. Standard & Poors' rating system takes several factors into account, including the track record of loan originators and the credit (FICO) scores of loan recipients. For a detailed description, see www.standardandpoors.com/ratings.

28. That is not to say that originators (or brokers) have *no* incentive to pay attention to the quality of loans sold to ABS or MBS issuers. Legal covenants applicable to some ABS or MBS issues require originators to take back loans in the event that defaults exceed some threshold level. Originators also face the risk that they will be removed from the list of approved brokers by major issuers – something that recently happened to several subprime mortgage brokers. The *Wall Street Journal* reported on 17 March 2007 that 'amid mounting defaults in the market for subprime mortgages, some big banks and mortgage companies are striking out in their efforts to wrest compensation from originators of those high-risk, high-return loans . . . [B]anks and larger mortgage lenders are trying to force smaller mortgage lenders to buy back some of the same loans that the larger entities eagerly purchased from the smaller mortgage originators in 2005 and 2006, by enforcing what the industry calls repurchase agreements.'

29. An HUD–Treasury Task Force on predatory lending was convened by HUD Secretary Andrew Cuomo and Treasury Secretary Lawrence Summers in April 2000. A report issued by the Task Force stated that '[i]n a predatory lending situation, the party that initiates the loan often provides misinformation, manipulates the borrower through aggressive sales tactics, and/or takes unfair advantage of the borrower's lack of information about the loan terms and their consequences. The results are loans with onerous terms and conditions that the borrower cannot repay, leading to foreclosure or bankruptcy' (p. 18). This report is available at www.hud.gov/library/bookshelf12/pressrel/treasrpt. pdf.

30. This figure comes from the Community Financial Services Association of America, a trade group representing the payday loan industry.

31. MyCashNow.com and Pay DayOK.com are two of the largest online outfits. Darryl Dahlheimer of Lutheran Social Service Financial Counseling in Minneapolis comments: 'With online loans, they're greasing the skids so people slide into boiling oil that much faster. The ease of access and the anonymity allow people to get into trouble with much less oversight' (quoted in Reinen 2006).

32. This is according to the consulting firm Stephens, Inc., as reported in Stegman (2007, p. 173).

33. According to Snarr (2002), when payday loan fees are converted to average percentage rates (APR), rates charged range between 400 and 1000 percent – and this does not account for rollovers.

34. The theoretical relationship between income distribution and effective demand is discussed in Chapter 4.

REFERENCES

Arrow, Kenneth (1971), *Essays in the Theory of Risk-Bearing*, Amsterdam: North-Holland Publishing.

Avery, R., R. Bostic, P. Calem and G. Canner (2000), 'Credit scoring: statistical issues and evidence from credit-bureau files', *Real Estate Economics*, **28** (3), 523–48.

Banner, P. (1958), 'Competition, credit policy, and the captive finance company', *Quarterly Journal of Economics*, **43** (2), 251–8.

Black, F. and M. Scholes (1973), 'The pricing of options and corporate liabilities', *Journal of Political Economy*, **81** (2), 637–59.

Brown, C. and J. Viar (1990), 'Centralized private sector planning and the allocation of automobile credit', *Journal of Economic Issues*, **24** (2), 597–604.

Chandler, Alfred (1988), 'The large industrial corporation and the making of the modern American economy', in T.K. McCraw (ed.), *The Essential Alfred Chandler*, Cambridge, MA: Harvard University Press, pp. 225–92.

Choudhry, Moorad (2004), *Structured Credit Products: Credit Derivatives and Synthetic Securitisation*, Hoboken, NJ: Wiley Publishing.

Davidson, P. (1986), 'Finance, funding, savings, and investment', *Journal of Post Keynesian Economics*, **9** (1), 101–11.

Edelberg, W. (2006), 'Risk-based pricing of interest rates for consumer loans', *Journal of Monetary Economics*, **53** (8), 2283–98.

Edwards, G. (2006), 'Debt trap or consumer need?', *Knight Ridder Business News*, 5 October, 1.

Enthoven, A. (1957), 'The growth of installment credit and the future of prosperity', *American Economic Review*, **47** (1), 913–29.

Fabozzi, F.J. (2005), 'The structured finance market: an investor's perspective', *Financial Analysts Journal*, **61** (3), 27–41.

Fox, J.A. (2004), 'Unsafe and unsound: payday lenders behind FDIC charters to peddle usury', Consumer Federation of America, http://www.consumerfed.org/pdfs/pdlrentabankreport.pdf (accessed 31 July 2007).

Giddy, I. (2005), 'New developments in asset-backed securities', ABS Research.com, http:giddy.org/abs-jhb.htm (accessed 20 March 2006).

Juster, Thomas (1966), *Household Capital Formation and Financing*, New York: National Bureau of Economic Research.

Kuhn, Arthur (1986), *GM Passes Ford*, College Park, PA: Pennsylvania State University Press.

Lee, S. (2003), 'Freddie hides in the hedges', *Wall Street Journal*, 15 July, A15.

Louis, E. (2003), 'Spitzer says out-of-state companies charge illegally high interest rates up to 780 percent a year on payday loans', *New York Sun*, 25 September, 3.

Luchetti, A. (2004), 'Indebted consumers reshape the bond market', *Wall Street Journal*, 14 September, C1.

Marron, D. (2007), ' "Lending by numbers": credit scoring and the constitution of risk within American consumer credit', *Economy and Society*, **36** (1), 103–33.

Ng, S. and R. Simon (2007), 'Ratings cuts by S&P's, Moodys rattle investors', *Wall Street Journal*, 11 July, A1.

Nugent, Rolf (1939), *Consumer Credit and Economic Stability*, New York: Russell Sage Foundation.

Olney, M. (1989), 'Credit as a production smoothing device: the case of automobiles, 1913–1938', *Journal of Economic History*, **49** (2), 377–91.

Pakulski, G.T. (2007), ' "Payday loan" sites jump in area, state', *Knight Ridder Tribune Business News*, 23 Febuary, 1.

Reinan, J. (2006), 'Payday loans rise online – and so does debt', *Knight Ridder Tribune Business News*, 23 October, 1.

Rubinstein, M. (1987), 'Derivative asset analysis', *Journal of Economic Perspectives*, **1** (2), 73–93.

Schwartz, S. (1994), 'The alchemy of asset securitization', *Stanford Journal of Law, Business, and Finance*, **1** (2), 133–53.

Sloan, Alfred P. (1964), *My Years with General Motors*, J. McDonald and C. Stevens (eds), New York: Doubleday & Company.

Snarr, R.W. Jr (2002), 'No cash 'til payday: the payday lending industry', Compliance Corner, 1st Quarter, Federal Reserve Banks of Philadelphia. http://www.phil.frb.org/src/srcinsights/srcinsights/q1cc1.html (accessed 22 July 2007).

Stark, J. (2006), 'Easy loans often come at high cost', *Knight Ridder Tribune Business News*, 10 December, 1.

Stegman, M. (2007), 'Payday lending', *Journal of Economic Perspectives*, **21** (1), 169–90.

Stiglitz, J. and A. Weiss (1981), 'Credit rationing in markets with imperfect information', *American Economic Review*, **71** (1), 393–410.

Thomas, L., R. Oliver and D. Hand (2005), 'A survey of issues in consumer credit modelling research', *Journal of the Operational Research Society*, **56** (9), 1003–5.

Wenske, P. (2007), 'Missouri demands reforms: the average loan has an annual interest rate of 422 percent', *Knight Ridder Tribune Business News*, 17 February, 1.

Whitehouse, M. (2005), 'How a formula ignited a market that burned investors', *Wall Street Journal*, 12 September, A1.

4. The saving puzzle: a closer examination

The collapse of the personal saving rate in the USA after 1993 makes it easy to forget that the long-run stability (or constancy of the trend value) of the saving-to-income ratio (or average propensity to save, in Keynesian terminology) was at one time an established (and stylized) empirical fact of macroeconomic analysis. Indeed, seminal postwar contributions to the theory of aggregate saving (and consumption) sought to reconcile the (apparent) contradiction between the short-run (or cyclical) and long-run behavior of the propensity to save.[1] According to standard Keynesian theory, the consumption-to-income (S/Y) ratio should behave pro-cyclically – that is, it should fall over the course of a business cycle contraction because people display a tendency, as a rule and on average, to resist drastic retrenchment in their lifestyles when their incomes are falling. Another logical implication of Keynes's fundamental law of consumption is that the S/Y ratio should climb in sympathy with a broad-based economic expansion.

Time series analysis of the S/Y ratio performed in the 1950s and 1960s revealed that, while the propensity to save did exhibit a pro-cyclical pattern during recessionary phases, there was otherwise a tendency of the S/Y ratio to converge to its long-run or trend value (approximately 0.078 for the 1947–69 era).[2] For example, the propensity to save remained remarkably stable through the protracted boom of the 1960s, an empirical fact at variance with the naïve Keynesian view. The relative constancy of the propensity to save amidst very large increases in real incomes is what we may term the inaugural saving puzzle.

The latter-day saving puzzle concerns not merely the stunning diminution of household saving (as it is conventionally measured) since 1993, though the phenomenon taken by itself has no historical precedent save for the worst months of the Depression. The truly baffling aspect of the problem is that household savings in the USA nosedived against a backdrop of relative economic prosperity. Table 4.1 tracks the behavior of three standard indices of macroeconomic health for 1993–2006. Note that the average growth rate of inflation-adjusted personal income was 2.5 percent. Moreover, the Great American Jobs Machine fired on all cylinders until

Table 4.1   The saving rate, unemployment, employment and personal income growth, 1993–2006

Year	Personal saving rate (%)	Unemployment rate [a] (%)	Change in payroll employment [b]	Growth of real personal income [c] (%)
1993	5.800	6.91	+2 124 000	0.676
1994	4.850	6.10	+3 435 330	2.449
1995	4.650	5.59	+3 024 170	2.429
1996	4.000	5.41	+2 392 250	2.962
1997	3.650	4.94	+3 068 000	3.629
1998	4.325	4.50	+3 157 000	5.708
1999	2.350	4.22	+3 068 250	2.856
2000	2.325	3.97	+2 800 080	4.520
2001	1.750	4.74	+39 830	0.658
2002	2.375	5.78	−1 484 920	0.210
2003	2.150	5.99	−356 750	0.872
2004	2.000	5.53	+1 433 330	3.422
2005	−0.375	5.08	+2 273 000	1.792
2006	−1.075	4.63	+2 478 330	2.962

Notes:
[a] Civilian labor force.
[b] Wage and salaried employment, change from previous year.
[c] Change from previous year.

Source: Bureau of Labor Statistics and Bureau of Economic Analysis.

2001. Net job creation between 1993 and 2000 was equal to 23 069 080 – a remarkable number. As was noted in Chapter 1, forecasting saving after 1993 using equations fitted to pre-1993 time series data produces large (negative) errors. As a thought-experiment, suppose that, in the year 1993, economists were asked to prepare a 15-year economic forecast with a single piece of information: the future saving rate would move steadily lower and break into negative territory during the year 2005. Is it unfair to say that many, if not most, economists would have feared a forthcoming economic calamity?

This chapter aims to unravel the saving mystery. It begins with an overview of recent theoretical explanations based on precautionary saving and the lifecycle hypothesis. In keeping with a main theme of this book, the chapter turns to the causal linkage of the S/Y ratio to income distribution. A simulation is performed to examine the effects of a change in income inequality on aggregate saving behavior. Empirical evidence on the distribution–saving relation is presented in a later section. Concluding remarks follow.

4.1 SHOULD SAVING INCLUDE UNREALIZED CAPITAL GAINS?

The national income and product accounts (NIPA) definition of saving includes employer and employee contributions to tax-deferred pension accounts such as 401(k)s.[3] It does not include unrealized capital gains, defined as 'increases or decreases in the value of assets yet to be sold [including] publicly traded stocks, pooled investment funds, the primary residence, other real estate, and the current tax basis of businesses' (Bucks et al. 2005, p. 9). Thus an individual could in practice have negative 'measured' saving but still be accumulating wealth at an enviable pace if asset holdings are considerable and if financial and real-estate markets cooperate. Gale and Sabelhaus (1999, p. 183) argue that 'over the past forty years, capital gains have dominated measured saving as a source of household wealth accumulation, and that, if all capital gains are included as saving, the household saving rate is at its highest level in the past forty years, not its lowest'.

The displacement of traditional 'defined benefit' pensions by defined contribution plans is probably responsible for a profound change in household behavior. The traditional pensioner anticipates receiving, based on career earning and/or years of service, a predetermined (or defined) annuity. The situation is different for the 401(k) holder, who is far more likely to count pension as a part of wealth. The proliferation of tax-deferred accounts has in effect tied the wealth (and unrealized capital gains) of a vastly larger number of households to stock or bond market performance. Quarterly reports and web portals provide a steady stream of information concerning changes in the monetary value of defined contribution accounts. Thus, while the switch to defined contribution plans may not, by itself, alter the true economic value of household pensions (where the value of defined benefit plans is equal to the present or discounted value of annuities expected to be realized from them), the very nature of these plans is such as to give the appearance of greater wealth. One aspect of the saving puzzle might be called a '401(k)-wealth effect' on consumer spending.[4]

The data in Table 4.2 show that unrealized capital gains are quite substantial, though disproportionately distributed to higher-income households. Changes in the 'stock' of realized capital gains between two years give an idea of the annual flow of saving replaced by asset appreciation. For all families, median unrealized capital gains were sufficient to replace about

Table 4.2   Median value of unrealized capital gains (2004 dollars)

Income percentiles	Year				
	1992	1995	1998	2001	2004
All families	9 900	6 800	12 500	16 000	23 000
Less than 20	†	†	†	†	†
20–39.9	1 400	400	2 100	1 500	3 000
40–59.9	4 100	4 600	10 400	10 100	12 100
60–79.9	21 200	16 400	23 400	29 800	46 700
80–89.9	32 400	33 200	39 600	58 600	70 000
90–100	122 600	80 000	112 500	170 400	221 900

Note: † Less than $50.

Source: Federal Reserve Board 2004, *Survey of Consumer Finances*, Table 9.

$1167 (2004 dollars) in measured saving per year between 1992 and 2004 – a figure adequate to give a median-income family ($46 326) with no measured savings an 'effective' saving rate (meaning inclusive of asset appreciation) of 2.4 percent. Mean unrealized capital gains (measured in 2004 dollars) increased by $69 400 between 1992 and 2004, an average annual increase of approximately $5783. By multiplying this figure by the number of households, we can estimate total unrealized capital gains in a particular year. Adding this total to measured saving and recalculating the saving rate yields a back-of-the-envelope estimate of the degree to which unrealized capital gains have replaced conventional saving. By reckoning the change in unrealized capital gains as saving in 2004, the saving rate increases from 2 to about 11 percent. Thus the solution to the saving puzzle might be found in what is clearly a heightened dependence among contemporary householders on market revaluations of financial assets or real estate. We need to bear in mind, however, that unrealized capital gains are nothing new – that is, adding them retrospectively to official saving would raise the saving rate several percentage points for most years since 1945. The hypothesis of one-to-one (or perfect) substitution of conventional saving with capital gains is valid only if it can be shown that, as a percentage of income, annual increases of (unrealized) capital gains have been equal to decreases in measured saving.

Another factor to consider is that a notional rise in the value of owner-occupied homes is fundamentally different from an increase in holdings of bank deposits, near monies, or bonds and equities – and not just in terms of liquidity. As shelter is an essential need, the realization of capital gains on an owner-occupied dwelling entails, in many cases at least, the purchase of a new home. In an environment of escalating real-estate values, a substantial capital gain from the sale of the current home may be necessary merely to afford a replacement home.

4.2   BUSINESS AND GOVERNMENT SAVING

Discussion of saving in this volume has, up to this point, been confined to personal or household saving. To the extent that saving is conceptualized as a critical activity that regulates the pace of capital goods production, there is no good reason to exclude business or government saving from the analysis. That is, there is no obvious reason to believe that the economic effects of business or government saving are different from those arising from household saving. Business saving is equal to the aggregate of net after-tax cash receipts of business units withheld from business owners (shareholders), while government saving is the excess of revenues over expenditures in a fiscal period, summed across public sector units. Aggregate saving is equal to the sum of household, business and government saving. The question arises: has overall saving in the USA fallen, or has there merely been a shift over time in the distribution of saving across household, business and government sectors? Figure 4.1 sheds light on the issue. We see that total net saving as a percentage of GDP in the USA actually rose considerably from 1991 to 1999. The key factor driving the saving rate higher was a major decline in the scale of new borrowing by the federal government. In fact, a federal deficit of $290 billion in 1992 morphed into a $236 billion surplus in the year 2000. The surge in household and federal borrowing since 2001 has driven the net saving rate to historic lows. All the while, corporate saving as a percentage of GDP has remained fairly stable.

4.3   PRECAUTIONARY SAVING AND LIFECYCLE EFFECTS

J.M. Keynes delineated several motives for saving (or the accumulation of wealth) in Chapter 9 of the *General Theory*. Among these was 'to build up a reserve against unforeseen contingencies'(Keynes 1936, p. 107). The precautionary motive figures prominently in the contemporary orthodox literature on the saving puzzle, where 'orthodox' denotes those contributions that build up aggregate saving functions from the intertemporal optimization problem of a representative agent.[5] For this class of models, the trick is to adjust the parameters facing the agent so as to generate a decrease

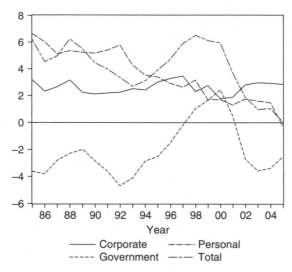

Note: Net saving is equal to gross saving minus consumption of fixed capital.

Source: *Economic Report of the President*, 2007, Tables B-1 and B-32.

Figure 4.1   Net saving as a percentage of GDP, by sector

in the utility-maximizing quantity of precautionary saving that, when summed over the population of agents, mimics the actual time path of the saving rate.[6] The technique ostensibly provides insight into the real-world forces at play if the readjustment of model parameters (initial endowments, constraints, or the degree of certainty about future income streams) corresponds to actual changes in the economic environment. A survey of the literature uncovers solid support for the view that fluctuations of aggregate saving are (partly) caused by shifting confidence levels about future income or job security.[7] The economic magnitude of the confidence–precautionary saving effect depends on: (1) the responsiveness of precautionary saving to a unit change in confidence; and (2) the importance of precautionary saving relative to total saving.[8]

Presuming that precautionary saving is a primary driver of the overall saving rate, recent saving behavior must be largely explained by a generalized buoyancy of views about future economic prospects.[9] Is there (or was there) an objective basis for such optimism? Structural changes in the employment mix could be one factor. Compared to 1985, the economy of today comprises far fewer (in both absolute terms and relative to total employment) manufacturing jobs in cyclical industries such as autos or heavy machinery. Whereas recurring layoffs were once a fact of life for a significant component of the labor force, they are less important in the major areas of job growth such as retail trade or healthcare. Changing workforce demographics may be implicated as well. Stiglitz notes that, with the aging of baby boomers, 'we now have a more mature labor force, with greater representation of age groups that have traditionally lower unemployment rates' (Stiglitz 1997, pp. 6–7). To the extent that lower unemployment rates correlate with higher job security, precautionary saving motivated by fear of imminent job loss may have diminished. However, a lifecycle approach predicts that *total* savings are positively related to the share of the labor force currently matriculating through the peak years of the earnings lifecycle, *ceteris paribus*.

It stands to reason that the strength of the precautionary motive would be greater if households' assets were comparatively illiquid and/or if households had limited borrowing options. One line of recent research looks for the decline in precautionary saving in the relaxation of liquidity constraints.[10] The innovations described in Chapter 3 are clearly a factor here. Li (2004) argues that improvements in credit-scoring techniques have given low-income, hitherto liquidity-constrained households a substitute for precautionary savings – that is, high-interest credit card and home equity loans. Those operating within the standard loanable funds (or time preference) theory of interest point to the global integration of financial markets. They argue that global integration, by enabling US households to tap foreign pools of financial capital, frees domestic borrowing from the constraint of domestic saving – an argument considered in Chapter 7.[11]

One would have thought that, in light of the events unfolding in the past 15 years, Modigliani's lifecycle hypothesis of saving (see Ando and Modigliani 1963) would be thoroughly discredited – at least where the USA is concerned. Cross-sectional evidence from the USA and elsewhere shows that, adjusting for differences in income, saving is strongly, and positively, related to age. Indeed, those 70 and older have the highest savings rates in the USA.[12] This should come as no surprise, given the arguments made in Chapter 2. Saving is not a function of age *per se*. Rather, it is a case of the older generation carrying a more deeply ingrained set of saving habits into retirement. Some argue that lifecycle effects are nevertheless part of the solution to the saving puzzle because they (partly) account for important changes in strategies of wealth accumulation.

The lifecycle view is that older workers are more likely to have accumulated assets that have the potential for capital gain and thus are more likely to rely on capital gains, as opposed to conventionally defined saving, for wealth accumulation. Home ownership rates, for example, are higher for middle-aged compared to younger workers. The profligacy of boomers (as evidenced by measured saving) might be exploded as a myth if it could be shown that, on average, unrealized capital gains have been large enough to offset decreases in officially measured saving.

4.4   INCOME DISTRIBUTION AND HOUSEHOLD SAVING: CAMBRIDGE AND KEYNESIAN VIEWS

The problem of income distribution – its measurement and underlying causes, as well as its economic and social ramifications – is the subject of a vast literature.[13] Yet surprisingly little attention has been paid to the question of its macroeconomic implications. The basic issue is straightforward enough: does the shape of the income distribution function matter for effective demand? Readers of Chapters 1 and 2 will anticipate the answer provided here: yes, it matters – but not in the way conventionally assumed. To revisit the position outlined earlier, rising income disparities, when projected into a consumerist social milieu featuring soft borrowing constraints, may act as a catalyst to aggregate spending. Surging inequality was identified as a significant factor in driving down the US saving rate (this hypothesis is submitted to econometric test in the next section). Thus we are asserting that aggregate saving is inversely related to income inequality, *ceteris paribus*. Some readers may find this claim counterintuitive. It is certainly incongruous with what we may term the Cambridge and Keynesian positions.

Income distribution does play a role in theories of consumption authored by economists affiliated to the Cambridge or post-Keynesian school.[14] Pressman (1997) notes that the dependence of aggregate consumption on the functional distribution of income is the distinctive feature of the Cambridge approach. For example, Kalecki divided total income between income of workers (W) and profit or income of capitalists (Π). Let α_1 denote the propensity to consume out of wage income and α_2 the propensity to consume out of profits. Thus aggregate consumption expenditure (C) is given by:

$$C = \alpha_1 W + \alpha_2 \Pi \qquad (4.1)$$

If α_1 is greater than α_2, then a change in functional shares in favor of labor income will boost consumption.

The Cambridge approach is well suited to a situation in which individual or household incomes are restricted to a single functional category – for example, people receive wages or profits, but not both. The methodological approach used in a forthcoming simulation follows more closely Keynesian lines. Income distribution matters for effective demand if, *ceteris paribus*, a change in the shape of the income distribution function, or the personal distribution of income, causes a change in the aggregate propensity to consume.[15] Keynes stated the essential principle as follows in a 1939 comment:

> Since I regard the propensity to consume as being (normally) as such to have a wider gap between income and consumption as income increases, it naturally follows that the collective propensity for the community as a whole may depend . . . on the distribution of incomes within it. (Keynes 1939, p. 129)

The Keynesian logic is as follows. Individuals confronting true uncertainty often wish to defer economic decision-making, and this is accomplished by the accumulation of wealth, or what is the same thing, the purchase of stores of value. But since agents generally prefer to hold wealth in intangible assets – that is, assets characterized by high liquidity, the demand for stores of value does not necessarily mean a corresponding demand for tangible, reproducible assets.[16] Although the desire to accumulate wealth is not specific to any income group or social class, the power to defer spending decisions is clearly connected to income level. The freedom to purchase stores of value expands in proportion to the difference between income and the cost of maintaining a material standard of living that is minimally satisfactory to the household. The effect of an upward redistribution of income is to place a greater share of total income under the control of households with power to defer spending. The net result for the average propensity to consume (or S/Y ratio) would be even more pronounced if the marginal propensity to purchase intangible stores of value were a geometric function of income.

4.5   MEASURING THE EFFECTS OF INCOME INEQUALITY ON SAVING: A SIMULATION[17]

In this section a simple model is developed for purposes of simulating the effects of changing income inequality on consumption expenditure and household saving based on Keynesian assumptions about consumer behavior. The model illustrates that the Keynesian logic is well founded so long as: (1) households are averse to borrowing to finance consumption or, alternatively, face 'hard' budget constraints; and (2) culturally sufficient buying routines remain unaffected by income redistribution.

The simulation yields an estimate of the maximum increase in household saving that could result if, *ceteris paribus*, income inequality were eliminated completely. The likelihood of producing estimates that are meaningful in a practical sense is greater if the model is a reasonably close facsimile of an actual economy in terms of population, GDP, income inequality, spending and saving behavior. Toward that end, the key parameters of the model described below have been selected so that they correlate as closely as possible to the US economy in the year 2005.[18] Specifically, the model assumes the following:

1. There are 114 984 000 households.
2. Mean household is equal to $63 344. Median income is equal to $46 326.
3. The initial distribution of income between persons approximates the actual distribution of income in the USA for the year 2005.
4. The household population is divided into 44 income groups. The simulation assumes that the distribution of income within these income groups is perfectly equal. So, for example, the average income for the fifth highest group of families is $98 658. We assume that all 854 000 families in this group have an income equal to $98 658.
5. The spending patterns of families at all income levels conform exactly to those of a 'representative' agent.

The consumption function specification for a representative agent incorporates the Marxian idea of a 'socially necessary minimum' level of consumption. More precisely, we assume that there is some level of planned or notional consumption expenditure that can be classified as exogenous in the sense of its being independent of current income. It is useful to think of the exogenous component of spending (denoted by the symbol φ) as the absolute minimum level of consumption necessary to maintain participation in the mainstream of economic and social life. It is the equivalent of what was earlier termed a 'culturally sufficient' level of expenditure.[19] The term 'notional' is used to describe it because there is no guarantee that the agent will have the purchasing power to achieve the socially necessary minimum level of spending.

Cross-sectional variations in the consumption-to-income ratio are explained by a variety of factors. These include variations in household size, differences in wealth or liquidity of assets held, as well as age and health factors. However, it is very likely that the single most important factor in explaining cross-sectional differences in the average propensity to consume is unevenness in the distribution of income among persons.

The consumption function of a single 'representative' agent (agent i) is described by the following equation:

$$C_i = \varphi_i + Y_i^a \tag{4.2}$$

where φ_i is the exogenous component of consumption and Y_i is income of individual i. Equation (4.2) obeys Keynes's fundamental psychological law so long as the following restriction holds: $0 < a < 1$. The non-linear specification given by (4.2) above makes the propensity to consume out the marginal increment of income a diminishing function of disposable income.

Computing aggregate consumption expenditure for the hypothetical economy is a matter of summing consumption functions across 114.984 million persons (i.e. $n = 114.984$ million). That is:

$$C = \sum_{i=1}^{n} (\varphi_i + Y_i^a) \qquad (4.3)$$

Attempting to specify, within the context of contemporary US society, an expenditure level equivalent to a socially necessary minimum unavoidably entails some degree of arbitrariness. One might argue that the Social Security Administration (SSA) official poverty line furnishes a reasonable measure of the socially necessary minimum.[20] But the SSA poverty index is an absolute standard – it makes no adjustments for a general increase in living standards. Chapter 2 used research findings from several disciplines (neuroscience, evolutionary psychology and anthropology) to give a scientific underpinning to the common observation that people's feelings about the satisfactoriness of their own material living standards are influenced by the consumption habits displayed by others.[21] Hence the desideratum for a poverty threshold that is *relative* in the sense of positioning the individual in unchanging (economic) proximity to the typical individual. Moreover, the most widely used relative poverty definition in cross-national studies is 50 percent of median household income, adjusted for differences in household size.[22] The preceding relative poverty definition is taken as the best available proxy for the socially necessary minimum level of income. The socially necessary minimum (φ_i) is thus defined as 50 percent of median income for a family in the year 2005, or \$23 163.[23]

The final problem for the simulation is to select a value of a (i.e., the power to which disposable income is raised in the consumption function) that makes equation (4.2) a reasonably close approximation of actual spending behavior in the USA. Data prepared by the Bureau of Economic Analysis for the year 2005 show that the ratio of aggregate consumption to disposable income was very close to 1.0 (thus the ratio of household saving to disposable income was 0.000). Thus the value of a satisfies the following equation when the fraction of total income accruing to persons within each of the 44 income groups in the model corresponds to the actual distribution of income for the year 2005:

$$\frac{\sum_{i=1}^{114\,984\,000} (\$23\,163 + Y_i^a)}{Y_T} = 1.00 \qquad (4.4)$$

where Y_T is total or aggregate income (equal to approximately \$7.2 trillion).[24] The value of a which satisfies the condition described by equation (4.4) subject to the condition described above is 0.9602. Thus we have:

$$C_i = \$23\,163 + Y_i^{0.9602} \qquad (4.5)$$

To examine the relationship between income inequality and the S/Y ratio more closely, it is helpful to select a specific measure of inequality. For the purposes of the following illustration we use the well-known Theil index (Theil 1967):

$$T = \frac{1}{n}\sum_{i=1}^{n} r_i \cdot \log r_i \qquad (4.6)$$

where r_i is the ratio between individual income (Y_i) and average income (μ_Y):

$$r_i = \frac{Y_i}{\mu_Y}, \ \mu_Y = \frac{\sum_{i=1}^{n} Y_i}{n} \qquad (4.7)$$

The Theil index (T) is a monotonically increasing measure of inequality, bounded by [0, log n].[25] The value of the Theil index for families in the USA in the year 2005 was 0.36094 $(T = 0.36094)$.[26]

Two simulations were performed. The first iteration assumes that households borrow as required to satisfy equation (4.5). The results show that, on this scenario, fully 65 percent of households engage in deficit spending – that is, have a saving-to-income ratio of less than zero. As the numbers in Table 4.3 attest, the simulation does not support the argument that income inequality imposes a significant drag on aggregate expenditure when budget constraints are soft (as defined above). The model estimates that a decrease of the Theil statistic from its 2005 value (0.36094) to zero would boost aggregate consumption expenditure by slightly less than 1 percent, or about \$69.6 billion.

The second model assumes that, initially, incomes are distributed evenly among households. Moreover, we impose the constraint that consumption expenditure cannot exceed income – that is, $C \leq Y$. The hard budget constraint means that a large number of households will be unable to reach the desired level of consumption as described by equation (4.5).

Table 4.4 displays results for the income-constrained model. They illustrate that, when income imposes a hard constraint on spending, income

Table 4.3   Simulated effects of an increase in income equality: soft budget constraint model (Theil statistic forced from 0.36094 to zero)

Change in consumption		C/Y	S/Y
$ (millions)	%		
+ 69 580 784.1	+0.96	1.00968	−0.00968

Table 4.4   Simulated effects of a decrease in income equality: hard budget constraint model (Theil statistic forced from zero to 0.36094)

Change in consumption		C/Y	S/Y
$ (millions)	%		
−1 013 456.3	−16.08	0.8694	0.1302

distribution can have very significant implications for effective demand. The hard budget constraint model predicts that the S/Y ratio would increase from zero to 0.1302 if the Theil statistic increased from zero to its actual level in 2005. Assuming that income is $7.2 trillion, this translates to a spending differential of approximately $1013.5 billion, or 16 percent.

The distribution–effective demand link illustrates that economic 'laws', in contrast to the laws of physics, are grounded in a particular socio-economic reality. The pre-theoretic conceptual reality implicit in the Kaleckian/Keynesian interpretation of the distribution–spending nexus is one in which the contents of culturally sufficient market baskets remain fairly stable over time, conservative attitudes to borrowing are the rule, and consumer financing arrangements are in their early stages. The simulation above illustrates, albeit in rather crude fashion, how causal relationships among economic variables can be fundamentally altered as a consequence of technological or institutional change.

4.6   DISTRIBUTION AND SAVING: EVIDENCE FROM THE USA

The purpose of this section is to determine if there is empirical support for the hypothesis that changes in the shape of the income distribution function have influenced the time path of saving in the USA since 1960. The methodology entails simple curve fitting, a Granger causality test, and time

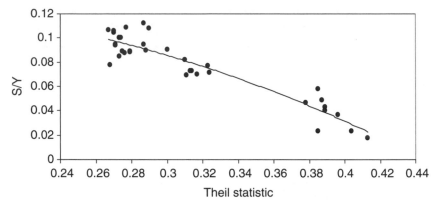

Sources: Bureau of the Census, Table IE-G and the Bureau of Economic Analysis.

Figure 4.2   Curve fitted to Theil statistic and saving ratio, 1967–2001

series estimation of a saving specification with a measure of income inequality included among the explanatory variables.

4.6.1   Curve Fitting

The scatter diagram labeled Figure 4.2 illustrates annual Thiel statistic–saving ratio pairs for 1967–2001. The polynomial function fitted to the data has a coefficient of determination (R^2) of 0.876. Note that the Theil statistic for households rose from 0.313 in 1991 to 0.413 in 2001. This would have been sufficient, according to the curve appearing in Figure 4.1, to reduce the saving ratio from 0.085 to 0.031, or a staggering 73 percent. While it is not wise to draw causal inferences based on statistical correlations among variables, the pattern illustrated in Figure 4.1 is not at variance with our main hypothesis.

4.6.2   Causality Testing

A time series X is said to Granger-cause Y if it can be shown, by a series of F-tests on lagged values of Y, that those X values provide statistically significant information about future values of Y (see Granger 1980). Granger causality tests were performed for two variables – the saving rate and the annual value of the Gini coefficient. The sample comprises 58 annual observations corresponding to the years 1947–2006. The Gini coefficient is a well-known measure of income inequality that is found by dividing the area beneath a Lorenz curve by the area below a line of equality.[27] Its value ranges from zero (perfect equality) to one.

Table 4.5   Pairwise Granger causality test (one lag)

Null hypothesis	F-statistic	Probability
Gini does not Granger-cause *PSR*	18.0085	0.000008
PSR does not Granger-cause Gini	1.29448	0.260616

The results are shown in Table 4.5. The null hypothesis – 'Gini does not Granger-cause the personal saving rate (*PSR*)' – can be rejected at the 0.00001 level. On the other hand, the F-statistic for the null hypothesis '*PSR* does not Granger-cause Gini' is quite low.

4.6.3   Time Series Estimation

To investigate the effects of income inequality on the time path of the personal saving rate, a simple model is specified. It posits the saving rate as a function of wealth, the opportunity cost of current consumption as measured by foregone future consumption (proxied by the interest rate), and income distribution. The following first-order autoregressive model was estimated using non-linear least squares:

$$\log PSR_t = \beta_0 + \beta_1 \log Stocks_{t-1} + \beta_2 \log TBill_t + \beta_3 \log Gini_t + \mu_t \quad (4.7)$$

$$\mu_t = \rho\mu_{t-1} + \varepsilon_t \quad (4.8)$$

where *PSR* is the personal saving rate in year *t*; *Stocks* is the inflation-adjusted value of the Dow Jones Stock Index at the end of the preceding year; *TBill* is the annual average of the 6-month Treasury bill rate; and *Gini* is the Gini coefficient described above.[28] The residuals obtained from ordinary least squares estimation of the model described by equation (4.7) revealed the presence of first-order serial correlation. The linear model described by (4.7) can be transformed to a first-order autoregressive model by the addition of equation (4.8). Substitution of equation (4.8) for the period *t* error term converts the specification into a non-linear one and therefore makes it possible to estimate the model using non-linear least squares. The technique used here is Marquardt's iterative algorithm (Marquardt 1963), which yields regression estimates that are asymptotically equivalent to maximum likelihood estimates and are asymptotically efficient. The model was estimated using annual US data for 1960–2005. The estimates are reported as follows (t-ratios in parentheses):

$$\log PSR_t = 2.405 - 0.516 \log Stocks_{t-1} + 0.059 \log TBill_t - 3.541 \log Gini_t$$
$$\quad\quad (2.23)\ (-5.69) \quad\quad\quad\quad\quad (0.82) \quad\quad\quad\quad (-6.14)$$

$R^2 = 0.933$ Inverted AR roots $= 0.45$ Sample: 1960–2005 ($n = 45$)

Many economists believe that, because home equity is far more evenly distributed among households than is financial wealth, housing prices have a tighter relation to spending behavior than financial asset prices. Non-proprietary data on annual changes in US housing prices are currently unavailable.[29] *Stocks* is therefore used as a substitute index of changes in household wealth. The estimates are consistent with a significant 'stock–price' effect on consumption.

The most important finding for our purposes is that income inequality, as proxied by the Gini coefficient, has a negative and statistically significant effect on the personal saving rate during the sample period. The estimate of the β_3 parameter may be interpreted as follows: a 1 percent increase of the Gini coefficient subtracted an average of 3.5 percent (not percentage points) from the saving rate over the sample period, *ceteris paribus.* Census Bureau figures show the Gini coefficient for households rising by nearly 11 percent between 1992 and 2005. The equation predicts that, holding all other variables constant, this should have reduced the saving rate by about 38 percent (the actual decrease was minus 114 percent).

NOTES

1. See Friedman (1957) and Duesenberry (1949).
2. Linear trend function estimated using Bureau of Economic Analysis (BSA) data for disposable income and consumption for 1947–69.
3. For the personal saving rate, meaning the percentage of monthly personal disposable income not used for consumption expenditure. Note that the BEA definition of saving includes employer contributions to tax-deferred pension accounts.
4. Defined benefit pensions are comparable to publicly funded retirement and healthcare programs. Very few people, for example, view future eligibility for social security or Medicare as a component of wealth, even though it would require a very sizeable portfolio (more than \$400 000) of financial assets to produce a flow of income equal to the average benefits received.
5. Sule (2006, p. 1105) writes that '[a] precautionary motive leads an agent to respond to a risk by making adjustments that will help to reduce the expected cost of the risk: Thus, precautionary saving arises when forward-looking consumers accumulate wealth today for the purpose of reducing the impact of future uncertainty on future consumption decisions'.
6. Carroll (1997) is representative. See also Turnovsky and Smith (2006) and Yi and Choi (2006). Kimball (1990) developed a technique to measure precautionary saving that subsequent researchers have relied on. Carroll has lately grown disenchanted with the representative consumer technique, as he writes that

   the theoretical conditions under which an economy composed of many individuals will behave exactly as though it contains a single representative agent ('exact aggregation holds') are very stringent. The most problematic requirement is that consumers can completely insure their income against idiosyncratic shocks. In reality, household-level income data that include information on the existing sources of insurance (such as unemployment insurance, government transfers, and support from family and friends) show large fluctuations in post-tax, post-transfer idiosyncratic income, and there is now a large literature showing that consumption responds strongly to uninsured income shocks. (Carroll et al. 2003, p. 111)

7. For example, Carroll et al. (2003) estimated the effect of job uncertainty on precautionary saving using Current Population Survey microdata and found that 'households in the lowest permanent income groups do not engage in precautionary saving, but as income rises, precautionary behavior becomes significant in both economic and statistical terms' (ibid., p. 600). See also Benito (2006).
8. There is substantial disagreement on this point. See Carroll et al. (2003).
9. Two well-known indices of consumer confidence, the Conference Board Consumer Confidence Index and the University of Michigan Index of Consumer Sentiment, fell very sharply during most of 2000 and 2001. Both indices have fluctuated since (though the Conference Board measure hit a five-year peak in February 2007). Note that both indices sample survey respondents about their future economic prospects. Thus, while the path of consumer confidence indices might give some support to the precautionary saving hypothesis before 2000, the same cannot be said for the years since 2000.
10. For example, see Sarantis and Stewart (2003), Bredin and Cuthbertson (2002), and Xu (1995). Fernandez-Corugedo (2002, p. 309) writes:

    [t]he literature finds at least three important implications of the inability to borrow (hard constraints) for consumption. First, hard constraints increase precautionary saving around levels of wealth where the constraints bind. Second, if consumers face the possibility of becoming constrained at any point in the future, they will behave as if they were constrained today, even in the absence of a current liquidity constraint. Finally, the introduction of further borrowing constraints does not necessarily lead to an increase in precautionary saving.

11. The logical extension of the time preference theory is that persistent US current account deficits are explained by cross-national differences in rates of time preference (or savings rates) as well as the willingness of surplus countries to purchase IOUs from deficit countries. For a discussion, see Mann (2002).
12. Source: Federal Reserve Board 2004, *Survey of Consumer Finances*, Table 9.
13. For a recent description of cross-national trends in income inequality, see Gottschalk and Smeeding (1997). See Acemoglu (2002) for a review of the literature on the question of technical change and income inequality.
14. The leading contributor is Kalecki (1991a, 1991b), but the group also includes Robinson (1954) and Kaldor (1960). See Pressman (1997) for a detailed discussion. See also Trigg (1994).
15. Keynes defined the 'propensity to consume' as the 'functional relationship . . . between . . . a given level of income . . . [and] the expenditure on consumption out of that level of income' (Keynes 1936, p. 90).
16. Davidson writes that '[T]he demand for a store of value, in an uncertain world, does not generate the demand to commit resources. Thus, the virtuous interaction between the supply of resources and the demand for resources which is succinctly expressed by Say's law is broken' (Davidson 1978, p. 145).
17. The techniques used in section 4.5 and subsection 4.6.3 are adapted from C. Brown (2004), 'Does income distribution matter for effective demand? Evidence from the United States', *Review of Political Economy*, **16** (3), 291–307, with permission from Taylor and Francis Journals (www.informaworld.com).
18. The assumptions of the model with respect to mean and median income, population and the distribution of income are based on the 2005 March Supplement (Annual

Demographic Survey) of the Current Population Survey, Table HINC-06, which can be viewed at http://pubdb3.census.gov/macro/032006/hhinc/toc.htm.

19.   The reader will notice that the concept of the 'socially necessary minimum', although it has largely the same meaning that Marx gave it, is used for a wholly different purpose here. Marx argued that compensation of labor could not fall below the minimum means of subsistence, or 'natural price of labor', or else 'the labor-power withdrawn from the market by wear and tear, and by death, that must be continually replaced, at the very least, by an equal amount of labor power, [will not be replaced]' (Marx 1977, p. 275). Marx relied on Torrens to define the natural price of labor: '[It] consists in such a quantity of necessaries and comforts of life, as, from the nature of the climate, and the habits of the country, are necessary to support the laborer, and enable him to rear such a family as may preserve, in the market, an undiminished supply of labor' (Torrens 1815, quoted in Marx, 1977, p. 275).

20.   The poverty threshold for a non-farm family of four in the year 2001 was $17960. The Social Security Administration poverty threshold is determined by measuring the cost of a market basket of food items that provide three minimally adequate meals per day and multiplying by three to obtain a 'daily' threshold. The poverty line is then determined by multiplying the daily figure by 365. The poverty threshold is adjusted for differences in family size. For a detailed description see Schiller (2001, Chapter 2).

21.   The reader will recall the importance of this principle in the work of Duesenberry (1949). More recently, Vaughan has written that people make judgments about the adequacy of their incomes based

> on the general level of material offerings available in their society at a given time. Thus in 1850, an urban New Yorker would hardly have felt deprived by not being able to afford a telephone, radio or television; as such goods did not exist, they were not part of the choice set of New York 140 years ago. For the same reason, the individual would hardly have felt diminished as a breadwinner because of an inability to acquire such items for his or her family. As a more relevant example of our own era, color television was not a part of the typical choice set . . . in the 1950s, but it most definitely is . . . in 1993. And simply because such consumption expectations exist, a consistent inability to meet them . . . is likely to take a heavy toll on individuals who see themselves as family providers. (Vaughan 1993, p. 23)

22.   For a discussion of relative poverty measures, and the 50 percent standard, see Ruggles (1990, Chapter 3). For recent examples of the use of the 50 percent of median household income poverty measure in cross-national studies, see Pressman (2002) and Burniax et al. (1998).

23.   The Gallup polling organization conducts an annual 'get-along' survey in which individuals are asked the minimum amount of income that a family of four needs to 'get along'. The average amount, expressed as a percentage of median income, was 68.3 percent for the period 1984–89. The estimate presented here appears conservative judged against the Gallup get-along standard. See Vaughan (1993, pp. 27–8).

24. Y_T is found by multiplying average income ($63 344) by the number of households (114.383 million). This figure is very close to total disposable income (current dollars) for the USA in the year 2005.

25.   For a description of the Theil index and instructions on how to compute it using widely available data sources, see Conceição and Galbraith (2000).

26.   For the purposes of this simulation, the Thiel statistic was computed using the 44-income group delineation for households described in CPS Table HINC-06 (see note 18 above). The true Theil statistic for US households in 2005 would exceed the value calculated for this simulation (0.036094) since the model assumes perfect equality within the income groups.

27.   For a good explanation, see Dorfman (1979).

28.   The sources for the data used in the times series estimation are as follows: *PSR*: Bureau

of Economic Analysis; *TBill*: Federal Reserve Bank of New York; *Stocks*: The Dow Jones Company; and *Gini*: Bureau of the Census.
29. The data can be purchased from the National Realtors Association.

REFERENCES

Acemoglu, D. (2002), 'Technical change, inequality, and the labor market', *Journal of Economic Literature*, **40** (1), 7–72.

Ando, A. and F. Modigliani (1963), 'The "life cycle" hypothesis of saving: aggregate implications and tests', *American Economic Review*, **52** (1), 55–84.

Benito, A. (2006), 'Does job security affect household consumption?', *Oxford Economic Papers*, **58** (1), 157–81.

Bredin, D. and K. Cuthbertson (2002), 'Liquidity effects and precautionary saving in the Czech Republic', *Applied Financial Economics*, **12** (6), 405–21.

Bucks, B., A. Kennickell and K. Moore (2006), 'Recent changes in U.S. family finances: evidence from the 2001 and 2004 Survey of Consumer Finances', *Federal Reserve Bulletin*, **92** (1), 1–38.

Burniax, J., T. Dong, D. Fore, D. Förster, M. d'Ercole and H. Oxley (1998), 'Income distribution and poverty in selected OECD countries', Organization for Economic Co-operation and Development, Economics Department Working Paper No. 189.

Carroll, C.D. (1997), 'Buffer stock saving and the lifecycle/permanent income hypothesis', *Quarterly Journal of Economics*, **62** (1), 1–55.

Carroll, C.D., K.E. Dynan and S.D. Krane (2003), 'Unemployment risk and precautionary wealth: evidence from household balance sheets', *Review of Economics and Statistics*, **85** (3), 586–604.

Conceição, P. and J. Galbraith (2000), 'Constructing long and dense time series of inequality using the Theil index', *Eastern Economic Journal*, **26** (1), 61–74.

Davidson, Paul (1978), *Money and the Real World*, 2nd edn, London: Macmillan.

Dorfman, R. (1979), 'A formula for the Gini coefficient', *Review of Economics and Statistics*, **61**, 146–9.

Duesenberry, James (1949), *Income, Saving, and the Theory of Consumer Behavior*, Cambridge, MA: Harvard University Press.

Fernandez-Corugedo, E. (2002), 'Soft liquidity constraints and precautionary saving', *Bank of England Quarterly Bulletin*, **42** (3), 309.

Friedman, Milton (1957), *A Theory of the Consumption Function*, Princeton, NJ: Princeton University Press.

Gale, W.G. and J. Sabelhaus (1999), 'Perspectives on the household saving rate', *Brookings Papers on Economic Activity*, **1**, 181–214.

Gottschalk, P. and T. Smeeding (1997), 'Cross-national comparisons of earnings and income inequality', *Journal of Economic Literature*, **35** (2), 633–87.

Granger, C. (1980), 'Testing for causality: a personal viewpoint', *Journal of Economic Dynamics and Control*, **2**, 329–52.

Kaldor, Nicholas (1960), *Essays in Value and Distribution*, London: Duckworth.

Kalecki, Michael (1991a), 'Studies in economic dynamics', in J. Osiatynski (ed.), *Collected Works of Michael Kalecki*, vol. 2, Oxford: Clarendon Press, pp. 117–90.

Kalecki, Michael (1991b), 'The theory of economic dynamics', in J. Osiatynski (ed.), *Collected Works of Michael Kalecki*, vol. 2, Oxford, Clarendon Press, pp. 207–338.

Keynes, John M. (1936), *The General Theory of Employment, Interest, and Money*, New York: Harcourt Brace Jovanovich.

Keynes, J.M. (1939), 'Mr. Keynes on the distribution of incomes and the "propensity to consume": a reply', *Review of Economics and Statistics*, **21** (3), 129.

Kimball, M.S. (1990), 'Precautionary saving in the small and in the large', *Econometrica*, **58**, 53–73.

Li, Ihsuan (2004), *An Essay on the Economics of Consumer Debt*, Ph.D. dissertation, Clemson University, Ann Arbor, MI: University Microforms, 312482.

Mann, C.L. (2002), 'Perspectives on the U.S. current account deficit and sustainability', *Journal of Economic Perspectives*, **16** (3), 131–52.

Marquardt, D. (1963), 'An algorithm for least squares estimation of nonlinear parameters', *Journal of the Society of Industrial and Applied Mathematics*, **11** (2), 431–41.

Marx, Karl (1977), *Capital*, volume I, New York: Vintage Books.

Pressman, S. (1997), 'Consumption, income distribution, and taxes: Keynes' fiscal policy', *Journal of Income Distribution*, **7** (1), 29–44.

Robinson, J. (1954), 'The production function and the theory of capital', *Review of Economic Studies*, **21** (2), 81–106.

Ruggles, Patricia (1990), *Drawing the Line: Alternative Poverty Measures and Their Implications for Public Policy*, Washington, DC: The Urban Institute Press.

Sarantis, N. and C. Stewart (2003), 'Liquidity constraints, precautionary saving, and aggregate consumption', *Economic Modelling*, **20** (6), 1151–75.

Schiller, Bradley (2001), *The Economics of Poverty and Discrimination*, 8th edn, Upper Saddle River, NJ: Prentice Hall.

Stiglitz, J. (1997), 'Reflections on the natural rate hypothesis', *Journal of Economic Perspectives*, **11** (1), 3–10.

Sule, A. (2006), 'Precautionary wealth accumulation: evidence from Canadian microdata', *Canadian Journal of Economics*, **39** (4), 1105–31.

Theil, Henri (1967), *Economics and Information Theory*, Chicago: Rand McNally and Company.

Trigg, A. (1994), 'On the relationship between Kalecki and the Kaleckians', *Journal of Post Keynesian Economics*, **17** (1), 91–109.

Turnovsky, S. and W. Smith (2006), 'Equilibrium consumption and precautionary saving in a stochastically growing economy', *Journal of Economic Dynamics and Control*, **30** (2), 243–61.

Vaughan, D. (1993), 'Exploring the use of the public's views to set income poverty thresholds and adjust them over time', *Social Security Bulletin*, **56** (1), 22–46.

Xu, X. (1995), 'Precautionary savings under liquidity constraints: a decomposition', *International Economic Review*, **36** (3), 675–91.

Yi, M.H. and C. Choi (2006), 'A GMM test of the precautionary saving hypothesis with nonexpected utility preferences', *Applied Economics*, **38** (1), 71–91.

5. Macroeconomic aspects of consumer credit dependence

That the market, industrialized economies have become increasingly reliant on consumer credit for the maintenance and growth of effective demand would seem to be confirmed by several statistics, including the secular rise in the ratio of household non-mortgage debt to consumption. The simulation performed in Chapter 4 (section 4.4) illustrated how consumer credit expansion may, at least for an unspecified time interval, mitigate or countervail the (potentially) detrimental impact of rising inequality with respect to aggregate spending. This chapter explores the macroeconomic pitfalls arising from the structural condition of 'consumer credit dependence'. Achieving something approximating full employment of resources necessitates expenditure flows adequate to give running validation to the preponderance of firm 'liability structures' and equity prices. The continuous extension and renewal of consumer loans is, in the context of the credit-dependent economy, a virtually irreplaceable gear in the machinery of effective demand. It is therefore important to identify and explicate a miscellany of phenomena that hold the potential to unsettle the pace of consumer borrowing or lending.

5.1 CONSUMER CREDIT AND THE 'ANIMAL-SPIRITED' CONSUMPTION FUNCTION

Much of life's drama originates in what G.L.S. Shackle labeled 'crucial' decision-making (Shackle 1979, p. 58). Decisions frequently have irreversible consequences because to act (and, sometimes, not to act) is irrevocably to alter the decision-making environment. Consider a lost hiker who must choose between two trails. If the hiker later decides a bad choice has been made, precious daylight will have been exhausted. The decision is a crucial one (in the Shacklean sense) because: (1) the hiker is ignorant of the consequences of either choice; and (2) to take action is to destroy the conditions under which the initial decision was made.[1]

The hiker's choice is trivial in the sense that it alters her reality, but no one else's. However, some crucial decisions can have permanent effects extending across a vast number of individuals and business enterprises. Completion of a light rail transportation system servicing greater Atlanta would transform the basis of millions of smaller decisions, from the purchase of cars to the location of restaurants. The creative or transformative power of human agency with respect to socio-economic reality is unleashed by crucial decision-making. Whereas physical reality is immutable (and describable in terms of probability functions), social reality is transmutable 'in the sense that future economic outcomes may be permanently changed in nature and substance by today's actions of individuals, groups (for example, unions, cartels, or governments), often in ways not even perceived by the creators of change' (Davidson 2002, p. 52). The transmutability of decision-making environments explains why uncertainty and risk should not be analytically conflated, since '[i]n the case of true uncertainty, today's decision makers believe that no expenditure of current resources in analyzing past data or current market signals can provide reliable statistical or intuitive clues regarding future prospects' (Davidson 1991, p. 130).[2]

If agents are regularly forced to make decisions based on 'unkowledge' (Shackle 1989, p. 49) or ignorance of future consequences, what motivates them to action? Keynes's position is well known:

> Most, probably, of our decisions to do something positive, the full consequences of which will be drawn out over many days to come, can only be taken as a result of *animal spirits* – a spontaneous urge to action rather than inaction, and not as outcome of a weighted average of quantitative benefits multiplied by quantitative probabilities. (Keynes 1936, pp. 161–3, italics added)

Animal spirits are a factor whenever crucial decisions are made. They are the source of the 'feeling of in-advance satisfaction . . . intense enough to overcome uncertainty' (Cardim de Carvalho 2002–03, p. 199). Decisions to take positions in long-lived capital goods are clearly in the crucial category, and discussions of animal spirits in the context of the theory of effective demand have up to now been confined mainly to investment. We shall argue that relaxation of the household liquidity constraint opens up space for crucial decision-making and therefore makes animal spirits more relevant to the theory of consumption.

The option to finance goods on credit transforms the spending decision into a more forward-looking activity than it would otherwise be. Like marriage or the purchase of reproducible capital goods, the decision to borrow is subject to uncertainty because: (1) the decision-maker is compelled to form conjectures about possible future states; and (2) such conjectures cannot be formed by recourse to the tools of actuarial science. In such situations, 'animal spirits, as much as calculation, have to play a decisive role' (Cardim de Carvalho 2002–03, p. 199). Note that a consumer who carries several department store charge cards and bank credit cards is never far removed from a crucial decision – that is, a spending decision with potentially long-lasting balance sheet or credit score repercussions. Moreover, the sweeping improvements in credit availability described in Chapter 3 have created for the household sector an augmented (aggregate) capacity to alter the economic environment. The decision-making horizon of today looks considerably different as a consequence of multitudinous crucial decisions to borrow. The animal-spirited consumption function comes into its own upon arrival at a state where a substantial share of consumption is executed by 'increasing debits' as opposed to 'reducing credits'.

To find a legitimate place in the theory of business cycle fluctuations, animal spirits must constitute an aspect of *Zeitgeist* – a prevalent and socially transmitted frame of mind. Feelings about the future vary. A collective state of confidence takes shape by the influence of a common set of factors on a plurality of individual psyches. If a change in borrowing behavior is one manifestation of wavering consumer confidence (and there is every reason to think it is), the US record shows that animal spirits may dissipate suddenly. For example, there is evidence of rather dramatic reversal in patterns of credit card usage during the first Persian Gulf War (1991), when a large number of cardholders switched from revolving use (carrying balances forward) to convenience use (retiring balances during the grace period to avoid interest charges).[3] As discussed in detail in Chapter 6, withering confidence has, on at least two occasions in US history (1930 and 1980), precipitated an abrupt spike in the ratio of repayments to outstanding consumer debt. Fears about the recent debt surge concern the possibility of a 'turning point' or episode during which consumers do not merely stop borrowing; they allocate a greater share of current income for repayment of existing debts. For reasons outlined below, a turning point could produce fearsome macroeconomic fallout. Thus animal spirits, set loose on a terrain of easy credit, may bring about conditions that make their sudden disappearance more consequential in terms of output and employment.

5.2   BALANCE SHEET OR 'MINSKY' EFFECTS

Writing in the midst of what appeared at the time to be an alarming build-up of household debt in the 1950s, J.K. Galbraith noted:

> As we expand debt in the process of want creation, we come necessarily to depend on this expansion. An interruption in the increase in debt means an

actual reduction in the demand for goods. Debt, in turn, can be expanded by measures which, in the nature of the case, cannot be indefinitely expanded. (Galbraith 1958, p. 174)

Galbraith was making the point that credit-driven consumption growth is not sustainable because credit expansion generally brings about conditions that make further credit expansion impossible. A debt contract is a legally enforceable claim to future income. As the stock of debt obligations expands, *ceteris paribus*, the proportion of future income earmarked for debt servicing rises concomitantly. From a macroeconomic perspective, consumer financing arrangements effectively turn expected future income streams into current consumption expenditure. But every new loan contributes to a diminution of expected income flows available for appropriation to the present.

Gramm (1978, p. 312) used the term 'credit saturation' to describe an individual state wherein anticipated income available for debt servicing has been completely exhausted – whether in the assessment of the individual, of lending agencies, or both. Is the concept of credit saturation meaningful in the aggregate sense? If 'meaningful' implies a state of all-inclusive credit saturation in the household sector, the answer is no. The household population will, even in the hardest of times, contain some number of units with room on their balance sheets for additional liabilities. However, a turning point – that is, a date at which the stock of consumer debt outstanding begins to decline – can have its origin in credit saturation which afflicts not all but merely a critical mass of households. The parameters of the consumption function cannot remain unaffected as a substantial number of households switch from deficit finance to a pay-as-you-go regime. The situation is made worse if households are seriously determined to discharge previously incurred debts, as this cannot be accomplished on a large scale without a redirection of spending power from product markets to debt servicing. Thus robust economic growth fueled by credit expansion may create favorable conditions for an episode of household debt liquidation.

Hyman Minsky (see Minsky 1986) claimed that a key determinant of investment (and hence the demand for funding) is the relationship between the firms' current flow of receipts from operations and their 'liability structures' – that is, contractual obligations to pay interest and principal on existing debt. Minsky's cash flow–debt principle can be extended to consumption if: (1) households carry substantial debts; and (2) a non-trivial share of household purchases is funded by the issue of IOUs. Under these conditions, the growth of consumption expenditure depends partly on the willingness of households to layer balance sheets with additional debt obligations and partly on the readiness of consumer lending agencies to accommodate credit demand. The willingness to borrow or lend is in turn conditioned by the sufficiency (or lack) of current income with respect to debt service.

Minsky developed the following taxonomy for borrowing units:

1. Hedge units: cash receipts (or income) are sufficient to repay interest and principal.
2. Speculative units: cash receipts (or income) are adequate to repay interest but not principal. These units must roll over existing debts.
3. Ponzi units: cash receipts (or income) are insufficient to repay interest or principal. Ponzi units must add debts (or sell assets) merely to pay interest on existing debt obligations.

The 'financial instability' hypothesis posits a tendency to decay of overall balance sheet quality in the course of business cycle expansions. A boom underpinned by debt must inevitably result in the migration of many spending units from 'hedge' to 'speculative' and 'Ponzi' status. Widespread financial deterioration may precipitate an episode of what Minsky terms 'debt deflation'. Debt deflation is potentially catastrophic because: (1) it chokes off new borrowing to finance spending for tangible, reproducible things (such as producer and consumer durables); and (2) it entails a massive redirection of income flows from product markets to debt servicing. The severity of economic contractions is thus intensified as a consequence of this process of balance sheet adjustment.

The following are among the issues explored in Chapter 6: does the US record give evidence of turning points or episodes of household debt deflation? To what extent have the innovations described in Chapter 3 (and especially the introduction of the asset-backed security) increased the risk of debt deflation by easing the borrowing constraint faced by the household sector? Applying the Minskian logic to the household sector, we may hypothesize that the likelihood of debt deflation is directly proportional to the fraction of households that at a particular point in time can be classified as speculative or Ponzi units. Is it possible to track changes over time in the division of household units among the three categories delineated above? Finally, what is the prospect for a turning point in the near future?

5.3 BANK LIQUIDITY PREFERENCE

Bank liquidity preference means the average preference of banks for assets that offer a high degree of liquidity. What properties of bank assets make some more liquid than others? One obvious factor is marketability – that is, can the asset be sold in a well-developed, orderly secondary market where residual buyers and sellers stand ready to 'make the market' in the event of an imbalance between buy and sell orders? The eligibility (or ineligibility) of receivables for discount at the Federal Reserve discount window is an important aspect of liquidity from banks' point of view. A third factor is less obvious, namely does the asset provide its holder with protection against what Joan Robinson (1979) described as 'capital uncertainty'? Robinson sought to analytically refine liquidity preference by differentiating financial assets in terms of

> uncertainty of future value, or capital uncertainty for short, due not to any fear of failure by the borrower but to changes in capital values owing to changes in the ruling rate of interest. (This is the main ingredient in Keynes's conception of liquidity preference. He regards the rate of interest as primarily as a premium against the possible loss of capital if an asset has to be redeemed before its redemption date.) (Robinson 1979, p. 140)

The factor that makes short-dated Treasury issues a nearer cousin to (narrowly defined) money than, say, shares listed on the New York Stock Exchange is not necessarily the superior marketability of the former asset. Rather, it is the lesser degree of capital uncertainty attached to Treasury bills *vis-à-vis* equities. Projected into the institutional context of contemporary bank portfolio management, rising bank liquidity preference means a shift in the desired composition of bank assets in favor of narrowly defined money and near monies such as government securities at the expense of less liquid assets such as agricultural, real-estate, mortgage, small business and consumer loans.

What factors might spur rising bank liquidity preference? Interest-bearing bank liabilities typically have short maturities and their yields move in line with rates offered by commercial paper, Treasury bills or other near monies. Given the normal maturity imbalance between bank holdings of securitized assets and liabilities, an increase in the spread between short- and long-term rates (a steepening of yield curve, in other words) would increase the return on holding securities and thus make marketable assets more attractive in comparison to loans. Deteriorating economic conditions will probably affect banks' assessment of the creditworthiness of current and prospective borrowers and therefore raise the (subjectively formed) appraisal of lenders' risk. Note that falling real-estate, farmland or securities prices damage profit prospects for existing loan packages, since these items are often pledged as collateral. Banks are likely to place greater emphasis on liquidity in reaction to heightened regulatory zeal. Also, bankers will naturally desire to have their portfolios heavily weighed with marketable securities and re-discountable notes if public confidence in the banking system is wavering.

The state of bank liquidity preference is subject to shifts that are largely independent of the prevailing course of monetary policy. In fact, a desire on the part of monetary authorities to ease credit conditions may be frustrated by a mounting appetite by banks for liquidity.[4] A fairly recent example of this phenomenon is provided by the US credit crunch of spring and summer 1991. Attempts by the Federal Reserve Open Market Committee to relax conditions were successful in pushing down yields of near monies. However, long-term rates did not fall in sympathy. Many banks simply rolled over their (short-term) liabilities at the new, lower rates and thus were able to realize improved margins on holding of Treasury securities.[5]

Banks are typically 'locked in' to sizeable positions in loans with remote maturity dates. Hence a decision to make portfolios more liquid requires time to carry out. The immediate effect of rising bank liquidity preference is a sharp reduction in new loan extensions. Modeled in a partial equilibrium framework, rising bank liquidity preference might be represented by a leftward shift of the 'supply of bank credit' function in interest rate–credit space. In theory, the price of bank credit (the rate of interest on loans) adjusts to clear the market. There is fairly wide agreement, however, that the loan rate is not a rationing device in markets for bank-intermediated finance.[6] As long as borrowers are heterogeneous in terms of their credit-worthiness, and so long as buyers face the possibility of default by the issuer of an IOU, there will always be an unsatisfied fringe of borrowers who wish to borrow more at the prevailing bank rate. Credit markets are characterized by extensive non-price rationing, or, in the case of households, rationing on the basis of credit scores.[7] It is useful to think of borrowing agents arranged in a hierarchy or queue, with relative positions being a function of credit ratings. Agents who occupy the bottom rungs never get credit (except perhaps in the 'predatory' segment), even if overall credit conditions are loose. Those in more favored positions, such as the Treasury or successful corporations, usually get their credit needs accommodated even in the midst of a crunch. As a practical matter, the most serious repercussion of rising bank liquidity preference is the crowding out of borrowing units that fall between those two extremes.

The relevance of bank liquidity to the scale of consumer lending is directly proportional to: (1) the share of secured and unsecured consumer receivables held by banks; and (2) the dependence of non-bank lending agencies (such as finance companies) on the commercial banking system to finance positions in consumer loans. Chapter 3 (section 3.4) described the structural transformation of the consumer lending industry following the introduction of the asset-backed security (ABS) – a marketable instrument collateralized by installment, home equity, credit card and student loan receivables. We saw that ABSs as a percentage of total consumer credit outstanding rose from

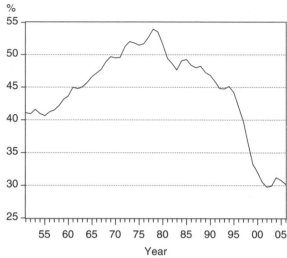

Source: Federal Reserve Board.

*Figure 5.1   Commercial bank holdings of consumer credit as a percentage
of total outstanding*

about 5 percent in 1990 to greater than 32 percent in 2003 (see Figure 3.3).
But we should not be tempted to think that the role of banks in the consumer
lending industry has been reduced to that of mere 'originator' or underwriter
of ABS issues. Figure 5.1 shows that, while the share of consumer debt outstanding held by banks has fallen since the mid-1970s, banks remain hugely
important. It is difficult to believe that a surge of bank liquidity preference
would not, given the scale of direct bank participation in the industry, exert
a restraining effect on consumer credit and consumption growth.

Assume that a less accommodative stance regarding loans to finance
companies (or discounts of finance company paper) is one aspect of rising
bank liquidity preference. A flight to liquidity by banks is capable, under
these circumstances, of roiling markets for wholesale and retail consumer
finance even if direct participation by banks in these markets is marginal.
We explained in Chapter 3 (section 3.1) that the captive finance company
leverages its ties to dominant firms (such as General Electric) to circumvent
bank intermediation. By the issue of bonds, commercial paper, or by borrowing from its parent, the captive finance unit may exercise a stabilizing
function under conditions of general credit restraint. The record shows
that, as the industry has grown more concentrated and the number of
finance companies has been greatly reduced, the reliance of finance companies on bank financing has diminished as well. Figures supplied by the

Federal Reserve Board indicate that, although there were about 1000 finance companies doing business in the USA in 2000, the largest 20 held 69 percent of total finance company receivables.[8] Bank loans accounted for a mere 2.6 percent of finance company liabilities in 2000.[9] Thus it is unlikely that bank liquidity preference could have more than a negligible impact on consumer spending (or saving) via the 'indirect' or finance company channel. The structure of the industry was very different in the 1920s and 1930s, however. The argument is made in Chapter 7 that bank liquidity preference was a key factor in prolonging the consumer durable goods slump in the Great Depression.

5.4 EFFECTS OF MONETARY RESTRAINT

One possible implication of credit dependence is that it grants to central bankers augmented power to stymie aggregate spending by means of monetary restraint. It is reasonable to think that the effects of a contractionary monetary regime would be more severe, *ceteris paribus*, if the health of consumer goods industries depended on regularized extensions of consumer credit. This conclusion presupposes that there are functioning channels through which monetary policy initiatives can alter hire purchase terms or the general availability of consumer credit. The purpose of this section is to articulate a post-Keynesian interpretation of the monetary transmission mechanism. We need to point out that the anatomy of the transmission mechanism is subject to change depending on several factors, including the structure of consumer finance markets, the capacity of banks to avoid disintermediation, and the sensitivity of rates paid on revolving credit balances to changes in short-term interest rates that the monetary authority may control.

A theory of the transmission mechanism is simply a formalization of views about the precise nature of power possessed by central banks. In a fractional reserve system, total reserves of the banking system (R) must be equal to:

$$R = \theta D \tag{5.1}$$

where θ is the amount of reserves banks must hold per dollar of deposit liabilities and D is deposit liabilities. Let c denote the fraction of liquid balances agents wish to hold in currency. The money supply (M) is defined by the following equation:

$$M = \frac{1}{[c + \theta(1 - c)]} H \tag{5.2}$$

where H is the quantity of high-powered money (or the monetary base – bank reserves on account plus currency). The evidence is consistent with the view that the parameter c is fairly stable, at least in the short run.[10] The reserve ratio (θ) is set by central bankers. Thus, if monetary authorities possess the power to control the variable H (at least within fairly narrow limits), the money supply (M) may be said to be exogenously determined – that is, determined independently of the demand for money or bank-intermediated credit. The standard view holds that the quantity of high-powered money (H) is a control variable for the Federal Reserve System. By the purchase (or sale) of securities on the open market, the Fed is able to force most banks into 'favorable' (or 'adverse') clearings with itself.[11]

The endogenous money theory, most closely associated with Moore (1986, 1988), but also with Wray (1992) and Lavoie (1984), derives from the view that, in the era of modern liability management, the capacity of central banks to target total reserves of the banking system is limited.[12] Banks innovated the negotiable certificate of deposit in 1962.[13] Responding elastically to the expanding credit needs of their major clients had, before this time, proven difficult for large banks given their reliance on local deposit markets. As Wojnilower explains:

> It was in response to such pressures that in early 1962 the negotiable certificate of deposit burst on the scene, spearheading a rapid and total transformation of financial practice . . . The new instrument – which from the standpoint of buyers was essentially a high-quality, more flexible, and higher yielding type of Treasury bill – suddenly enabled well-known banks to bid for deposits all over the world. At a price, funds would be available. (Wojnilower 1980, pp. 284–5)

By issuing negotiable CDs (and other techniques), banks can adjust their liabilities (and reserves) as needed to accommodate loan demand.[14] We should not conclude that liability management has left monetary authorities prostrate, however. The power of the Federal Reserve remains formidable, and finds its source in the Fed's extensive holdings of a strategic financial asset – short-dated Treasuries. The Treasury bill rate, owing to the superior creditworthiness of its issuer relative to all other (domestic) issuers of short-term securities, furnishes the lower limit for the complex of yields for interest-bearing assets of all types – including certificates of deposit, commercial paper, asset-backed securities and longer-dated bonds.[15] The first step in our specification of the transmission mechanism is to explain how open market operations alter the terms on which banks can roll over their short-term liabilities.

The Federal Reserve Open Market Committee (FOMC) dispensed with 'reserve-targeting' in favor of 'interest rate-targeting' in the 1980s. In the latter approach, the FOMC issues a policy directive which specifies a target for the federal funds, or interbank reserve, rate. The sale of government securities, initiated by the Fed's New York trading desk pursuant to an FOMC directive, will have the predictable effect of forcing banks into adverse clearings, thus producing a situation of excess demand for borrowed reserves (federal funds) at the prevailing federal funds rate. Bear in mind that engineering any substantial change to the federal funds rate (say, 25 basis points or more) requires the sale (or purchase) of Treasury securities on a scale sufficient to cause a change in the price and yields of treasuries. The Fed's dominance in the market for short-term Treasury debt is such that it cannot make a quasi-significant change in its holdings without roiling prices.[16] Professional forecasting of short-term interest rates is for this reason mainly a problem of predicting the future course of monetary policy or of specifying and estimating a 'reaction function' of monetary authorities. Thus open market operations do not merely affect the price of reserves obtained in the interbank market. To fund their operations, banks rely on the rollover of large CDs by institutional depositors. Taking into account the ultra-high elasticity of substitution between large CDs and other near monies (including Treasury bills), the CD rate must move in sympathy with the Treasury bill rate – otherwise banks will see deposits go elsewhere when the bill rate rises.[17] Interest paid on liabilities is, from the point of view of banks, a component (and a highly significant one) of cost. Open market operations thus produce what we may term 'cost' effects.[18] Is it possible for the monetary authority to control total reserves by its influence over short-term interest rates? Yes, in theory. In practice, central bankers have seen their main responsibility as one of ensuring the stability of the banking system and financial markets. As reserve-targeting regimes can require frequent, erratic and disquieting interest rate adjustments to be effective, central bankers as a rule have eschewed them.

Policy-induced cost effects are not limited to banks – they impinge on other consumer lending agencies as well. We previously explained that the major finance companies fund operations by the regular issue of short-dated commercial paper – instruments that clearly belong in the 'near-money' class. The commercial paper rate is among a cluster of short-term rates (along with the CD rate) that move in step with the Treasury bill rate.[19] Access to the commercial paper market requires issuers to maintain back-up lines of credit with banks. The cost of maintaining these is (partly) based on banks' cost of funds, as measured by the CD rate. Thus monetary contraction may exert an indirect influence on the total cost of raising funds via the commercial paper route by their effect on the CD rate.

The market for ABSs has matured to the stage where monthly flows of new offerings are a mere fraction of previously issued ABSs. Thus the decisive factor regulating the terms on which new ABSs can be floated off is the prices prevailing in the secondary market. After all, there is no point in purchasing a newly issued ABS if a previously issued one (a perfect substitute) can be bought at a lower price. Presuming ABSs are substitutable with near monies, it stands to reason that a sufficient narrowing of the spread between the yields of (previously issued) ABSs and near monies would precipitate a shift of portfolio capital out of ABSs and into Treasury bills, commercial paper or CDs. As arbitrage can be relied on to quickly eliminate any price gap between new and old ABS issues, prices fetched by new issues cannot remain invariant with respect to falling prices in the secondary market. Consequently, the cost of providing consumer loans by the securitization technique is also affected by the prevailing course of monetary policy.

Rising interest (financing) costs erode profit margins realized on existing portfolios of fixed-rate consumer loans. Our main concern here, however, is the effect of monetary restraint on volume of new loan extensions. The problem ostensibly presents the opportunity for the application of partial equilibrium analysis. We can think of a consumer credit demand function which is downward sloping in interest rate–credit space. The monetary restraint-induced cost effects discussed above should cause the credit supply function to shift up to the left. Comparison of the new equilibrium with the initial one will reveal a higher price of consumer credit and a reduced volume of new consumer loans. As I have argued elsewhere (Brown 2003–04), partial equilibrium analysis is a defective platform for the analysis of credit markets. For one thing, credit money is something institutional or intangible – its creation involves a minimal employment of real resources. What shape should a credit supply function take? A vertical function makes sense for a commodity money system (i.e., the supply of money is limited by the quantity of a non-augmentable, producible commodity) or if the quantity of high-powered money is exogenously controlled. The familiar textbook supply curve derives its shape from diminishing returns, which makes no sense for non-producible items such as credit money. That leaves one other possibility: the horizontal credit money supply schedule. Some leading lights have embraced the 'horizontal' option as a device for articulating the endogenous money position. Moore (1988), for example, argues that rates on bank loans are administered based on a markup over lenders' cost. Thus we may picture a horizontal credit supply function shifting up or down in nearly exact proportion to a change in the federal funds or CD rate. The problem with this interpretation is that there is no evidence that the markup over lenders' cost is a stable magnitude – at least in the case of consumer loans.

Figure 5.2 tracks the spread between the federal funds rate (a proxy for lenders' cost) and three bank-administered interest rates over the period

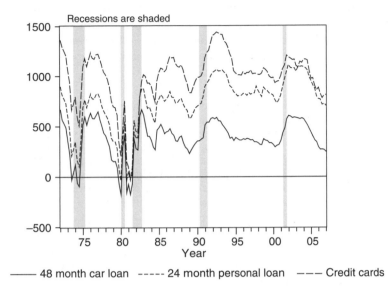

Source: Federal Reserve Board.

Figure 5.2   *Interest rate spreads, commercial bank loans and the federal funds rate (in basis points)*

1971–2007. The evidence is consistent with the view that bank profit margins on consumer loans are quite variable and tend to move inversely with changes in federal funds or CD rates, though Ausubel (1991, p. 71) notes that, '[e]mpirically, interest rates on loans have an asymmetric response to the cost of funds: they are quicker to move upward in response to increases in the cost of funds than to move downward in response to decreases in the cost of funds'. Why the rigidity of bank-administered rates with respect to changes in lenders' cost? The answer coming from the new Keynesian literature is 'adverse selection' – that is, as the price of credit increases, the mix of credit applicants changes adversely (Akerlof 1970).

Stiglitz explains why expected loan profitability is a decreasing function of the interest rate, at least beyond some threshold level:

> Assume that as the bank increases the interest rate, the 'quality' of those who apply decreases; that is, those who, on average, have a higher probability of defaulting, of not repaying their loans. The safest borrowers are unwilling to borrow at higher interest rates. Then, the expected return on a loan . . . may actually decrease as the interest rate . . . increases. (Stiglitz 1987, p. 6)[20]

The claim that consumer credit markets are characterized by substantial non-price rationing is hardly controversial, although opinions as to its causes may differ. The comments of former Federal Reserve Governor Ralph Young seem to have retained their relevance amid the myriad changes in the industry through the decades:

> [C]hanges in interest rates in the credit markets have a less than corresponding effect on the charge for credit to consumers. Nevertheless, the interest cost is one important element of lender's cost, and the general tightness or ease tends to be transmitted to consumer credit through its influence on the strictness or leniency of credit standards applied by consumer-credit granting institutions. Alterations of credit standards is a method by which lenders in this area control other elements of cost, namely collection costs and the costs of default. (Young 1953, pp. 225–6)

Figure 5.3 encapsulates the arguments made to this point. The term 'modern transmission mechanism' should be understood to mean that the interpretation of causality presented is applicable to a monetary system containing the features previously delineated – that is, widely practiced techniques of liability management and mature markets for securitized consumer receivables. One aspect of the transmission mechanism we have neglected up to now is the impact of monetary restraint on interest payments on existing credit balances. The fine print of many credit card agreements contains a proviso that permits the issuer to alter the average percentage rate on outstanding balances. In some cases, the credit card rate (on existing balances) adjusts automatically to changes in some benchmark rate (such as the prime rate). This is especially true in the so-called 'subprime' credit card market. Rising interest rates are blamed for the recent rash of defaults on subprime, adjustable-rate mortgages (see Hagerty et al. 2007). However, a Wall Street research firm warned that, as of February 2006, approximately 5 percent of households would face higher minimum payments on their existing credit card balances should interest rates rise.[21] By forcing subprime borrowers into higher interest payments, the monetary authorities are visiting a negative income effect on a segment of the population that is not well positioned to absorb it. Nevertheless, adjustable rates open up a pathway for monetary restraint to reach consumer behavior.

5.5   RISKS RELATED TO FINANCIAL ENGINEERING

Chapter 3 explained how innovations such as credit scoring and asset-backed securities have greatly expanded borrowing opportunities for indi-

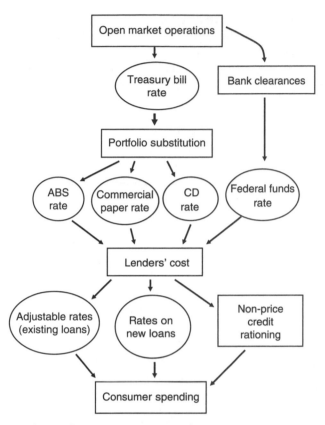

Figure 5.3   The modern transmission mechanism

viduals at virtually all stations of creditworthiness.[22] The post-1987 restructuring of the consumer credit industry has linked the supply of credit (and thus consumer spending) to the smooth operation of primary markets for debt-collateralized securities. Difficulties in placing newly issued securities backed by consumer loans will surely reverberate back to consumer spending. Thus we are obliged to ask: are there factors intrinsic to derivatives markets or trading strategies that raise the risk of a major disruption of consumer lending activity?

One would think at first blush that the main problem with the securitization of consumer loans is that it opens a new channel through which speculative activity may perturb effective demand. That is, one would think that J.M. Keynes's admonition about speculation in securities markets would apply here as well.[23] Fluctuating prices of previously issued ABSs, an effect of buying and selling decisions of agents in pursuit of windfall capital gains realized through such price changes, must, given the substitutability among old and new issues, alter the terms on which new ABSs can be floated. The reality is, however, that secondary markets for debt-collateralized securities are extremely thin and feature virtually no speculative activity. The more pressing danger is the looming potential for market illiquidity.

Liquid securities markets provide fertile ground for speculation. Liquidity (and orderliness) issue forth when financial asset ownership is widely dispersed and specialists stand ready to stabilize market price by acting as residual buyers and sellers. In the case of credit derivatives, ownership is tightly concentrated in giant private equity and hedge funds. Moreover, reliable market-making mechanisms are lacking. In contrast to widely held equities, derivatives are held for yield, not capital gain.[24] Andrew Large writes:

> A macro-environment of sustained low nominal interest rates and accommodatory fiscal policy in big economies has . . . encouraged financial institutions and investors generally to increase their holdings of less liquid assets [including ABSs], in an effort to sustain nominal returns by taking on higher risks. This 'search for yield' . . . could increase the prospect of one-way markets developing and market liquidity evaporating in response to a shock. (Large 2004, p. 10)

The 'search for yield' reached an apogee in the subprime mortgage lending segment – with tragic consequences.[25] A one-way market in securities backed by subprime mortgages appeared in the spring and summer of 2007, drying up mortgage money available to low-income and/or high-risk borrowers.[26]

The subprime debacle also cast an unfavorable light on the practices of hedge funds – that is, highly leveraged, lightly regulated, professionally managed funds open only to qualified investors. Valuing a portfolio containing a large position in thinly traded derivatives is problematic because values cannot be readily 'marked to market'. Investment funds rely instead on complicated in-house valuation models (for a description, see Cheng 2001). For hedge fund managers, 'the incentives to abuse the murkiness of the market can be huge, because they are compensated by fees based on the value of their portfolios' (Ng et al. 2007, p. A10). Critics charge that standard valuation models employ faulty assumptions concerning credit risk correlation and thus yield inflated estimates of value (see Jarrow and Yildirim 2002, for example).[27] The *Wall Street Journal* reported that a 'study by a Paris risk management firm Risk-data shows that roughly 30 percent of hedge funds that invest in illiquid securities smooth out returns with price estimates for these securities that are potentially self-serving' (Patterson 2007, p. C1). Why should embellished hedge funds valuations be a worry? When a secondary market does appear (usually as a result of distress selling), it exposes the disparity between the market price and the theoretical price of derivatives, putting pressure on hedge funds managers to mark down values. They are loath to do this because a revaluation of illiquid derivative holdings to more realistic levels risks provoking a run to the exits by hedge fund patrons. Shrinking capitalization among these units would severely cripple their capacity to absorb new ABS issues (and other debt-collateralized securities).[28]

The greatest source of unease springs from the highly leveraged status of hedge funds as well as the symbiotic relationship of these units with core financial institutions. Hedge funds depend on loans from money center commercial and investment banks to take positions in derivative securities marketed by the same institutions. Thus hedge funds are a source of both interest and fee income to banks. Federal Reserve Chairman Ben Bernanke recently spoke on the dangers inherent in this arrangement:

> All else being equal, highly leveraged investors are more vulnerable to market shocks. If leveraged investors default while holding positions that are large relative to the markets in which they have invested, the forced liquidation of those positions, possibly at fire-sale prices, could cause heavy losses to counterparties. These direct losses are of concern, of course, particularly if they lead to further defaults or threaten systemically important institutions; but, in addition, market participants that were not creditors or counterparties of the defaulting firm might be affected indirectly through asset price adjustments, liquidity strains, and increased market uncertainty. (Bernanke 2006)

The nightmare scenario is financial contagion, 'characterized by rapid spillover of falling prices, rising volatility, declining market liquidity, and a significant increase in the co-movement of prices and quantities among firms, conditional on a crisis occurring in one firm or market' (Halstead et al. 2005, p. 65). Hedge funds may in such an environment be faced with a flood of margin calls (prompted by a decline in the market value of assets pledged as collateral). Note that the triggering event need not be endogenous to the complex of markets in which hedge funds participate.[29]

Nevertheless, the drive by hedge funds to unwind massive positions to meet margin calls would exacerbate the crisis and expose the commercial banking sector to potentially huge loan losses. What about portfolio insurance – that is, the use of instruments such as credit default swaps or interest swaps to hedge risks attached to collateralized debt obligations? It is well understood that counterparties to hedging contracts can meet their obligations only so long as credit events remain localized, such as was the case with the downgrade of General Motors debt in March 2005.[30] After all, risk buyers tend to be highly leveraged units whose strategies are predicated on the assumption that credit events are not contagious.

The case of the hedge fund Long-Term Capital Management (LTCM) provides a cautionary tale. The fund saw its capitalization fall sharply after a series of negative events starting with the devaluation of the ruble and a moratorium on Russian debt repayment declared on 21 August 1998. Shortly thereafter, LTCM lost $500 million 'due to increased volatility in stock markets' (Halstead et al. 2005, p. 67). With its leverage ratio at 26 to 1, it seemed that LTCM would have no other choice to avoid default on its debts than to liquidate holdings of thinly traded securities. Key figures in the financial community quickly determined that such a course would have disastrous effects, as Alan Greenspan explained:

> [T]he act of unwinding the LTCM portfolio in a forced liquidation would not only have a significant distorting impact on market prices but also in the process could produce large losses, or worse, for a number of creditors and counterparties, and other participants that were not directly involved with LTCM . . . Had the failure of LTCM triggered the seizing up of markets, substantial damage could have been inflicted on many market participants . . . and could have potentially impaired the economies of many countries, including our own. (Greenspan 1998, p. 1)

LTCM was bailed out on 23 September 1998 with a $3.65 billion cash infusion from 15 financial institutions – Barclays, Crédit Suisse, First Boston, J.P. Morgan, Goldman Sachs and UBS AG among them.

Another potential problem concerns the adequacy (or lack) of international clearance and settlement arrangements for over-the-counter derivatives. Bank of England official Nigel Jenkinson (2007, pp. 3–4) explained that 'market participants rely on such infrastructure to implement their desired portfolio allocation; to execute risk management strategies; to raise liquidity, both in normal times and in times of stress; and to manage contingent exposures and cash flows', but the '[r]ising volumes (and values) and the development of new, and often more complex, products, have placed a strain on existing arrangements, exposing capacity constraints in existing procedures'.[31]

Financial engineering has transformed the systems by which household IOUs are monetized. The overall effect has been to increase the ease with which various types of consumer loans may be obtained. At the same time, the exotic new securities, and the leveraged trading units that have assumed such importance in the aftermath of their introduction, have made the provision of consumer credit more vulnerable to derangement as a consequence of a shock emanating from any firm, industry or market located virtually anywhere in the world. The true terms of the tradeoff will not be fully understood until a real crisis develops, something most agree has yet to occur. Until then, derivatives merit the closest scrutiny by academics and regulators.[32]

NOTES

1. 'A course of action . . . declares itself to be *crucial*, indeed *self-destroying*, experiment, an inherently and essentially once-for-all, all or nothing throw of the die' (Shackle 1979, p. 50, italics in original).

2. Davidson has explained the requirement for measuring uncertainty with the use of a probability function, as is common practice in economics. Data used for decision-making purposes must be 'part of a times series realization generated by an ergodic stochastic process' (Davidson 2002, p. 50). If a stochastic process is ergodic, 'then statistics calculated from past time-series or cross-sectional data are statistically reliable estimates of space statistics that will occur at any specific future data' (ibid., p. 51). Davidson argues that transmutable realities are non-ergodic (see Davidson 1991).

3. Consumer credit outstanding dipped through much of 1991. Madelyn Hochstein, President of DYG Inc., a consumer research firm, commented that 'the consumer's agenda is all about getting out of debt' (quoted in the *Wall Street Journal*, 10 September 1991, p. A2). Numerous stories about changing consumer borrowing and saving behavior appeared in the financial press during 1991. See, for example, Wessel (1991) and Mitchell (1991). Commenting on a recrudescence of household thrift in 1990–91, Graven (1991, p. A1) wrote that 'It may be too early to declare the 1990s the Saving Decade.'

4. Bernanke and Lown (1991, p. 237) note that monetary policy can be rendered ineffective 'if banks refuse to lend (that is, if banks accommodate deposit expansion only by holding more securities)'.

5. See Greenspan (1991) and Bernanke and Lown (1991).

6. Stiglitz and Weiss (1981) developed a model where non-price credit rationing is an equilibrium phenomenon. They define the equilibrium interest rate as the rate that maximizes profits per dollar lent. They reason that because lenders have incomplete information about prospective borrowers, the interest rate charged may affect the riskiness of the entire loan portfolio. As such, lenders use the interest rate as a screening device: 'The interest rate which the individual is willing to pay may act as [a] screening device: Those who are willing to pay a higher interest rate may be, on average, worse risks . . . As the interest rate rises, the average "riskiness" of those who borrow increases, possibly lowering bank profits' (Stiglitz and Weiss 1981, p. 393). Thus the interest that equates the demand and supply of credit may diverge from the interest rate that maximizes bank profits.

7. We noted in Chapter 3 that consumer loan pricing has lately become more complex, with banks charging multiple rates based on borrowers' credit scores. Under the old, 'single price' system, credit was denied to those individuals with credit scores below the 'cutoff' level. Risk-based pricing makes it easier for persons with low credit scores to obtain bank loans.

8. See Dynan et al. (2002, p. 2).

9. This figure comes from Dynan et al. (2002, p. 8), Table 6, 'Sources of finance company funding, June 30, 2000'. Commercial paper accounted for 17.8 percent of finance company liabilities as of this date; loans due to the parent 7.6 percent; debt not classified elsewhere 38.4 percent; and other 22 percent.

10. Some expected the c ratio to rise with the advent of electronic currency cards. In contrast to a debit (ATM) card, balances on electronic currency cards are a liability of the central bank, not the banking system. Owen and Fogelstrom (2005) estimated a probit model with 2001 *Survey of Consumer Finances* data and found that smartcard holders (only 3 percent of households in 2001) had higher average balances in their checking accounts. There is some evidence that credit card use leads to a decrease in desired holdings of cash and checkable deposits, particularly among low-income households (see Duca and Whitesell 1995). However, there is no obvious reason why credit cards might cause a change in the c parameter.

11. Suppose that on a particular day a single monetary transaction occurs in which a check drawn on Bank A is deposited into an account in Bank B. Bank A will, as an effect of

the transaction, sustain a debit to its reserve account or suffer what is known as an 'adverse' clearing. Bank B, on the other hand, will see its reserve balance rise or have a 'favorable' clearing. A central bank is, by definition, a bank so immense in terms of asset holdings that it has the power (by the sale of assets) to force all other banks into adverse clearings with itself.

12. The main outlines of endogenous money theory are summarized as follows: (1) in a credit-money system – that is, in a system in which the money supply is not tied to the quantity of a tangible commodity (like gold) such that the creation of new money requires a negligible employment of real resources – money is created when banks make loans and is destroyed when loans are retired or not renewed; (2) banks have substantial off-balance-sheet loan commitments in the form of pre-negotiated overdraft privileges granted to firms and individuals. The money supply expands automatically (endogenously) when agents draw on these lines of credit. The measured money supply is a statistical echo of successful efforts to buy goods/make factor payments; (3) credit money is like electricity in that there can be no excess supply of it. Thus agents have no cause to rid themselves of redundant money balances as the scale of transactions recedes because credit money never materializes except when it is needed; and (4) the familiar vertical supply of money schedule gives a misleading analogy of the real-world process of money creation and destruction.

13. Other key innovations of the 1960s (including eurodollars and repurchase agreements) assisted banks in avoiding disintermediation – that is, a surge of withdrawals provoked by a rise in 'open market' interest rates above the maximum rates allowed on bank liabilities under the Federal Reserve's Regulation Q.

14. The Treasury bill rate has from time to time moved above the bond rate – a phenomenon known as an 'inverted yield curve'. However, such episodes have proved to be transitory and have coincided with Fed tightening measures, such as in late 1979 and early 1980.

15. Moore (1986, pp. 448–9) explains that 'Previously bankers passively accepted whatever deposit liabilities the public wanted to hold with them, and allocated these funds among potential borrowers. Liability management has enabled banks to target rates of asset growth, then adjust liabilities to suit their needs for funds, rather than accepting their liability structure and tailoring their assets accordingly.'

16. In this sense, the Fed's situation is comparable to giant pension or mutual funds. Managers of these funds have complained they are 'too big' – that is, managers encounter difficulty in adding to or subtracting from positions without affecting market valuations.

17. Under a 'mark-to-market' accounting standard, falling government securities prices can have a deleterious effect on the status of bank balance sheets. In the aftermath of the Fed–Treasury Accord of 1951, the Fed failed to accommodate a large flotation of long-term bonds by the Treasury in 1953. Wojnilower describes the fallout: 'Prices of outstanding long term bonds fell correspondingly. It is difficult to recapture today the shock felt in the financial community at the startling devaluation of a major part of its assets . . . Bank credit became scarce. Within just a few weeks, observers could take for granted that a recession was now unavoidable; it began shortly after midyear' (Wojnilower 1980, pp. 281–2).

18. This is precisely the set of circumstances which caused the credit crunch of 1966. Specifically, the Treasury bill rate moved above the ceiling rate on bank-issued CDs.

19. To test the 'lock-step' hypothesis, partial correlation coefficients were computed using monthly Federal Reserve Board data for the following interest rates: (1) the 6-month Treasury bill (secondary market); (2) the 6-month CD rate (open market); and (3) the 6-month commercial paper rate. The sample period: 1985:1 to 2007:3 (n = 267). The correlation coefficient for the Treasury bill–commercial paper pairing is 0.9936. For the Treasury bill–CD rate pairing it is 0.9962.

20. Ausubel (1991) and Calem and Mester (1995) have emphasized the role of search costs and switching costs in limiting price competition in the credit card segment.

21. The firm is CIBC World markets. See Collins (2006).

22. A standard argument in defense of derivatives is that these products serve to 'complete' markets and thus push economic reality into closer conformity with the idealized Arrow–Debreu system. A complete market is one in which the complete set of possible gambles on future states-of-the-world can be constructed with existing assets. Federal Reserve Governor Kevin Warsh recently remarked that '[f]inancial innovation, by definition, makes markets more complete by expanding the set of available types of securities reducing transactions costs' (Warsh 2007, p. 3).

23. Keynes defined speculation as 'the activity of forecasting market psychology', whereas enterprise is 'the activity of forecasting the prospective yield of assets over their whole life' (Keynes 1936, p. 158). Commenting on the former, Keynes wrote that 'when the capital development of a country becomes the by-product of the activities of a casino, the job is likely to be ill-done' (ibid., p. 159).

24. Lahart and Luchetti explain that: 'illiquid assets can be lucrative when investors with long time horizons, who don't have to worry about creditors suddenly calling in loans' (Lahart and Luchetti 2007, p. A13).

25. For an account of the role of unscrupulous mortgage brokers in the subprime market, see Simon and Hagerty (2007). Low-income, previously redlined neighborhoods in cities are prime targets of subprime mortgage brokers: 'In 2006 alone, subprime investors from all over the world injected more than a billion dollars into 22 zip codes in Detroit . . . Fourteen zip codes in Memphis, Tenn. attracted an estimated \$460 million. Seventeen zip codes in Newark, N.J. pulled in about \$1.5 billion' (Whitehouse 2007, p. A14). The *Wall Street Journal* reported that seven out of 26 home owners on a single residential block in Detroit (the 5100 block of W. Outer Dr.) took out subprime loans. Of these, three were in foreclosure and the status of two others was 'uncertain' (see ibid.).

26. Illiquidity in the subprime market also contributed to the failure of two big hedge funds – Bear Stearns High Grade Credit Strategies Structured Credit Fund and High Grade Structured Credit Strategies Enhanced Leverage Fund.

27. Credit risk correlation is low if risk factors are unique or borrower-specific. On the other hand, if the likelihood of default is largely a function of factors common to the population of borrowers, then credit risk correlation is high. Hull and White, creators of a widely used derivatives pricing model, note that 'Like most other approaches, ours assumes that default probabilities, interest rates, and recovery rates are mutually independent. Unfortunately, it does not seem to be possible to relax these assumptions without a considerably more complex model' (Hull and White 2000, p. 30). A summary of findings is presented in a recent paper by Abel Elizalde:

> Using bond prices for a sample of 14 U.S. firms during 2001–2003 . . . [w]e find that credit risk correlations, measured by the impact of a few common factors on the firms' credit risk, explain a large part of such risk. In particular, a single common factor affecting the credit risk of all firms is found to explain between 15% and 91% of the firms' credit risk, with an average of 68% across firms. (Elizalde 2005, p. 43)

28. Patterson writes:

> [i]f and when these new funds are ultimately forced to put an accurate price on the holdings, the results could be messy. Fears of just such an outcome shot through Wall Street recently when the mortgage-backed securities of two Bear Stearns hedge funds briefly came to market at fire-sale prices. The chief concern was that hedge funds holding similar assets would need to adjust the value of their holdings sharply downward. (Patterson 2007, p. C1)

29. The finance literature differentiates between fundamentals-based contagion and non-fundamentals-based or 'pure' contagion: 'Under the first category, the infected firm or market is linked to other via trade or finance, and the shock to one firm or market affects only that that share some common characteristics' (Halstead et al. 2005, p. 65).

30. The *Financial Times* reported on 11 May 2005 that

[f]ears of hedge fund troubles in the wake of last week's General Motors' downgrade rattled stock and bond markets yesterday as investors worried that some funds may be struggling to meet margin calls. Investment banks' stocks slipped and Treasury bonds rose as investors shifted into safe haven assets. The complex trades struck by many hedge funds mean any troubles risk drawing in the counterparties, particularly banks, with which they conducted the trades. (Drummond and Hughes 2005, p. 1)

31. The Federal Reserve of New York recently held a meeting with major derivative markets participants (Credit Suisse, Goldman Sachs, Lehman Brothers, Citigroup and others) to push for 'Standardization and automation in derivatives trading markets in response to a massive backlog of unconfirmed trades, which risked causing disruptions that could have spread to broader markets' (reported in the *Wall Street Journal*, 22 November 2006, C4).
32. Academic literature on derivatives trading has up to now been largely confined to practitioner outlets such as *Mathematical Finance* and the *Journal of Derivatives*.

REFERENCES

Akerlof, G.A. (1970), 'The market for "lemons": quality uncertainty and the market mechanism', *Quarterly Journal of Economics*, **84** (3), 353–74.

Ausubel, L.M. (1991), 'The failure of competition in the credit card market', *American Economic Review*, **81** (1), 50–81.

Bernanke, B. (2006), 'Hedge funds and systemic risk', Speech delivered at Federal Reserve Bank of Atlanta's Financial Markets Conference, 16 May, Sea Island, Georgia (www.bis.org/review/r06522a.pdf, 21 December 2007).

Bernanke, B. and C. Lown (1991), 'The credit crunch', *Brookings Papers on Economic Activity*, (2), 205–39.

Brown, C. (2003–04), 'Toward a reconcilement of endogenous money and liquidity preference', *Journal of Post Keynesian Economics*, **26** (2), 323–37.

Calem, P.S. and L.J. Mester (1995), 'Consumer behavior and the stickiness of credit-card interest rates', *American Economic Review*, **85** (5), 1327–36.

Cardim de Carvalho, F.J. (2002–03), 'Decision-making under uncertainty as drama: Keynesian and Shacklean themes in three of Shakespeare's tragedies', *Journal of Post Keynesian Economics*, **25** (2), 189–218.

Cheng, W. (2001), 'Recent advances in default swap valuation', *Journal of Derivatives*, **9** (1), 18–27.

Collins, B. (2006), 'CIBC report claims borrowers squeezed', *Origination News*, **15** (5), 39.

Davidson, P. (1991), 'Is probability theory relevant for uncertainty? A Post Keynesian perspective', *Journal of Economic Perspectives*, **5** (1), 129–44.

Davidson, Paul (2002), *Financial Markets, Money, and the Real World*, Cheltenham, UK and Northampton, MA: Edward Elgar.

Drummond, J. and J. Hughes (2005), 'Hedge funds under scrutiny as fears grow of fall-out from GM downgrade', *Financial Times*, 11 May, p. 1.

Duca, J. and W. Whitesell (1995), 'Credit cards and money demand: a cross-sectional analysis', *Journal of Money, Credit, and Banking*, **27** (2), 604–23.

Dynan, K.E., K.W. Johnson and S.M. Slowinski (2002), 'Survey of finance companies, 2000', *Federal Reserve Bulletin*, January, 1–14.

Elizalde, A. (2005), 'Do we need to worry about credit risk correlation?', *Journal of Fixed Income*, **15** (3), 42–61.

Fisher, I. (1933), 'The debt-deflation theory of Great Depressions', *Econometrica*, **1** (4), 337–57.

Galbraith, John K. (1958), *The Affluent Society*, Boston: Houghton Mifflin.

Gramm, W. (1978), 'Credit saturation, secular redistribution, and long run stability', *Journal of Economic Issues*, **12** (2), 307–27.

Graven, K. (1991), 'Americans save more and have reason to in a tough economy', *Wall Street Journal*, 22 April, A1:5.

Greenspan, A. (1991), 'Statement before the Committee on Ways and Means, U.S. House of Representatives, March 6, 1991', *Federal Reserve Bulletin*, **77** (4), 300–305.

Greenspan, A. (1998), 'Private sector refinancing of the large hedge fund, Long-Term Capital Management', Testimony before the Committee on Banking and Financing Services, US House of Representatives, 1 October (www.federalreserve.gov/BoardDocs/Testimony/1998/19981001.htm, 21 July 2007).

Hagerty, J.R., R. Simon, M. Corkery and G. Zuckerman (2007), 'At mortgage lender, rapid rise, faster fall', *Wall Street Journal*, **58**, 12 March, A1–A12.

Halstead, J.M., S. Hegde and L. Schmid Klein (2005), 'Hedge fund crisis and financial contagion: evidence from Long-Term Capital Management', *Journal of Alternative Investments*, **8** (1), 65–84.

Hull, J. and A. White (2000), 'Valuing credit default swaps I: no counterparty default risk', *Journal of Derivatives*, **1**, 29–40.

Jarrow, R. and Y. Yildirim (2002), 'Valuing default swaps under market and credit risk correlation', *Journal of Fixed Income*, **11** (4), 7–20.

Jenkinson, H. (2007), 'Promoting financial system resilience in modern global capital markets: some issues', *BIS Review*, **77**, 1–10.

Keynes, John M. (1936), *The General Theory of Employment, Interest, and Money*, New York: Harcourt Brace Jovanovich.

Lahart, J. and A. Luchetti (2007), 'Wall Street fears Bear Stearns is tip of the iceberg', *Wall Street Journal*, 25 June, A1.

Large, A. (2004), 'Why should we worry about liquidity?', *Financial Times*, 11 November, 19.

Lavoie, M. (1984), 'The endogenous flow of credit and the Post Keynesian theory of money', *Journal of Economic Issues*, **18** (3), 771–98.

Minsky, Hyman (1986), *Stabilizing an Unstable Economy*, New Haven, CT: Yale University Press.

Mitchell, C. (1991), 'Homeowners rush to repay mortgages, causing chill in mortgage markets', *Wall Street Journal*, 9 May, C1.

Moore, B. (1986), 'How credit drives the money supply: the significance of institutional developments', *Journal of Economic Issues*, **20** (2), 443–52.

Moore, Basil (1988), *Horizontalists and Verticalists: The Macroeconomics of Credit Money*, Cambridge, UK: Cambridge University Press.

Ng, S., K. Kelly and D. Reilly (2007), 'Two big funds at Bear Stearns face shutdown', *Wall Street Journal*, 20 June, A1.

Owen, A.L. and C. Fogelstrom (2005), 'Monetary policy implications of electronic currency: an empirical analysis', *Applied Economics Letters*, **12** (7), 419–23.

Patterson, S. (2007), 'Subprime flu sheds light on derivatives', *Wall Street Journal*, 2 July, C1.

Robinson, Joan (1979), *The Generalization of the General Theory*, New York: St Martin's Press.

Shackle, G.L.S. (1979), *Imagination and the Nature of Choice*, Edinburgh, UK: Edinburgh University Press.

Shackle, G.L.S. (1989), 'What did the General Theory do?', in J. Pheby (ed.), *New Directions in Post Keynesian Economics*, Aldershot, UK: Edward Elgar, pp. 48–58.

Simon, R. and J.R. Hagerty (2007), 'Mortgage mess shines light on brokers' role', *Wall Street Journal*, 5 July, A1.

Stiglitz, J. (1987), 'The causes and consequences of the dependence of quality on price', *Journal of Economic Literature*, **25** (1), 1–48.

Stiglitz, J. and A. Weiss (1981), 'Credit rationing in markets with incomplete information', *American Economic Review*, **73** (5), 912–27.

Warsh, K. (2007), 'Financial intermediation and complete markets', Speech delivered to the European Economics and Financial Centre, 5 June (www.bis.org/review/r 070606f.pdf, 18 August 2007).

Wessel, D. (1991), 'Consumers hesitate to spend, impeding recovery', *Wall Street Journal*, 22 September, A1:6.

Whitehouse, M. (2007), ' "Subprime" aftermath: losing the family home', *Wall Street Journal*, 30 May, A1.

Wojnilower, A. (1980), 'The central role of credit crunches in recent financial history', *Brookings Papers on Economic Activity*, (2), 277–339.

Wray, L.R. (1992), 'Alternative approaches to money and interest rates', *Journal of Economic Issues*, **26** (4), 1145–78.

Young, R. (1953), 'Influence of credit and monetary measures on economic stability', *Federal Reserve Bulletin*, **39** (3), 219–34.

6. Balance sheet (Minsky) effects: an empirical analysis

The previous chapters have attempted to explain how the emergence of social habit structures amenable to the use of credit to buy things such as consumer electronics, clothing, travel, food and entertainment has, in conjunction with financial innovations such as the asset-backed security (ABS), pushed consumer spending to unexpected levels in the past two decades – or more precisely, to levels that would not have been anticipated based on the contemporaneous performance of fundamental factors such as income and employment. We argued that a key implication of consumer credit is that it tends to diminish the structural dependence of consumption on current income and thus makes it reasonable to think in terms of an animal-spirited consumption function. As credit extended its range of importance, the prevailing mood of the household sector assumed greater power to disturb aggregate spending. A funk that envelops a substantial share of households can, in the context of the credit-dependent economy, have devastating consequences. Resistance to taking on new debt obligations is a predictable reaction among those suffering heightened distress about economic security. The parameters of the consumption function cannot remain unaffected if a great number of households are determined to shift from deficit finance to a pay-as-you-go regime (or in Minskian terms, a shift from speculative and Ponzi positions to hedge positions). The situation is made worse if individuals on average earmark an increased share of income for servicing of previously incurred debt obligations. The latter phenomenon was defined in Chapter 5 as the balance sheet or 'Minsky' effect, and is most likely to occur near the terminal point of a business cycle expansion – one characterized by rapid build-up of household debt. The Minsky effect – that is, the headlong migration of balance sheet units to more conservative locales – is the cumulative consequence of a protracted dependence on credit expansion to stimulate effective demand.

This chapter investigates the following issues. First, does the US record give evidence of Minsky-type household debt reversals? Second, given the recent household debt build-up described in the preceding chapters (especially Chapter 1), is the US economy vulnerable to balance sheet-related shocks in the near future?

6.1   1930: PORTENT OF DISASTER?[1]

Joseph Schumpeter described industrial capitalism as 'an engine of mass production, which unavoidably means also production for the masses' (Schumpeter 1942, p. 67). Large-scale or Fordist production methods delivered impression reductions in unit production costs – but only when the immense fixed costs entailed by these techniques could be spread over a vast number of units. The viability of units such as Ford Motor, Singer or Westinghouse was contingent upon the capture of a consumer market extending across several socio-economic strata.[2]

It is no exaggeration to say that big-ticket items such as autos, gas ranges or washing machines would have never made it into the mainstream of American life without the easy payment plan. Throughout the 1920s, consumer goods manufacturers and retailers came to rely increasingly on point-of-sale credit as a marketing tool. Consumer credit outstanding doubled between 1923 and 1929, a period of explosive growth in durable goods industries.[3]

The quarterly behavior of the consumption series during 1926–35 is displayed in Figure 6.1. The interpolated series estimated by Gordon and Balke (1986, p. 822) indicates that consumption expenditure fell by roughly \$24 billion (1972 dollars) or 11 percent between September 1929 and December 1930. The credit-sensitive durable goods sector was hit particularly hard during the same stretch. Durable goods sales decreased by 26 percent in real terms.

There is fairly broad agreement among economic historians that the behavior of the consumption series in the Depression is more plausibly interpreted as a 'shift' of the simple Keynesian consumption function, as opposed to a benign movement down along a short-run schedule in income–consumption space, although there are differing views as to causes of the shift.[4] Robert Hall (1986), operating within the standard microtheoretic framework, claims that a large proportion of the change in consumption during the Depression can be explained by the voluntary substitution of leisure for work.[5] Others have emphasized the importance of the stock market crash and related effects.[6] The aim here is to convince the reader that the rapid buildup of debt on household balance sheets during the late 1920s contributed to an environment in which heightened insecurity assumed greater power to destabilize output and employment.

Hyman Minsky has written:

[T]he more severe depressions in history occur after a period of good economic performance, with only minor cycles disturbing a generally expanding economy.

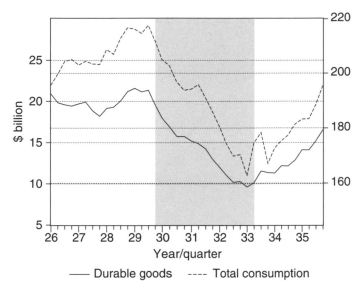

Source: Gordon and Balke (1986, Appendix B).

Figure 6.1   Consumption expenditure, 1926–35 (billions of 1972 dollars)

As the economy expands and is interrupted by only minor downturns, the liability structures of firms, households, and financial institutions change so that payment commitments on liabilities increase relative to cash flows derived from income.

As a result of such an evolution of the financial environment, a shortage of cash flows from the income stream, which in a low indebted environment is readily contained, can, in a highly indebted environment, reach and break through barriers so a cumulative and interactive debt deflation process takes place. (Minsky 1995, p. 85)

The year 1929 marked the terminal year of what Minsky has described as a 'long wave of financial relations' (ibid.). The long wave of the post-World War I era was characterized by the rapid accumulation of household debt on household balance sheets (or liability structures). Household debt grew faster than income between 1923 and 1929 (see Juster 1966). Martha Olney (1991, pp. 87–90) estimated that consumer debt as a percentage of disposable income increased from 4.68 percent in 1920 to 9.34 percent in 1929. According to Frederic Mishkin (1978, p. 921), total household debt obligations rose (in real terms) by 12 percent in 1928 and 20 percent in 1929. Seeking to put things in historical perspective, Mishkin commented that the 'increase in liabilities [in 1928–29] not only is three times the average

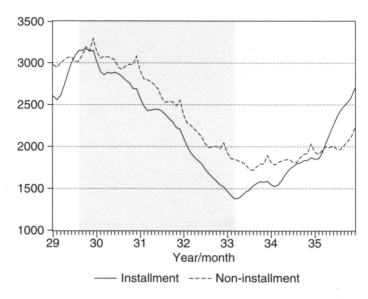

Source: Federal Reserve Bulletin, April 1953, Table 7, p. 354.

Figure 6.2   Consumer credit outstanding, 1929–35 (in millions of dollars)

annual increase from 1952–1975, but also exceeds the largest year-to-year 1952–1975 increase' (ibid.).

Figure 6.2 depicts the time profile of consumer credit outstanding during our period. Installment credit outstanding shrank by 15 percent in nominal terms in the year 1930. Total consumer credit owed decreased by $1.73 billion (current dollars) from 1929 to 1931. No cyclical contraction is even roughly comparable in terms of the falloff in household debt. A jagged reversal in the time series path of debt outstanding constitutes one piece of evidence supporting the hypothesis of a sudden but widely diffused push by households to reduce indebtedness starting in the autumn of 1929. However, it is also possible that the behavior of the debt series during this time reflects factors operating on the supply side of consumer credit markets (in fact, the claim is made in Chapter 7 that the recovery of consumer durable goods industries in the 1930s was stalled by a curtailment in the availability of dealers' inventory financing and point-of-sale consumer credit). A sudden reversal of household attitudes toward debt should produce a distinctive time series signature – specifically, a sharp increase in the ratio of monthly or quarterly debt repayments to existing debt obligations. A surge in this ratio is catalyzed by an increase in 'discretionary' repayments, defined as repayments of interest and principal exceeding those that are just sufficient to meet the contractual terms of existing debt obligations.

6.1.1 Uncovering the Minsky Effect

Households disburse a stream of money payments each period to pay interest and to retire principal amounts specified in installment debt contracts. Payments of principal can be subdivided into two components. First, there is the minimum payment of principal in a given time interval sufficient to comply with the terms of the installment debt contract. Let this amount be designated by ϕ_t. In addition, there is any repayment of principal in excess of the minimum required. Let this discretionary component be denoted by δ_t. Thus the total principal repaid in period t (symbolized by ρ_t) is given by:

$$\rho_t = \phi_t + \delta_t \tag{6.1}$$

To reiterate the point made above, the Minsky effect should manifest itself by an increase in the ratio of discretionary to total repayment of principal amounts owed on debt obligations. Let

$$\theta_t = \delta_t / \rho_t \tag{6.2}$$

A rise in the quarterly value of θ_t gives evidence that the household sector is attempting to reduce its indebtedness. It would also indicate that, *ceteris paribus*, an increasing share of personal income is being absorbed by debt servicing.

There are, unfortunately, no data available on installment debt extensions and repayments for 1929–33. Nevertheless, it is possible to construct an estimate of the quarterly values of the θ_t ratio using data on installment debt outstanding and consumer durable goods sales. A simple model is developed for this purpose. It is based on the following assumptions: (1) installment loans are used primarily for the purpose of financing consumer durable goods;[7] (2) two-thirds of all newly purchased durable goods are bought on installment contracts;[8] (3) the average down-payment is 20 percent;[9] (4) the quarterly default rate on installment loans is 1 percent;[10] and (5) the average maturity of installment debt contracts is 12 months.[11]

The results are reported in Table 6.1 (a complete description of the methodology is contained in the appendix to this chapter). The reader will notice the rise in repayments in the fourth quarter of 1929 and the first quarter of 1930. The most striking result is the increase (both in absolute terms and relative to total repayments) of the 'discretionary' component of

Table 6.1   Estimates of total and discretionary repayments on installment loans, 1929–32 [a]

Year/ quarter	Change in durable goods sales (in $ millions) [b]	Change in new installment loans (in $ millions) [b]	Total repayments (in $ millions)	Discretionary repayments (in $ millions)	Ratio of discretionary to total repayments
1929–2	−115	−68	948	296	0.312
1929–3	30	18	1199	449	0.374
1929–4	−180	−106	1246	457	0.367
1930–1	−240	−142	1395	607	0.435
1930–2	−72	−43	1034	320	0.309
1930–3	−197	−116	1040	318	0.306
1930–4	90	53	1104	406	0.368
1931–1	−302	−177	1080	408	0.378
1931–2	40	24	833	225	0.270
1931–3	−145	−85	873	262	0.299
1931–4	−105	−62	830	246	0.296
1932–1	−177	−104	881	329	0.374
1932–2	−108	−58	667	186	0.284
1932–3	−80	−64	656	207	0.316
1932–4	−78	−52	558	150	0.269

Notes:
[a] Data on consumer durable expenditures were taken from Gordon and Balke (1986, Appendix B, pp. 822–3). Data on consumer debt outstanding were taken from the *Federal Reserve Bulletin*, April 1953, Table 7, p. 354.
[b] From the previous quarter.

Source: Adapted from *Journal of Post Keynesian Economics*, vol. 19, no. 4 (summer 1997), 632. Copyright © by M.E. Sharpe, Inc. Used by permission.

debt servicing. Estimated discretionary repayments on installment debt contracts increased by $311 million, or 51 percent, between the second quarter of 1929 and the first quarter of 1930. Thus the estimates indicate that, ignoring the payment of interest, about $3.10 out of every $10 paid out in installment debt service in the spring of 1929 could be classified as discretionary. By the winter of 1930, the amount had increased to $4.35 out of every dollar.

While the estimates give a rough approximation of the spending power absorbed by debt servicing, they understate the full extent of leakages from the income–expenditure stream associated with the Minsky effect since they fail to take account of changes in the discretionary repayment of non-installment debt. A switch from revolving to convenience use of open accounts (accounts that permit flexibility with respect to repayment) is a clear indication of a change of attitude toward borrowing. Although our period pre-dates the introduction of the universal credit card, the 1920s was the liberalization of charge account policies at retail establishments.[12] The practice of carrying forward open account balances had become more the rule than the exception by the end of the 1920s. Thus the 20 percent decrease ($321 million) in charge account balances almost certainly reveals a swing of the pendulum back in favor of financial conservatism.[13] In summary, there is no reason to believe that the drive to rein in debt was restricted to installment balances.

Among the multifarious lessons that may be drawn from the Depression, two deserve special emphasis here. First, extreme income inequality impedes the growth of demand for many types of consumer goods and services.[14] Second, the proliferating use of credit, while it can act as a powerful stimulant to economic growth, is also capable of producing harmful aggregate demand shocks. To get an idea of just how powerful these credit-related (negative) spending shocks might be, we pose the following question: suppose that, in the year 2007, there is a surge in discretionary repayments of installment and revolving balances that is equivalent in relative magnitude to the change estimated for 1929–2 to 1930–1 (as reported in Table 6.1, θ_t increased from 0.312 to 0.435) – what would the change in aggregate consumption be, assuming that a $1 increase in repayments is equivalent to a $1 decrease in consumption expenditure? Based on the Federal Reserve Board's estimates of revolving and installment debt outstanding in April 2007, the increase in repayments would result in an initial change in consumption of $298.76 billion (current dollars), or 3.11 percent of annual consumption based on Bureau of Economic Analysis estimates for the first quarter of 2007. A spending shock of this order would certainly be sufficient to ignite a recession. Also bear in mind that our calculations ignore any increase in repayments on home equity loans that would probably take place in a debt reduction environment. As was explained in Chapter 1 (section 1.4), many have switched from conventional consumer loans to home equity loans to capture the tax advantages associated with the latter type.

6.2 MEASURING STRESS ON HOUSEHOLD BUDGETS FROM DEBT SERVICE

The risk of balance sheet-triggered consumption shocks is a function of overall or average balance sheet quality, where balance sheet quality is primarily a matter of the adequacy of cash flows in relation to contractually

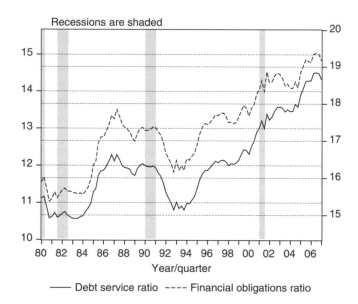

Source: Federal Reserve Board.

Figure 6.3   Debt service and financial obligations ratios (percent)

obligated payments of interest and principal on previously incurred debt
obligations. Thus we are interested in statistics that track changes over time
in the capacity of households to service their debts. It is not possible (at
least without arbitrary assumptions) to give precise estimates of the distribution of household units in a given year between the categories of hedge,
speculative and Ponzi finance. There are statistics that enable one to make
reasonable inferences about the general direction and sinew of movement
among these divisions.

The debt service ratio (DSR) is the Federal Reserve's estimate of the
required minimum payment on consumer borrowing. It is determined by
the amount of debt outstanding (excluding home equity and mortgage
debt) and hire purchase terms (payment schedules, interest rates and other
fees). The financial obligations ratio (FOR) adds other consumer obligations (automobile lease payments, rental payments on tenant-occupied
property, home owners' insurance and property tax payments) to the
DSR. Both measures track closely with personal bankruptcy filings.
A report prepared by the Congressional Budget Office shows that DSR is
an excellent predictor of future changes in the non-business bankruptcy
rate.[15]

The generally pro-cyclical movement of these indices is consistent with the Minsky story. The Federal Reserve Board began publishing these measures in 1980. Since then, the turning points of the DSR and FOR have been located in fairly close proximity to national Bureau of Economic Research (NBER)-designated business cycle peaks and troughs. The decline of these time series after 1986 is an important nonconformity, and is partly explained by the substitution of home equity loans for conventional consumer loans after the elimination of the tax deductibility of interest paid on the latter type of debt. But the record shows a more or less uninterrupted rise in these ratios between 1994 and 2002, followed by a brief moderation and then another surge beginning in the autumn of 2003. Both indicators are presently near their peak levels, and well above historic averages.

The behavior of these variables certainly does not serve to falsify the hypothesis that a large cohort of families is more financially distressed today than ten years ago. The debt service and financial obligations ratios are nevertheless of limited usefulness for our purposes. For one thing, they omit home equity debt. Second, they are aggregate ratios and thus give no information about the underlying distribution of debt or income across households.[16] We know, for example, that most of the income growth of the last few years has accrued to those with very high incomes. The distribution of debt, on the other hand, has been far more egalitarian. Given these facts, it is possible that what appears to be a slight increase in the DSR or FOR ratios might in fact signal a serious deterioration in financial condition for a large segment of the population.[17]

6.3 EVIDENCE FROM MICRODATA

Microdata extracted from the *Survey of Consumer Finances* were used to compute mean debt-to-income ratios by income quintile (as well as the top 5 percent) for the years 1983, 1989, 1995, 2001 and 2005. These are displayed in Table 6.2. Note that debt includes credit card debt, installment loans, personal loans, student loans and home equity loans. It does not include mortgage debt. The overall debt-to-income ratio reached 0.304 in the year 2004. It was equal to 0.181 in 1983. Probably the most striking aspect of Table 6.2 is the large increase in the debt-to-income ratios of the bottom two quintiles between 1989 and 2004. These figures support the view that financial engineering has exerted powerful effects on the spending behavior of low- and middle-income groups especially. Sadly, these units are most vulnerable to financial ruin as a result of borrowing.

Table 6.2   Debt-to-income ratios by quintile [a]

Quintile	Year				
	1983	1989	1995	2001	2004
Bottom	0.384	0.236	0.291	0.491	0.427
Second	0.153	0.179	0.200	0.258	0.354
Middle	0.150	0.239	0.180	0.250	0.282
Fourth	0.140	0.221	0.160	0.206	0.260
Top	0.138	0.178	0.092	0.140	0.145
Top 5%	0.126	0.201	0.047	0.107	0.088
All	0.181	0.215	0.192	0.264	0.304

Note: [a] Debt includes consumer and home equity debt.

Source: Author's calculations from the *Survey of Consumer Finances*, adapted from *Journal of Post Keynesian Economics*, vol. 29, no. 3 (spring 2007), 450. Copyright © by M.E. Sharpe, Inc. Used by permission.

Even within income quintiles, debt and income are distributed unequally. Every income stratum includes a slice of households (mainly older) that are conservative in their use of credit. Thus a matriculation of units from hedge to speculative or Ponzi status might be uncovered by measuring the proportion of households with debt-to-income ratios exceeding some threshold level.

Table 6.3 provides estimates for various years of the fraction of households within income quintiles (and the top 5 percent) with debt-to-income ratios exceeding 0.4 and 0.6. Note that for the entire population, slightly more than 10 percent had debt-to-income ratios greater than 0.4. The number was 12.4 percent in 1995 and then rose to 23.2 percent in 2004. Note also that debt-to-income ratios for the top quintile and top 5 percent actually decreased in the same period. This is not surprising given that the top quintile (and top 5 percent) saw its share of total income increase from 44.7 to 50.1 (16.4 to 22.4) percent from 1983 to 2001.[18] The story is very different for the remaining 80 percent of households, and especially the bottom two quintiles. Notice for example that the proportion of units within the lowest quintile with a debt-to-income ratio exceeding 0.4 rose from 14.5 to 40 percent between 1995 and 2004. Notice also that while approximately 9 percent of second-quintile units had debt-to-income ratios in excess of 0.6 in 1995, the comparable figure in 2004 was 26.2 percent.

The numbers presented above give the impression of a society embarked on a great economic experiment. It is apparent that many individuals are

Table 6.3 *Proportion of households with debt-to-income ratios exceeding 0.4 and 0.6, by quintile*

Quintile	Year									
	1983		1989		1995		2001		2004	
	≥ 0.4	≥ 0.6	≥ 0.4	≥ 0.6	≥ 0.4	≥ 0.6	≥ 0.4	≥ 0.6	≥ 0.4	≥ 0.6
Bottom	0.124	0.088	0.164	0.118	0.145	0.118	0.182	0.145	0.400	0.382
Second	0.110	0.056	0.137	0.074	0.173	0.088	0.217	0.142	0.300	0.262
Middle	0.096	0.045	0.207	0.109	0.140	0.058	0.220	0.130	0.200	0.145
Fourth	0.082	0.042	0.169	0.085	0.106	0.044	0.165	0.069	0.170	0.120
Top	0.095	0.052	0.075	0.037	0.036	0.007	0.088	0.048	0.065	0.038
Top 5%	0.106	0.053	0.081	0.033	0.016	0.003	0.059	0.033	0.038	0.029
All	0.102	0.057	0.164	0.118	0.124	0.065	0.174	0.109	0.232	0.196

Source: Author's calculations from the *Survey of Consumer Finances*, adapted from *Journal of Post Keynesian Economics*, vol. 29, no. 3 (spring 2007), 452. Copyright © by M.E. Sharpe, Inc. Used by permission.

determined to test the limits to which debts can be expanded in relation to income receipts (Chapter 2 attempted to bring the cultural and psychological forces driving such bold experimentation into relief, while Chapter 3 described the innovations which have broadened the opportunity for it). The ABS era may have brought forth a lasting structural change in which debt-to-income ratios remain at levels considerably higher than was considered prudent not long ago.

6.4 SUSTAINABILITY OF CURRENT TRENDS

Income distributed in factor markets (earned income) and cash transfer payments provide the bulk of purchasing power available to meet periodic payments of interest and principal stipulated in debt contracts. A substantial increase in the share of income claimed by debt servicing should raise concerns. As a general principle we may state that, holding the underlying distribution of income and debt among income groups constant, the growth rate of household debt is sustainable if the ratio of debt service to income is stable (or decreasing) as the time axis shifts forward. A rise in this ratio does, however, cast serious doubts on whether the current growth rate of debt (and spending) can be maintained.

The purpose of this section is to ask the following question: if consumer and mortgage debt expand according to trends established since 2001, should we expect a worrisome change in the relationship between income and debt servicing? The short answer is: it depends. Specifically, the capacity of the household sector to continually expand its debts depends on many factors, including income growth, interest rates, the average maturity of debts, and the distribution of income and debt obligations. Several estimates of the future course of the debt service to disposable income ratio are provided below. The estimates differ based on assumptions made about the growth rate of disposable income as well as the interest rates for the forecast horizon – specifically, the third quarter of 2008 through the fourth quarter of 2009.

6.4.1   Forecast Technique

The following symbols are used for purposes of the forecasts:

Service$_t$: Debt service in quarter t;
DPI$_t$: (Nominal) personal disposable income in quarter t;
τ_t: Equal to Service$_t$/DPI$_t$;
Revolve$_t$: Revolving debt outstanding in quarter t;
Nrevolve$_t$: Non-revolving debt outstanding in quarter t;
Mdebt$_t$: Mortgage debt outstanding in quarter t (includes home equity loans);
Interest$_t$: Minimum interest owed in quarter t;
Principal$_t$: Minimum principal owed in quarter t;
Maturity$_{C1}$: Average maturity of revolving debts (in quarters);
Maturity$_{C2}$: Average maturity of non-revolving debts (in quarters);
Maturity$_M$: Average maturity of mortgage debts (in quarters);
R_{C1}: Average interest rate paid on revolving debts;
R_{C2}: Average interest rate paid on non-revolving debts; and
R_M: Average interest rate paid on mortgage debts.

Assumptions are as shown in Table 6.4.

The growth of consumer and mortgage debt is forecasted using a trend component obtained from quarterly observations for these variables for the period 2001–1 to 2007–1. Having obtained trend growth rates for household debt, the next step is to estimate quarterly debt service, or:

$$\text{Service}_t = \text{Interest}_t + \text{Principal}_t \qquad (6.3)$$

Quarterly interest payments are estimated using the following equation:

$$\text{Interest}_t = \{[(\text{Revolve}_t)(R_{C1})] + [(\text{Nrevolve}_t)(R_{C2})] + [(\text{Mdebt}_t)(R_M)]\}/4$$
$$(6.4)$$

Table 6.4 Forecast assumptions of λ_t

Forecast	DPI$_t$ [a]	M_{C1} (QTRs)	M_{C2} (QTRs)	M_M (QTRs)	R_{C1} (%)	R_{C2} (%)	R_M (%)
1	Trend [b]	14.8	33.6	67.5	14.64	7.74	6.2
2	Trend [b]	14.8	33.6	67.5	15.14	8.24	6.7
3	0	14.8	33.6	67.5	14.64	7.74	6.2
4	2.5	14.8	33.6	67.5	15.14	8.24	6.7
5	−1.0	14.8	33.6	67.5	15.14	8.24	6.7
6	−1.0	14.8	33.6	67.5	14.14	7.24	5.7

Notes:
[a] Expressed in percent per year.
[b] Approximately 4.92 percent per year.

The estimate of minimum principal owed is obtained from:

$$\text{Principal}_t = (\text{Revolve}_t/\text{Maturity}_{C1}) + (\text{Nrevolve}_t/\text{Maturity}_{C2}) +$$
$$(\text{Mdebt}_t/\text{Maturity}_M) \tag{6.5}$$

Equations (6.4) and (6.5) are substituted into (6.3) to estimate quarterly debt service.

Six sets of estimates of the fraction of quarterly disposable income claimed by debt servicing (λ_t) for the years 2008 and 2009 are presented in Table 6.5. The forecasts use the technique above but differ according to assumptions about future quarterly values of income growth and interest rates (see Table 6.4). Forecast 1 is based on 'status quo' assumptions about the future time paths of DPI, R_{C1} and R_{C2}. The trend growth rate of (nominal) diposable income, computed from 25 quarterly observations (2001–1 to 2007–1) is 4.92 percent per year.

Forecast 2 attempts to model the effect of a change in Federal Reserve policy that fails to dislodge the economy from its trend growth rate. Fed tightening is manifest in a 50 basis point increase in the average mortgage and consumer loan rate. The presence of 'lock-in' effects (many existing loan agreements have fixed nominal repayment schedules through 2008) means that it requires a very substantial increase in rates charged on new loans to drive up the average rate on all loans by 50 basis points. The following example will illustrate the point. Assume that (nominal) consumer debt outstanding remains unchanged at $100 billion over a three-year period. If the average maturity of a consumer loan is 12 quarters, it will take three years for the debt to roll over. Thus, given a 'once and for all' increase in rates of 100 basis points (from say, 9 to 10 percent), the average

Table 6.5   Forecasted values of λ_t

Yr/qtr	Forecast					
	1	2	3	4	5	6
2008–1	0.2084	0.2154	0.2165	0.2108	0.2184	0.2042
2008–2	0.2096	0.2167	0.2188	0.2186	0.2226	0.2080
2008–3	0.2109	0.2180	0.2209	0.2198	0.2268	0.2120
2008–4	0.2121	0.2193	0.2231	0.2210	0.2310	0.2160
2009–1	0.2133	0.2205	0.2252	0.2221	0.2352	0.2198
2009–2	0.2144	0.2217	0.2273	0.2232	0.2395	0.2238
2009–3	0.2156	0.2229	0.2293	0.2243	0.2437	0.2277
2009–4	0.2167	0.2240	0.2130	0.2254	0.2480	0.2317

rate will rise by 20 basis points after one year, 57 after two, and 100 basis points after the debt is completely rolled over.

The results for forecast 1 indicate that the current pace of household indebtedness might be sustainable throughout 2008 – so long as income growth stays strong and interest rates remain unchanged. Forecast 4 assumes a more modest growth rate of 2.5 percent and higher interest rates. The fraction of income claimed by debt servicing is projected to rise from 21.1 to 22.5 percent, which may seem trivial to some. However, the technique deployed here suffers from the same defects as the financial obligations and debt service ratios discussed in section 6.2 above. That is, the macroeconomic effects depend not only on the absolute flow of debt service payments relative to income, but also on the distribution of debt service across income groups. A debt build-up would be less worrisome (in terms of the potentially dampening effects on future consumption) if the debt burden were disproportionately distributed to the balance sheets of high-income, high-net-worth individuals. Conversely, the time path of λ_t may conceal the fact that a sizeable number of lower- and middle-income households (which account for a big share of total consumer spending) is at or near the point of financial distress. Thus, even a slight increase in λ_t may be cause for concern.

Forecasts 5 and 6 indicate that the current growth rate of consumer indebtedness would not be sustainable should a recession develop. Under the 'worst case' assumptions of forecast 5 (negative income growth of 1 percent and a 50 basis point increase in interest rates), the value of λ_t rises from 0.2184 to 0. 2480 in the span of eight quarters. Given the historical relation between debt service ratios and bankruptcy filings, an increase of this magnitude would almost certainly be accompanied by a surge in the bankruptcy rate. The forecast 6 results show that the debt servicing ratio (λ_t) will rise considerably if the economy slides into recession – even if the Fed pursues an expansionary policy.

6.5 CONCLUDING REMARKS

The household balance sheet data presented above give the impression of a society embarked on a grand, but potentially dangerous, economic experiment. Many individuals are testing the limits to which their debts can be expanded. This process of experimentation has fueled a protracted consumption boom, the likes of which would not have materialized had more conservative attitudes to borrowing held sway. The penetration of the SUV, the passenger truck, the home computer, the digital camera, the flat-screen TV, the iPod and other expensive items deep into the market space occupied by middle- and lower-income households would have been well-nigh impossible if not for the concomitant debt surge documented earlier. This would seem to be (in terms of effective demand) all to the good. Viewed through the Fisher–Minsky lens, however, the debt surge contains the seeds of recession. For reasons explained in Chapter 5 (section 5.2), the severity of business cycle contractions is strongly influenced by the quality of balance sheets in the waning months of the preceding expansion.[19] The evidence presented above suggests that, if balance sheet quality is judged by the ratio of income receipts to total debt or debt servicing, the US economy is vulnerable to a deep, prolonged slump.

NOTES

1. Section 6.1 is adapted from *Journal of Post Keynesian Economics*, vol. 19, no. 4 (summer 1997), 617–39. Used by permission of M.E. Sharpe, Inc.
2. Robert Averitt has argued that Fordist techniques are 'only economically feasible if a high volume of output is assured . . . [Hence], marketing is paramount. Unit costs will automatically fall until existing plants are operated quite near their engineering capacity . . . [F]irms will engage in heavy advertising expenditures to create and sustain a viable demand for their product' (Averitt 1968, pp. 30–31).
3. Edwin Seligman, the authoritative source on the consumer credit industry in the 1920s, wrote that '[t]he colossal growth of the automobile business and the multiplication of the finance companies during the [period] finally led to the application of the instalment system to many other lines of industry. As a consequence durable goods . . . that are not sold on instalment plan today form the exception and not the rule' (Seligman 1927, p. 54).
4. Thomas Mayer (1980) is a dissenter on this point. Peter Temin writes that '[t]he American economy experienced . . . a fall in consumption in 1930 that was too large to be easily explained. This autonomous fall in consumption . . . is still an important part of the American story' (Temin 1989, p. 43). Temin estimated consumption functions

using 1919–49 data and then inferred the magnitude of the shift in the year 1930 based on the negative 'residual' for 1930 and the average residual for the study period (see Temin 1976, pp. 64–75). Commenting on Temin's technique, Robert Hall said, 'Temin considerably understates the power of his case by looking for departures from the historical relation between consumption and income . . . Temin looks only at the excess in 1930 over the usual amount of the shift, when his argument logically involves the whole amount of the shift' (Hall, 1986, p. 240).

5.   Hall writes: [T]he story of the Depression is told by these results: . . . [R]eal GNP [1972 dollars] fell by $227 billion in 1929–30, $171 billion in 1930–31, and $243 billion in 1931–32. Of this, $140 billion can from a random shift in household behavior toward less work and less consumption, $97 billion in 1930–31, and $148 billion in 1931–32' (Hall 1986, p. 252).

6.   J.K. Galbraith (1961) is perhaps best known among those who attribute great significance to the Crash in causing the subsequent decline in real activity. Temin (1991) notes that 'Time has not been kind to the school of thought that blames the Depression on the stock market crash . . . If the crash of 1929 was an important independent shock to the economy, the crash of 1987 should have been equally disastrous' (ibid., pp. 43–4). Christina Romer (1990) argues that, although the wealth effect is overrated, the Crash did adversely affect aggregate demand by intensifying job and income uncertainty.

7.   Based on figures contained in Edward Seligman's study of installment selling in the 1920s, contracts collateralized by autos accounted for 56 percent of total installment extensions in the year 1925; furniture 17 percent; pianos 4 percent; radios 3 percent; and washing machines 2 percent. See Seligman (1927, p. 117, Table XVI).

8.   This figure is slightly below the estimate of Milan Ayres (1926) and slightly above the estimate of Seligman (1927).

9.   This figure is taken from Seligman (1927, p. 100, Table XII).

10.   The assumed default rate probably overstates the actual default rate – even during the worst months of the Depression. GMAC loan losses on retail installment paper never reached 1 percent (per annum) of holdings between 1929 and 1933. The retail loss ratio (percent of paper in default) peaked at less than 1 percent in 1933. This figure was reported in Alfred P. Sloan (1964, p. 304).

11.   According to data supplied by Juster (1964, Table 6), the average maturity of installment contracts was 13 months in 1928 and edged up slightly to 14.2 months by 1933. Thus the use of the 12-month assumption guards against underestimating compulsory repayments (ϕ_t) and overstating discretionary repayments (δ_t).

12.   Rolf Nugent reported that 'from 1923 to 1929 a rise in receivables in relation to sales appears to have been common to all types of open-book credit merchants and to many types of service creditors. Collection percentages indicate clearly a gradual increase in the period of liquidation . . . The most liberal policies tended to become the rule' (Nugent 1939, p. 101).

13.   The trend illustrated in Figure 6.2 generated considerable commentary at the time. Economist Franklin Ryan, for example, noted in regard to the steep decline in household debt between 1930 and 1932 that '[though] these declines reflect the increase in the value of the dollar as well as the falloff in buying power . . . [t]he most potent influences here were the real desire of individuals to get out of debt . . . The getting out of debt process is going on with accelerated momentum' (Ryan 1933, pp. 320–21).

14.   It is well known that the distribution of income in the 1920s and 1930s was highly skewed – at least by contemporary standards of most OECD nations. For example, the data show that in 1929, the top 5 percent of individuals received 30 percent of personal income and the top 20 percent received 54.4 percent. The bottom 40 percent received on 12.5 percent of personal income. These data are reported in Dowd (1993, p. 214, Table 5.2).

15.   Dynan et al. warn that the interpretation of the DSR 'is subject to several caveats', including that 'this measure expresses the debt service obligations of the population as a whole but not necessarily the obligations of the typical household' (Dynan et al. 2003, p. 417).

16. See Kowalewski (2000, p. 10, Figure 3), 'Growth in the personal filing rate and the debt service burden of the household sector'.
17. It is easy to demonstrate that the DSR or FOR of most individual households can increase, even when aggregate ratios are falling, given certain (not very unrealistic) assumptions about the distribution of debt and income across income groups.
18. These data are taken from the Bureau of the Census Historical Income Tables, IE-3.
19. The severity of a business cycle contraction is a function of its duration (in months or quarters) and its depth (typically measured by the percentage decrease peak to trough in real GDP, employment, or other measures of aggregate activity, from their peak or trend values). See Brusca (1992).

REFERENCES

Averitt, Robert (1968), *The Dual Economy*, New York: W.W. Norton.
Ayres, M. (1926), 'Instalment selling and financing', paper presented at the Third National Automotive Financing Conference, Chicago, November.
Brusca, R. (1992), 'Recession or recovery?', *Challenge*, July–August, 4–15.
Dowd, Douglas (1993), *U.S. Capitalist Development since 1776*, Armonk, NY: M.E. Sharpe.
Dynan, K., K. Johnson and K. Pence (2003), 'Recent changes to a measure of household debt service', *Federal Reserve Bulletin*, (10), 417–26.
Galbraith, John K. (1961), *The Great Crash*, Boston, MA: Houghton Mifflin.
Gordon, Robert J. and Nathan Balke (1986), 'Appendix B: historical data', in R.J. Gordon (ed.), *The American Business Cycle: Continuity and Change,* Chicago, IL: University of Chicago Press, pp. 781–850.
Hall, Robert (1986), 'The role of consumption in economic fluctuations', in R.J. Gordon (ed.), *The American Business Cycle: Continuity and Change*, Chicago, IL: University of Chicago Press, pp. 237–66.
Juster, Thomas (1966), *Household Capital Formation and Financing*, New York: National Bureau of Economic Research.
Kowalewski, K. (2000), 'Personal bankruptcy: a review of the literature', Washington: Congressional Budget Office, http://www.cbo.gov/ftpdocs/24xx/doc2421/Bankruptcy.pdf (accessed 23 July 2007).
Mayer, T. (1980), 'Consumption in the Great Depression', *Journal of Political Economy*, **86** (2), 139–45.
Minsky, H. (1995), 'Longer waves in financial relations: financial factors in the more severe depressions II', *Journal of Economic Issues*, **29** (1), 83–96.
Mishkin, F. (1978), 'The household balance sheet and the Great Depression', *Journal of Economic History*, **38** (4), 918–37.
Nugent, Rolf (1939), *Consumer Credit and Economic Stability*, New York: Russell Sage Foundation.
Olney, Martha (1991), *Buy Now, Pay Later*, Chapel Hill, NC: University of North Carolina Press.
Romer, C. (1990), 'The great crash and the onset of the Great Depression', *Quarterly Journal of Economics*, **105** (3), 597–624.
Ryan, Franklin (1933), 'Short-term personal debts', in E. Clark (ed.), *The Internal Debts of the United States*, New York: Macmillan, ch. 11.
Schumpeter, Joseph (1942), *Socialism, Capitalism, and Democracy*, New York: Harper & Row.

Seligman, Edwin (1927), *The Economics of Instalment Selling*, New York: Harper and Brothers.
Sloan, Alfred P. (1964), *My Years with General Motors*, (eds) T. McDonald and C. Stevens, New York: Doubleday.
Temin, Peter (1976), *Did Monetary Forces Cause the Great Depression?*, New York: W.W. Norton.
Temin, Peter (1989), *Lessons from the Great Depression*, Cambridge, MA: MIT Press.

APPENDIX 6A   TECHNIQUE FOR ESTIMATING DISCRETIONARY REPAYMENTS ON INSTALLMENT DEBT, 1929–33

Definitions

d prefix indicating change in variable from the previous quarter;

$Debt_t$ consumer installment credit outstanding in quarter t;

$Loans_t$ new extensions of installment credit in quarter t;

$Used_t$ installment loans used to purchased used goods in quarter t;

DUR_t consumer durable goods sales in quarter t;

β ratio of $Used_t$ to New_t;

ρ_t total repayments of principal on installment loans in quarter t;

ϕ_t minimum repayments of principal on installment loans in quarter t;

δ_t discretionary repayments of principal on installment loans in quarter t; and

γ_t charge-offs taken by installment lenders due to defaults in quarter t.

Method

The net change in the stock of debt from the previous quarter appearing on balance sheets must be equal to additions to the stock of debt during the quarter resulting from new loans minus subtractions from the stock of debt during the same period due to repayments of principal or defaults. That is:

$$dDebt_t = Loans_t - \rho_t - \gamma_t \qquad (6A.1)$$

Households borrow to finance the purchase of used goods as well as newly produced goods. There are no quarterly data available on the value of used goods sold during the period. New installment loans made for the purchase of used goods is set equal to some fraction of loans made for the purchase of new durable goods. Thus we have:

$$Loans_t = New_t + Used_t \qquad (6A.2)$$

where:

$$Used_t = \beta\ New_t \qquad (6A.3)$$

Based on the estimates of Milan Ayres (reported in Seligman 1927, p. 101) for the year 1925, installment extensions collateralized by used goods (mainly cars and trucks) were equal to 15 percent of new installment paper collateralized by new consumer durables. As the estimates of repayments (both total and discretionary) are sensitive to the value of β, the estimates reported in Table 6.1 above are based on a conservative assumption about β – specifically, $\beta = 0.10$. Equation (6A.3) is rewritten:

$$Used_t = 0.10\ New_t \qquad (6A.4)$$

As noted in section 6.2, the model is based on the assumption that two-thirds of new durable goods are purchased on installment contracts and the average down-payment is 20 percent. Thus new loan extensions are given by:

$$New_t = 0.67[(0.80)(DUR_t)] \qquad (6A.5)$$

Substituting equation (6A.5) into (6A.4) yields:

$$Used_t = 0.10\{0.67[(0.80)(DUR_t)]\} \qquad (6A.6)$$

Quarterly installment extensions are estimated by substituting (6A.5) and (6A.6) into (6A.2):

$$Loans_t = 0.67[(0.80)(DUR_t)] + 0.10\{0.67[(0.80)(DUR_t)]\} \qquad (6A.7)$$

Assuming a quarterly default rate of 1 percent (assumption 4 in section 6.2), we have:

$$\gamma_t = 0.01 \cdot Debt_{t-1} \qquad (6A.8)$$

Total repayments on installment loans are equal to minimum (compulsory) repayments and 'discretionary' repayments, or:

$$\rho_t = \phi_t + \delta_t \qquad (6A.9)$$

The average maturity of an installment debt contract is assumed to be 12 months. Thus 3/12 (or 25 percent) of outstanding installment debt must be repaid each quarter to meet terms stipulated in debt contracts. Minimum repayments are thus given by:

$$\phi_t = 0.25 \cdot Debt_{t-1} \qquad (6A.10)$$

Substituting (6A.10) into (6A.9) yields:

$$\rho_t = (0.25 \cdot Debt_{t-1}) + \delta_t \qquad (6A.11)$$

Substituting equation (6A.9) into (6A.1) and rearranging yields:

$$\delta_t = Loans_t - (dDebt_t + \phi_t + \gamma_t) \qquad (6A.12)$$

Using equations (6A.7), (6A.9) and (6A.10), respectively, solutions are obtained for $Loans_t$, γ_t and ϕ_t. The discretionary repayments variable (δ_t) is then computed as a residual.

7. Consumerism, inequality and globalization

The term 'globalization' is invoked in connection with a variety of phenomena. These include the expanding scale of international trade in merchandise and services, the removal of barriers to the transnational movement of resources and financial capital, as well as the relocation of production activity to so-called less developed countries (LDCs). The area of overlap between the elements subsumed under 'globalization' and the subject matter addressed in the preceding chapters is extensive. The analysis here is restricted to some salient points of intersection. We shall be concerned first of all with appraising the view that persistent US trade deficits are largely explained by 'overconsumption' or, equivalently, a shortage of saving by US households. Next, we shall take up the issue of the implications of globalization, and more specifically what is commonly called the global dis-integration of production, for inequality and household saving within the industrialized nations. We shall argue that the rising economic inequality, the debt surge and the decline of household saving are closely connected to the far-reaching push by US-based corporations to improve earnings by shifting production to LDCs.

We have argued that the surprising muscularity of the US consumer is partly the result of financial innovations and practices that have effectively shifted the demand for household IOUs. Given that a substantial faction of new securities backed by credit card, installment, student loan, home equity, or other consumer receivables is placed in foreign-owned portfolios, is it accurate to claim (as some have) that US lifestyles are somehow underpinned or enabled by the comparatively stronger habits of thrift which prevail among the peoples of its major trading partners? A basic principle of post-Keynesian economics is that, so long as reserve production capacity and sophisticated financial institutions are present, income does not impose a hard constraint on spending. This must be true, or how could spending grow? Implicit in the view that deficit spending (negative saving) of the household sector in one nation is impossible without voluntary abstinence in other nations is the belief that global effective demand is limited by global income. Our task is to explain why foreign saving *per se* has little to do with the pace of domestic credit expansion. At the same time, decisions with respect to the allocation of foreign portfolio capital (or accumulated saving) can and do have a significant impact on local credit conditions.

The transition of the USA to debtor nation status raises a number of concerns. There is considerable support for the view that, in the aftermath of a sustained run of capital account surpluses, the preference of foreign-based wealth controllers for dollar-denominated financial assets has assumed enlarged power to influence domestic credit (and economic) conditions. Thus a discussion of the potential fallout in the consumer credit industry arising from a flight from the dollar is in order.

7.1   CONSUMERISM AND THE TRADE DEFICIT

The issues of the causes, consequences and sustainability of ballooning US current account deficits (see Figure 7.1) have produced a voluminous literature.[1] Inspection of Figure 7.2 leaves no doubt that household spending is a main driver of import growth. Olivier Blanchard recently wrote the following about the US trade deficit:

> I believe that there is now a broad consensus about the following proximate causes: first, low U.S. saving, reflecting primarily low private saving, but also budget deficits; second, high foreign saving, particularly for Asia; third, low foreign investment, in both Europe and Asia; and fourth, a strong preference for U.S. over foreign assets. (Blanchard 2007, p. 198)

While Blanchard's comments imply that trade imbalances can be largely explained by cross-national differences in saving rates, we shall argue that it is more accurate to state that variations in saving rates between countries originate from several of the same causes that produce trade imbalances.[2]

The salient features of modern consumerism were discussed in previous chapters. Among these is the common use of goods as a system of communication about class. We argued that consumerism should be understood as a social or cultural accommodation to exigencies of big business and, indirectly, to the share and bondholding classes. Consumerism is a cultural manifestation of a particular form of material provisioning – one in which (private) capital (and other resources) may be withheld from use and the continuous recycling of income receipts for the purchase of producibles provides the best insurance against it. Its relative importance depends on a number of economic and non-economic factors. The strength of old habits and institutions in forestalling the movement to more unadulterated forms of consumerism will vary according to time and place. Thus at any given point in time the world consists of societies exhibiting lesser or greater

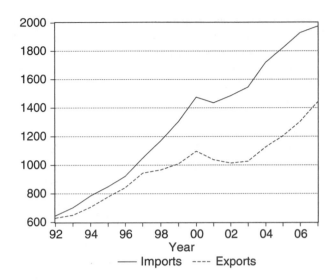

Source: Bureau of Economic Analysis (www.bea.gov).

Figure 7.1   Imports and exports of the USA (billions of chained 2000 dollars)

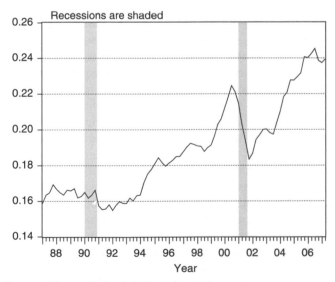

Source: Bureau of Economic Analysis (www.bea.gov).

Figure 7.2   Ratio of imports to consumption

degrees of consumerism, as measured by objective criteria such as the saving rate, per capita consumer debt or cars per household. The integration of culturally heterogeneous societies in a global trading system raises a number of important questions. For example, do current trade regimes allow nations with poorly developed consumption sectors to 'free-ride' on those nations that do?

The constitution of a social unit capable of generating the kind of unfailing expenditure levels required to keep corporatism flourishing does not happen automatically, and should not be taken for granted. It requires first of all the emergence of institutions that facilitate a somewhat level distribution of liquid claims to goods across individuals, households or social classes. The assertion that a robust market for mass-produced consumer items cannot emerge out of conditions of extreme income skewness will find no disconfirmation in the historical record. The onset of the American Age of Affluence (Galbraith 1958) was, not coincidentally, contemporaneous with the arrival of a *bona fide* middle class. It is certainly true that the shared prosperity of the 1950s and 1960s was enabled by improvements in technology, infrastructure, business organization and education. However, the appearance of a vast and prosperous middle class had its origins in social and political movements that aimed to alter the balance of power between labor and capital.

Institutionalists (and post-Keynesians) reject the standard (marginal productivity) theory of income distribution.[3] Observed income disparities do not, according to the institutionalist view, arise from differential contributions to value at the margin of production.[4] Rather, such disparities emerge from institutionally rooted asymmetries in the distribution of political and economic power. These asymmetries spring mainly from the concentration of control over property, as well as the nature of modern property rights.

Power is the capacity to give effect to the will and, importantly, to prevail against those with opposing wills. A contest of wills usually turns on which party is best positioned to sustain (actual or potential) injuries that other parties may inflict upon it. Property confers the privilege to withhold. With the rise of public ownership, and the systematic replacement of markets with organizational hierarchies, property morphed into a shape quite unlike anything found in the writings of John Locke. Its domain is now coextensive with production systems, the continuous operation upon which a great number of jobs depends. Absentee ownership, vertical integration, horizontal consolidation – while these innovations may have been beneficial in terms of expanded production possibilities, they also delivered fearsome powers of coercion to the controllers of business enterprises (and, by extension, to the shareholder class) *vis-à-vis* labor. That the actual or potential loss of employment or livelihood is a potent despoiler of labor truculence has shown forth time and again. An equable, and macro-efficient, division of the material gains arising from the new methods of economic organization was only achieved after society took protective measures against the coercive powers of big business.

Social technologies such as collective bargaining, the closed shop and legalized strikes are of equal importance to innovations such as continuous process manufacturing in explaining broad-based improvements in material welfare. Reforms of the working rules applicable to labor market transactions did, in many cases, eradicate the gross power disparities indicative of the wage bargain and thus were vital in making the fruits of modern capitalism obtainable for working people. These reforms were not achieved without a protracted and violent struggle, however. What is too often overlooked is the critical importance of labor legislation and unionism in bringing forth a macro-efficient division of income receipts – efficient in the sense of facilitating the return of income receipts to the expenditure stream.

Trade deficits occur when agents affiliated with surplus nations withhold liquid claims to goods earned through exports from the purchase of foreign-made goods and services. Surplus nations such as Japan and China purchase dollar-denominated financial assets, an activity often described in the financial press as 'financing the US trade deficit' (we shall subsequently explain why this idea harbors a fundamental misunderstanding of trade deficits). What is often missed is the fact that if surplus countries had exercised liquid claims to buy US-made goods, instead of dollar-denominated debt and equity, there would be no trade deficit to begin with. That is, the USA would not have experienced the kind of massive current account deficits seen in the new millennium if agents based in its principal trading partners had exhibited a greater preference for Chevrolets, Budweiser, Disney entertainment and Arkansas long-grain rice, and a lesser preference for Treasury bills, mortgage-backed securities or Wal-Mart shares. Viewed in the framework of utility theory, foreign-based agents with the wherewithal to purchase US-made goods and services evidently judge themselves better off by holding intangible, liquid assets instead. However, as Keynes was at pains to point out, a ravenous appetite for non-producible assets can exert a major drag on effective demand.

Blanchard (2007, p. 193) has noted that '[t]oday's current account deficits are . . . quite different from their predecessors. The countries in deficit are rich countries.' The annualized US current account deficit through the first three quarters of 2007 was $803 billion – a record high both in absolute terms and as a percentage of GDP. The data contained in Table 7.1 show that slightly less than 40 percent of the deficit in merchandise and services

Table 7.1   Contributions of trading partners to the US current account
              deficit, 2007[a]

Trading partner	Deficit (millions of current dollars)	Deficit as a percentage of total
Canada	49 392	8.20
China	187 597	31.15
European Union	77 237	12.83
Japan	61 119	10.15
Mexico	52 713	8.75
Others	174 177	28.92
Total	602 235	100.00

Note: [a] January to September.

Source: Bureau of the Census, International Trade Statistics, Exhibit 14
(www.census.gov/foreign-trade).

is accounted for by two less developed countries – China and Mexico. These
nations are similar in important respects. Both feature extreme economic
inequality, extensive poverty, vast reserve armies of cheap labor, and powerful, cohesive, authoritarian and fabulously wealthy elite political castes.
Moreover, both countries serve as low-cost manufacturing platforms for
transnational corporations that realize the bulk of their revenues from sales
in high-income (developed) countries.

It is not a simple matter to conceptualize the circumstances under which
the disposition of income receipts earned from export activity to purchase
financial assets, as opposed to foreign-made goods or services, is welfare
improving. This would seem to be particularly true in the case of impover-
ished nations where the use of hard currency to procure tangible things
(such as infrastructure or medicines) holds the potential to improve so
many lives. And this begs the question: why have trading partners such as
China accumulated vast stores of dollar-denominated financial assets?
There are at least four possible explanations: (1) to manage the lack of
perfect coordination between cash inflows and outflows arising from international transactions; (2) to protect the domestic currency against speculative attack; (3) a large share of national income has been allocated to a
political/economic elite characterized by a high propensity to save and a
strong preference for securities dominated in foreign currencies; and
(4) government policy which leverages reserve holdings to gain power and
influence, whether domestically or versus foreign governments.

With respect to point (1) above, Davidson has written:

> Once uncertainty and the impossibility of perfect coordination of cash inflows and outflows is recognized as inherent characteristics of all trading relations, it is obvious that an increase in international reserve holdings (liquidity) becomes a necessary condition for expanding trade. (Davidson 2002, p. 166)

China's current account transactions with the USA increased about threefold between 2000 and 2006 (from $118 to $344 billion), but its holding of US securities multiplied nearly ninefold ($92 to $809 billion) in the same period.[5] Dollar reserves controlled by the State Administration of Foreign Exchange (the Chinese central bank) amounted to $1455 billion in October 2007. There is simply no basis for believing that the need for reserves to manage trade-related cash flow problems should rise more than proportionately to the scale of trade. As such, the main factors underpinning the dollar reserve buildup must fall into one or more of the other categories delineated above.

The 'impossible trinity' pertains to the futility of attempts by nation-states to simultaneously maintain a fixed exchange rate, economic policy autonomy, and the free movement of foreign portfolio capital into and out of assets denominated in the home currency (capital mobility).[6] It is possible to pursue any combination of two out of three objectives, however. Intent on attracting foreign investment, and in some cases bowing to pressure brought by the international agencies such as the International Monetary Fund (whose policy advice/dictates to client states followed the 'Washington Consensus'), many nations of the developing world refrained from imposing effective controls on (financial) capital mobility.[7] This choice left some nations vulnerable to 'capital flight' or the risk of a sudden exit of the global portfolio management community from the local currency. The devastating effects of 'hot money' were felt in the case of the Mexican peso, which came under speculative attack in late 1994, and later during the Asian crisis of 1997–98, which saw a precipitous decline in the values of the Korean won, the Malaysian ringgit, the Thai baht and other currencies.[8]

The necessary conditions for capital flight are: (1) the absence of capital controls; and (2) extensive foreign ownership of domestic securities. If both conditions hold, it makes sense from a policy point of view to maintain large foreign currency reserves that can be deployed as needed to neutralize capital outflows. But neither conditions (1) or (2) is met in the case of China. In fact, China 'maintains extensive control over portfolio investment, including equities, bonds, bank loans, currencies, commodities, and derivative instruments' (Hu 2005, p. 359). Moreover, China is interested in controlling hot money mainly because it threatens to drive the value of the renminbi above its longstanding government peg against the dollar (¥8.276–8.28 to $1). Many have argued that the renminbi is artificially, and substantially, undervalued against the dollar, the pound and the euro. Nearly everyone agrees that a relaxation of capital controls would, in the short term at least, cause a major upward revaluation of the Chinese currency. In summary, the argument that China must maintain immense dollar reserves as a safeguard against currency speculation does not stand up to scrutiny.

China, with its explosive income growth and vast population, would seem a potential gold mine for suppliers of consumer goods and services. But the efforts of US-based companies to find markets in China have up to now yielded mostly disappointment. China joined the World Trade Organization (WTO) in December 2001, so exporters are no longer required to deal through designated national trading companies. Daunting bureaucratic and logistical obstacles remain. US trade officials bemoan difficulties encountered by US firms in obtaining distribution licenses from the Chinese government. There is also the well-publicized issue of intellectual property theft.[9]

Even if non-tariff barriers were diminished and intellectual property rights were enforced, are lucrative Chinese consumer markets there to be tapped? Western businessmen regularly complain about the meager spending power of the Chinese consumer. The Chinese consumer faces a 'hard' budget constraint due to the poor development of (formal) consumer lending institutions. The improvement in market robustness that might have been expected in light of sustained double-digit growth rates of real output has thus far not materialized. The lamentable fact about the Chinese economic boom is the limited extent to which the majority of its peoples have benefited from it. In terms of forging a truly broad-based consumerism, the Chinese economic miracle has been a failure. The big winners are coteries of political officials, their families, or entrepreneurs possessed of the good *guanxi* necessary to thrive in the Chinese system. The income streams generated by China's awesome manufacturing platform accrue in large share to a comparatively tiny, spectacularly rich and parsimonious slice of society – a factor that goes some distance in explaining the inchoate status of its consumer markets.

Chinese officials must believe there are advantages in accumulating foreign credit balances; otherwise a larger share of these balances (accumulated through trade surpluses) would be spent for imports or foreign direct investment. Ironically, the Communist Party has metamorphosed into a twenty-first-century *rentier*. The Chinese central bank is one of the largest single holders of US Treasury securities ($396 billion in September 2007). The Party has lately sought to diversify its asset holdings away from

Treasuries by constituting a sovereign wealth fund (an entity that aims to improve returns on foreign currency reserve holdings through the purchase of a range of assets including equities).[10]

The Chinese regime has profited greatly by its open access to the great engine of effective demand that is the US household sector. At the same time, China, by seeking a 'resting place for savings other than reproducible assets' (Hahn 1977, p. 31), contributes to US unemployment. The US body politic should not allow this situation to continue indefinitely. A new set of trading rules should be evolved that make surplus countries responsible for correcting trade imbalances. Mechanisms should be developed that create incentives for creditor nations to disgorge excessive foreign reserve balances.[11] Some will object that any action to force China to reduce its international reserves will have deleterious effects on US securities prices and perhaps jeopardize the status of the dollar as international reserve currency. Given the immense size of Chinese dollar holdings, these fears are well founded. To avoid this possibility, no sanctions should be imposed on reserve balances accumulated before the date when the new rules become effective. It is difficult to envision how the majority of Chinese people are not made better off by a policy that puts constraints on the ability of its leaders to withhold the spending power that its people have earned.

Consumerism, for all its distastefulness, its harmful psychological, social and environmental effects, does keep the factories humming and the malls flourishing. The view that US trade deficits result from 'overconsumption' fails to acknowledge that, if not for the overspent American, the gap between the world's production possibilities and its actual production would be greater than it already is.[12] That is, the US consumer is doing the job that surplus countries are failing to do. At the same time, some of the institutions that make a vibrant consumerism sustainable have been severely eroded in the past three decades and stand in need of major repair.

7.2 OFFSHORING AND DOMESTIC INCOME INEQUALITY

The increased openness of the US economy (as measured by the increase in the sum of imports and exports relative to GDP) is a major factor in explaining structural changes of employment within the country – most importantly the loss (both in absolute terms and relative to total employment) of manufacturing jobs. Even the most ardent defenders of free trade do not dispute the fact that the flood of imported autos and parts, consumer electronics, machine tools, cameras, heating and cooling equipment, computers, apparel and shoes, toys and other goods is implicated in the elimination of hundreds of thousands of well-paying domestic manufacturing jobs. And, as Blanchard (2007, p.. 37) has noted: 'Traditional concerns about the impact of trade on blue collar manufacturing industries have evolved to new concerns about the impact of offshoring on high-tech services that have previously been considered less susceptible.' United Airlines planes now receive routine maintenance in China. Indian software engineers do extensive work for Microsoft at wages far below those received by their counterparts in Redmond, WA. Tax preparers now face cut-throat competition from tax preparation outsourcing centers located in India.[13]

On the other side of the equation, growth of employment in export-related industries in the USA has grown substantially. Moreover, the record on total job creation in the USA is very good (especially when compared with European countries) – trade deficits notwithstanding. Enough jobs have been created to more than replace those lost due to trade. The question remains: how does the average quality of new jobs compare with those lost due to globalization/offshoring? The evidence supports the view that, although globalization has created remunerative opportunities for many entrepreneurs and those owning a range of specialized skills, the overall effect of global economic integration on the quality of US jobs has been negative. In fact, the evidence is consistent with the view that global economic integration has contributed mightily to the 'hollowing out' or loss of density of the US distribution function.[14]

The mushrooming US trade deficit is partly the efflux of a transformation in the vertical structure of US-based firms. The factors underpinning this transformation include: (1) a decrease in international shipping costs, largely due to the innovation of containerization;[15] (2) higher-quality, cheaper telecommunications; (3) trade agreements that permit US companies to export equipment and materials to offshore locations for manufacturing or assembly and then re-export products (typically back to the originating country) that are subject to tariffs only on the value-added component; (4) systems that tie the compensation of top corporate officials to share prices ('value-based' compensation) and thereby establish powerful incentives to reduce costs/improve margins through the relocation of production offshore; and (5) pressures on vendors reliant on dominant distribution channels such as Wal-Mart to conform to the 'China price'.[16]

The global dis-integration of production by US corporations is evidenced by the shifting composition of traded goods – specifically, the increased share of total trade flows accounted for by intermediate goods as well as the increase in imports of manufactured goods from developing countries. The growth of the US trade deficit is in good measure the manifestation of a broad-based drive by corporations to take cost out of supply chains by the relocation of production abroad – either through direct foreign investment or through partnerships with foreign-based manufacturers.[17] Offshoring (the practice of shifting of manufacturing and service activities to foreign-based affiliates or unaffiliated firms) is economically efficient because the resulting cost saving (from lower wages, profit taxes or reduced regulatory compliance costs) more than offsets tariffs or transportation costs.

The relocation of production by US firms to Mexican *maquilidoras*, Saipan or China's Guandong Province has reshaped the personal distribution of domestic income by way of effects both direct and indirect. The permanent loss of good-paying jobs has shoved a significant fraction of the labor force away from the center of what was once a more densely compacted income distribution function (the statistical representation of the middle class). Job losers have frequently seen their economic status decline – even when they have found new employment. One study reported that, during the 1980s and 1990s, 65 percent of manufacturing workings displaced by trade were employed two years later. However, most took a pay cut. A quarter of these workers suffered pay losses of 30 percent or more.[18] Concurrently, executive pay soared.[19]

The validity of the NAIRU (non-accelerating inflation rate of unemployment) hypothesis became increasingly tenuous through the 1990s as the unemployment rate fell well below levels that many of its advocates felt certain would trigger a price spiral, but no such development occurred.[20] In fact, unit labor cost remained remarkably stable (1.4 percent average annual growth) as the unemployment rate fell from a peak of 7.8 percent in 1992 to 4.2 percent in 1999.[21] One factor explaining this 'nonconformity' is obviously strong productivity growth (private sector labor productivity grew at an impressive 2.31 percent annual rate between 1995 and 1999).[22] However, a significant factor restraining wage growth was a loss of job security experienced by workers in occupations vulnerable to cross-border relocation. In case after case, employees (both blue- and white-collar) have seen their bargaining power denuded – even when they have been able to retain their jobs. One report told of the experience of workers at Ford Motor's Focus assembly plant in Wayne, Michigan. Ford built a sister plant (a virtual duplicate of its Wayne facility) to assemble its Focus model in Hermosilla, Mexico (a *maquiladora*). With negotiations under way between Ford and the United Auto Workers, employees came to work one day to discover equipment taken from the plant shrink-wrapped, stamped 'Mexico' in large letters, and loaded on to rail road cars. This type of scenario has played out countless times.

Collective bargaining can produce good results, at least in terms of employee wages and benefits, when the employer is a dominant firm that

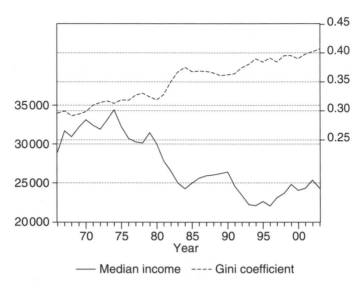

Source: Author's calculations from public use micro data.

Figure 7.3   Median income, Gini coefficient for males, aged 22–34 (income in 2000 dollars)

enjoys considerable pricing power. A diminution of market power, suffered as a consequence of competition from cheap imports, narrows the discretion of management in the collective bargaining process. Marina Whitman (1999) has written persuasively on the importance of globalism in making the paternalistic corporation extinct.

The deleterious income distribution effects of trade are most evident in the case of young men. With the negative growth of manufacturing jobs, and remaining high-wage manufacturing jobs unavailable due to union seniority rules, a great many young men (especially those without post-secondary education or training) have been forced to settle for low-paying service sector jobs. Figure 7.3 illustrates a 'double movement' – a decline in median real incomes coupled with a surge in within-group inequality (as measured by the Gini ratio) for males aged 22–34 years.[23] Real median income for this group fell by about 13 percent between 1990 and 1997. A broad consensus formed among labor economists during the 1990s that rising wage inequality resulted from the effects of globalization on the 'skill premium' – that is, the differential compensation received by those with more skill (usually measured by education).[24] The second wave of dislocations, usually attributed to improvements in worldwide telecommunications, has placed many highly trained workers at risk of job loss – not just telephone solicitors.

Viewed through the Schumpeterian lens, the relocation of production activity to LDCs by transnational corporations is simply part of the process of creative destruction – a process that, if left unfettered, can bring forth amazing improvements in the quality of life for all people. The problem with this view is that it overlooks the vital importance of effective demand. Production relocation is not a strategy to increase profits through product innovation or by increased sales of existing products. Rather, it is an attempt by firms to raise profit margins by squeezing out labor costs. The fallout of such cost-cutting measures by a single firm – even a very large firm – for the economy-wide distribution of income is, of course, negligible. However, given the scale of production relocation or offshoring by the US business community at large, the cumulative effects are quite extensive.

We have argued throughout this volume that the negative macroeconomic consequences (including negative effects on profits) of sharply rising income inequality have thus far been largely avoided because income inequality has not been accompanied by an equivalent surge in consumption inequality. The reason for this is that households have borrowed more heavily than ever before to finance their consumption expenditures. The new, ruthless brand of shareholder capitalism has seriously undermined the viability of institutions that both protect against extreme economic inequality and limit the reliance on credit expansion for consumption growth. One (indirect) repercussion of the aggrandized power of employers is an unsustainable buildup of debt on household balance sheets.

7.3 FOREIGN SAVING AND DOMESTIC BORROWING

A main purpose of Appendix 1A was to explain why the capacity of the banking system to provide finance (by expanding its liabilities) has nothing to do with the proportion of income saved (not spent) or the saving rate. We also attempted to explain that the production of non-consumables such as factories, durable equipment, bridges or aircraft carriers must necessarily result in the distribution of a residual income stream that is (at the aggregate level) just sufficient to provide long-term funding for non-consumables, a principle condensed in the statement 'investment creates the saving to fund itself'.

Some have argued that massive US current account deficits are necessary, and even welcome, given the insufficiency of domestic saving in relation to the financing or funding needs of domestic households, firms and government units. Had US investment been constrained by the domestic supply of saving since the great saving shortfall that began around 1993, so the argument goes, the pace of capital accumulation actually achieved during the period would have been impossible. A trade deficit gives foreigners the wherewithal to purchase dollar-denominated financial assets – a fact that is reflected in the capital account surplus. Paul Krugman recently commented:

> I think we would have more protectionism if it wasn't for the fact that at least the financial community is acutely aware on how much we depend on those treasury purchases by the [Chinese] central bank. We hate the Chinese trade deficit but we love the capital account deficit. (Quoted in Eliot 2005, p. 125)

Krugman's reasoning is built on an (implicit) assumption that merits close scrutiny. Specifically, Krugman's comments suggest that, if not for the trade deficit, the total stock of liquid assets available to purchase treasuries (or other dollar-denominated IOUs) would decrease. That is, trade deficits do not merely alter the cross-national distribution of saving but contribute positively to its flow per unit of time. This idea is firmly rooted in the classical view that aggregate saving is ultimately regulated by volitional abstinence of income recipients. Looked at in this light, trade imbalances act to redistribute income from low-saving nations to high-saving nations and thus facilitate a higher rate of new investment (or household or public sector borrowing) than could otherwise be achieved.

The standard view may be articulated by use of national income identities. Consider the following national income identity (truism):

$$S + T + M \equiv I + G + X \qquad (7.1)$$

Equation (7.1) simply states that the sum of the 'leakages' (income receipts not spent for final goods in the domestic product market – comprising saving (S), net taxes (T) and imports (M)) into the circular flow of national income and product are necessarily equal to the sum of 'injections' (expenditures for final goods in domestic product markets other than consumption – including investment (I), government expenditure minus transfers (G) and exports (X)) to the circular flow. The two sides of equation (7.1) must be equal because of the way in which the various artificial components of the equation are (heuristically) defined.[25] Given (7.1), the following must also be true by definition:

$$S + (M - X) + (T - G) \equiv I \qquad (7.2)$$

Understood in the loanable funds context, there are three sources or pools of saving available to fund investment: private domestic saving (S), public saving $(T - G)$ and foreign saving $(X - M)$.[26] If the public sector is in deficit, it is best to rewrite (7.2) as follows:

$$S + (M - X) \equiv I + (G - T) \tag{7.3}$$

If saving is assumed to be determined independently of investment (including public investment), then, by equation (7.3), an increase in the public sector deficit must result in an equivalent decrease in private investment – that is, unless foreign saving comes to the rescue. The deductive basis of Krugman's statement should now be transparent. Given low domestic saving and surging public borrowing, a mushrooming trade deficit is required to generate a net increase in the stock of unexercised liquid claims to goods (measured by the left-hand side of equation (7.3)) sufficient to absorb the greater flow of public sector IOUs without upsetting the complex of yields – otherwise, investment will be crowded out (and debt servicing costs will soar).

Having explicated the standard view of trade deficits, we must now explain why it is terribly misguided. We explained in Appendix 1A that aggregate saving is a residual – that is, its value is largely, though not completely, determined by the scale of factor payments distributed for the production of non-consumables.[27] Saving in excess of the value of goods produced in the current period but not available for consumption (non-consumables) can be properly called volitional or 'discretionary'. Discretionary saving must be matched by (positive) unplanned inventory investment on the right-hand side of equation (7.3).[28] Discretionary saving is equal to zero in macroeconomic (but not necessarily full-employment) equilibrium – and so is unplanned inventory investment. The important point is that, so long as producers of investment goods are successful in obtaining finance, and if they are able to gain disposal over real resources, we can be confident that sufficient saving will materialize to provide long-term funding. We explained, moreover, that the capacity of the banking system to accommodate the financing needs of capital goods producers does not depend on the fraction of income saved – because saving, while it alters the distribution of bank deposits across balance sheets, does not change their total quantity – at least not immediately.

From the principles explicated above we may deduce the following: trade deficits have no direct effect on total saving per unit of time but do impinge on the distribution of new (net) liquid claims between domestic and foreign balance sheets. Krugman's position should be modified as follows: the US capital account surplus is not a good thing; but at least those countries with negative capital account balances *vis-à-vis* the USA have exhibited a high preference for dollar-denominated portfolio assets (such as Treasuries).

China is, for obvious reasons, a valued client of Wall Street. It therefore should come as no surprise that one of society's major power centers has deployed all of its political and opinion-shaping might to deflect criticism about the current state of USA–China economic relations. The idea that trade deficits supply a remedy for a (phantom) domestic saving shortage persists because its serves a powerful vested (and narrow) interest – not because the idea rests on a sound intellectual footing.

7.4   FALLOUT OF A FLIGHT FROM THE DOLLAR

One concern about the trade-induced build-up of external debt (or foreign ownership of dollar-denominated equity) is the possibility of a run on the dollar provoked by the exit of the international community of portfolio controllers from dollar-denominated securities. Discussion on this issue is apparently based on the view that, in terms of the comparative propensity to seek a fast exit from the dollar, a real difference exists between domestic and foreign-based portfolio controllers. The validity of this view is not questioned here. However, it should be pointed out that extensive foreign ownership of debt and equity issued in the home currency is not a necessary condition for capital flight. If capital controls are minimal, and if liquid securities markets exist, a quick exit from the domestic currency can develop even if foreign ownership is trivial. The main thing is that there exists a real possibility that portfolio controllers, whether foreign or domestic, will coalesce around the view that US current account deficits are not sustainable and, as such, a major devaluation of the dollar against other major currencies (such as the renminbi, the euro or the yen) is inevitable.

The worst-case scenario would be the loss of the dollar's post-1914 hegemonic status. Already the euro's share of known official foreign reserves had risen to 26.4 percent in the third quarter of 2006. The dollar's share of known official reserves fell to 63.8 percent from 66.5 percent in the same three months of 2006,[29] prompting the *Financial Times* to opine that

> the primacy of the dollar is no longer to be taken for granted. Should wealth-holders (both foreign and domestic) come to doubt the determination of the Federal Reserve to preserve the dollar's domestic purchasing power, they might dump it, with devastating effects on its external value, long-term US interest rates and the US economy. (*Financial Times*, 27 December 2007, p. 10)

The dollar's vulnerability was revealed on 7 November 2007, when its value spiked downward in reaction to public comments made by a pair by mid-level Chinese officials about the need to diversify China's $1.4 trillion reserve portfolio away from dollars.[30]

Taking into account the structure of the modern consumer credit industry, and in particular the dependence of consumer credit expansion on the capacity of underwriters to find a market for synthetic securities collateralized by household IOUs of all types, the fallout of a flight from the dollar could prove calamitous. We explained in Chapter 5 (section 5.5) that secondary markets for securities backed by consumer, student and home equity loans are very thin, and it takes little selling pressure for one-way markets to develop. The illiquidity of these instruments thus acts as a *de facto* capital control. The problem arises when underwriters attempt to place new issues in an environment in which the prices of old issues have reached rock-bottom levels.

The subprime crisis furnishes a preview of what can be expected in the event of a full-fledged retreat from the dollar. The write-downs recently taken by Merrill Lynch, USB, Bear Stearns, Goldman Sachs, Barclay's Capital, Citigroup and other underwriters happened because these firms were carrying large inventories of (subprime) collateralized mortgage obligations when the appetite for new issues abated. The result was the virtual disappearance of subprime lending. Underwriting of subprime mortgages simply stopped altogether. As of January 2008, the effects were being felt in the residential construction industry.

It stands to reason that a quasi-permanent change in the average preference for dollar-denominated securities has the potential to substantially alter the terms on which new, greenback-denominated asset-backed securities (ABSs) can be placed. The result is likely to be a US consumer credit crunch of some magnitude. Consumer credit is not so fungible as to be unaffected by the disappearance, in part or in whole, of the primary issue market for ABSs. If the pattern of previous consumer credit crunches (most conspicuously in spring and summer of 1980) is repeated, we can expect the captive finance affiliates such as Ford Motor Credit or Sears Holdings to move aggressively to stabilize the market. The capacity of these units to perform the lender of last resort function on behalf of their parent corporations will depend largely on the market for their own IOUs – including commercial paper backed by consumer receivables. However, the effects of dollar flight are likely to be diffused across asset classes – even gilt-edged issues. The placement of new issues collateralized by household debt on reasonable terms – that is, on terms that would provide a decent profit margin for originators and underwriters – may entail an increased emphasis on credit quality. Thus it is likely to be the case that individuals with credit scores in the middle and lower ranges will find consumer credit much harder to get, and more expensive, as compared with the halcyon era of 1993–2006.

NOTES

1. See, for example, Hubbard (2006), Roubini (2006), Mann (2002), Feenstra (2001), Cooper (2001), and Hervey and Merkel (2000).
2. It is noteworthy that Blanchard failed to mention 'currency misalignment'. We can take it as a tacit acknowledgment by a responsible economist that a revaluation of the dollar is not likely to help the US situation very much – even if trade theory textbooks tell us it should. After all, Treasury Secretary James Baker's 'talk down the dollar' campaign of 1986–87, informed as it was by the view that currency realignment is the corrective for trade imbalances, proved wholly ineffective. The persistence of trade imbalances in the post-Bretton Woods era of flexible, market-determined exchange rates has driven home the reality that the Marshall–Lerner conditions (upon which the classical adjustment process rests) are rarely met in practice. The Marshall–Lerner principle states that for a change in the exchange rate to improve a country's balance of trade, the sum of the price elasticities of demand for exports and imports must exceed unity. If this condition is not met, then a devaluation of the domestic currency can actually cause an increase in the trade deficit. See Appleyard and Field (1986) for further explanation.
3. See Peach (1994) and Brown (2005). The critiques of Pierra Sraffa (1960) and Joan Robinson (1953–54) will be known to some readers. They showed that it was not possible to find an index number measuring capital independent of (or without prior knowledge of) the distribution of income between wages and profits. G.C. Harcourt noted that

   > such independence is necessary if we are to construct an iso-product curve showing the different quantities of labor and capital which produce a given level of national output . . . The slope of this curve plays a key part in the determination of relative prices of capital and labor and therefore of factor rewards. However, the curve cannot be constructed and the slope measured unless the prices it is intended to determine are known beforehand. (Harcourt 1969, p. 371)

4. That is not to say that 'market forces' are unimportant in establishing compensation levels for fast-food cooks, nurses, machinists, football coaches, website designers, cotton farmers or business executives. Markets are socially approved, mutually understood practices or working rules that regulate exchange. Yvnge Ramstad explained that 'the "price mechanism" is mentally inseparable from the *instituted* working rules of which it is but an active description. Indeed, without an understanding of the specific rules themselves, one cannot understand how the "mechanism" functions' (Ramstad 2001, pp. 258–9). Working rules 'operate by placing certain limits or by opening up certain enlargements for the choices and powers of the individuals, who are parties to the transactions' (Commons 1924, p. 68).
5. The trade data are taken from the US International Trade Commission. Data on Chinese dollar holdings are taken from the US Treasury, Foreign Holdings of US Long-Term Securities, 31 March 2000 and 30 June 2006.
6. Ostfeld and Taylor (1998) alternatively refer to it as the 'open economy trilemma'. See Rodrik (2000) for a good explanation.
7. For a critique of the Washington Consensus, see Stiglitz (2002).
8. Mexican President Zedillo's decision to devalue the peso in October 1994 apparently provoked a run on peso-denominated assets. The peso lost 40 percent of its value against the dollar in the first three months of 1995. The ringgit price of the US dollar rose from 2.5 to 4.4 ringgits between July 1997 and February 1998. The won and baht suffered similar declines.
9. Dollar estimates of the loss of revenue by US companies due to pirating vary. US Trade Representative Robert Portman estimated that US losses from piracy of copyrighted materials ranged between $2.5 billion and $3.8 billion annually. In addition, US Customs and Border Protection seized $134 million of Chinese knockoffs of trademarked goods, such as brand-name batteries, pharmaceuticals and auto parts of such Chinese products

at US ports in 2004 (reported in Spearshott 2005, p. 1). The Motion Picture Association claims that movie pirating in China costs the big studios almost $300 million a year (reported in Hernandez 2005, p. 1).
10. See Sasso (2007).
11. This recommendation borrows from the 'trigger mechanism' proposal of Paul Davidson. Under his proposal, trading nations are organized into 'clearing unions'. Surplus countries can spend excessive credits (i.e., foreign reserves deemed excessive by clearing union members) in three ways (imports, foreign direct investment or unilateral transfers) or else face a 100 percent tax on excessive reserve holdings, the proceeds of which would be used to adjust current account balances via a unilateral transfer to deficit countries. 'The important thing is to make sure that continual oversaving by surplus nations in the form of international liquid reserves is not permitted to unleash depressionary forces and/or a building up of international debts so encumbering as to impoverish the global economy of the twenty-first century' (Davidson 2002, p. 234).
12. An *Economist* editorial recently blamed the US trade deficit on 'American profligacy' (*Economist*, 19 May 2007, p. 9).
13. Other examples can be found in Thomas Friedman (2005).
14. A 1996 report of the Council of Economic Advisors conceded that 'trade may have some adverse impact on wage inequality' (Council of Economic Advisors 1996, p. 232). A widely cited empirical paper by Ravegna reported 'significant effects of import penetration on both employment and wages in manufacturing' (Ravegna 1992, p. 256). Bivens (2007) estimates that 'In 2006, the impact of trade flows increased the inequality of earnings by roughly 7%, with the resulting loss to a representative household (two earners making the median wage and working the average amount of (household) hours each year) reaching more than $2,000.' See also Freeman (1995), Richardson (1995) and Wood (1998).
15. Containerization is a system of intermodal cargo transport using isocontainers that can be loaded intact into container ships, railroad cars, planes and trucks. Herod (1998, p. 181) writes that 'loading 11,000 tons of cargo might take a total of 10,585 [work] hours. Containerization allows for the same tonnage to be loaded with 546 work hours.'
16. Robert Scott (2007) writes that

Wal-Mart accounted for approximately 9.3% of total U.S. imports from China between 2001 and 2006. This estimate is based on widely reported statistics, including Wal-Mart's own estimates of its imports from China. U.S. imports from China increased $185 billion between 2001 and 2006 . . . Wal-Mart's imports increased from $9.5 billion in 2001 to $26.7 billion in 2006, an increase of $17.2 billion (181%). As they are a retailer and not a manufacturer, Wal-Mart exports only a negligible amount to China, accounting for at most 0.2% of total U.S. exports to China.

17. A distinction is to be made between 'market-seeking' production relocation which 'involves a replication of production capacity in the foreign location, presumably for sales there' and 'efficiency-seeking' offshoring, which means the shifting of activity offshore 'with the aim of lowering costs' (Milberg 2004, p. 45).
18. See the *Economist*, 20–26 January 2007, p. 33.
19. The *Economist* observed in a 20 January 2007 editorial that '[i]f you look back 20 years, the total pay of the typical top American manager has increased from roughly 40 times the average – the level for four decades – to 110 times the average now'.
20. According to the NAIRU hypothesis, the inflation rate will tend to accelerate when unemployment falls below a threshold, full-employment level – typically estimated in the range from 5.5 to 6.5 percent.
21. These figures are taken from the *Economic Report of the President*, 2007, Tables B-50 and B-42.
22. This is according to the *Economic Report of the President*, 2001, Table 1-2.
23. For a more detailed look at wage inequality in the USA, see Gottschalk and Danziger (2005).

24. Freeman's views are representative: 'Since the U.S. imports that make heavy use of low-skilled labor, and exports goods that make heavy use of high-skilled labor, trade with developing countries reduces the relative demand for less-skilled labor in the U.S.' (Freeman 1995, p. 23). In contrast, Autor et al. (1998) argued that computerization shifted the relative demand for college graduates and thus contributed strongly to the widening educational pay differentials.
25. Davidson (2002, p. 137) reminds us that '[f]or the most part, aggregate income measures can have no meaning other than that assigned to them by aggregate accounting theory. The aggregate (social) accounts do measure conventionally existing items. Rather, they are a way of accounting for particular abstract theoretical concepts.'
26. As was explained earlier, the loanable funds (time preference) theory of interest makes no distinction between funding and finance.
27. There is a qualification to this argument in the case of unplanned inventory investment. Production of many capital goods (e.g. aircraft, electrical generating equipment) is done on a 'for contract' basis so that the manufacturer is assured of a sale at the point in time when production begins. Production of consumer items, on the other hand, is mainly 'for market' so that firms may, when demand forecasts are inaccurate, accumulate unwanted inventories. Total saving may therefore exceed the amount just sufficient to fund all new capital goods produced during the period – a disequilibrium situation that will bring about a change in the scale of output.
28. Note that discretionary saving can also be negative, in which case there is a corresponding amount of unplanned inventory depletion.
29. This is according to the International Monetary Fund.
30. The *Economist* (8 November, 2007) recently reported that

> The dollar fell sharply on November 7th [2007] after mid-ranking Chinese officials, not actually responsible for foreign-exchange policy, made remarks that were seized upon by already jittery markets. A Chinese parliamentarian called for his country to diversify its reserves out of 'weak' currencies like the dollar and another official suggested that the dollar's status as a reserve currency was 'shaky'.

REFERENCES

Anonymous (2007), 'Ready for a rout? The dollar', *Economist*, 8 November, **385** (8554), 116.
Appleyard, D. and A. Field, Jr (1986), 'A note on teaching the Marshall–Lerner condition', *Journal of Economic Education*, **17** (1), 52–6.
Autor, D., L. Katz and A. Krueger (1998), 'Have computers changed the labor market?', *Quarterly Journal of Economics*, **113** (4), 1169–213.
Bivens, L.J. (2007), 'Globalization, American wages, and inequality', Economic Policy Institute Working Paper 279, Washington, DC (http://www.epi.org/content/cfm/wp 279, accessed 23 November 2007).
Blanchard, O. (2007), 'Current account deficits in rich countries', *IMF Staff Papers*, **54** (2), 191–220.
Brown, C. (2005), 'Is there an institutional theory of distribution?', *Journal of Economic Issues*, **39** (4), 915–31.
Commons, John (1924), *Legal Foundations of Capitalism*, Clifton, NJ: Augustus Kelley.
Cooper, R. (2001), 'Is the U.S. current account deficit sustainable? Will it be sustained?', *Brookings Papers on Economic Activity*, **1**, 217–26.

Council of Economic Advisors (1996), *Annual Report*, Washington, DC: US Government Printing Office (www.gpoaccess.gov/usbudget/fy97/pdf/erp.pdf, accessed 24 October 2007).

Davidson, Paul (2002), *Financial Markets, Money, and the Real World*, Northampton, MA: Edward Elgar Publishing.

Eliot, L. (2005), 'In conversation with Professor Paul Krugman', *Public Policy Research*, **12** (2), 123–30.

Feenstra, R. (2001), 'Is the U.S. trade deficit sustainable?', *Journal of Economic Literature*, **39** (2), 584–6.

Freeman, R. (1995), 'Are your wages being set in Beijing?', *Journal of Economic Perspectives*, **9** (3), 15–32.

Friedman, Thomas (2005), *The World is Flat*, New York: Farrar, Straus & Giroux.

Galbraith, John K. (1958), *The Affluent Society*, Boston, MA: Houghton Mifflin.

Gottschalk, P. and S. Danziger (2005), 'Inequality of wage rates, earnings and family income in the United States, 1975–2002', *Review of Income and Wealth*, **51** (2), 231–56.

Hahn, F.H. (1977), 'Keynesian economics and general equilibrium theory', in G.C. Harcourt (ed.), *The Microfoundations of Macroeconomics*, London: Macmillan, pp. 77–108.

Harcourt, G.C. (1969), 'Some Cambridge controversies in the theory of capital', *Journal of Economic Literature*, **7** (2), 369–405.

Hernandez, G. (2005), 'CD, DVD piracy makes billions in China', *Knight Ridder Business News*, 22 November, 1.

Herod, A. (1998), 'Discourse on the docks: containerization and inter-union disputes in U.S. ports', *Transactions of the Institute of British Geographers*, **23** (2), 177–91.

Hervey, J. and L. Merkel (2000), 'A record current account deficit: causes and implications', *Economic Perspectives*, **24** (4), 2–13.

Hu, F. (2005), 'Capital flows, overheating, and the nominal exchange rate regime in China', *Cato Journal*, **25** (2), 357–66.

Hubbard, G. (2006), 'The U.S. current account deficit and public policy', *Journal of Policy Modeling*, **28** (6), 665–82.

Mann, C. (2002), 'Perspectives on the U.S. current account deficit and sustainability', *Journal of Economic Perspectives*, **16** (3), 131–52.

Milberg, W. (2004), 'The changing structure of trade linked to global production systems: what are the policy implications?', *International Labour Review*, **143** (1/2), 45–91.

Ostfeld, Maurice and Alan Taylor (1998), 'The Great Depression as a watershed: international capital mobility over the long run', in Michael D. Bordo, Claudia D. Goldin and Eugene N. White (eds), *The Defining Moment: The Great Depression and the American Economy in the Twentieth Century*, Chicago, IL: University of Chicago Press, pp. 353–402.

Peach, James (1994), 'Distribution theory', in G. Hodgson, W. Samuels and M. Tool (eds), *The Elgar Companion to Institutional and Evolutionary Economics*, vol. 2, Brookfield, VT: Edward Elgar Publishing, pp. 166–71.

Ramstad, Y. (2001), 'John R. Commons' reasonable value and the concept of just price', *Journal of Economic Issues*, **35** (2), 253–78.

Ravegna, A. (1992), 'Exporting jobs: the impact of import competition on employment and wages in U.S. manufacturing', *Quarterly Journal of Economics*, **107** (1), 255–84.

Richardson, J. (1995), 'Income inequality and trade: how to think, what to conclude', *Journal of Economic Perspectives*, **9** (3), 33–55.

Robinson, J. (1953–54), 'The production function and the theory of capital', *Review of Economics and Statistics*, **21** (2), 81–106.

Rodrik, D. (2000), 'How far will international economic integration go?', *Journal of Economic Perspectives*, **14** (1), 177–86.

Roubini, N. (2006), 'The unsustainability of the U.S. twin deficits', *Cato Journal*, **26** (2), 343–57.

Sasso, L. (2007), 'New trends in China's foreign investment strategy', *International Spectator*, **42** (3), 399–407.

Scott, R. (2007), 'The Wal-Mart effect: its Chinese imports have displaced nearly 200,000 jobs', Issue Brief No. 235, Washington DC: Economic Policy Institute (www.epi.net, accessed 8 January 2007).

Sparshott, J. (2005), 'Trade nominee would take harder line on China', *Knight Ridder Tribune Business News*, 22 April, 1.

Sraffa, Pierra (1960), *Production of Commodities by Means of Commodities*, Cambridge: Cambridge University Press.

Sraffa, Pierra (ed.) (1951), *The Works and Correspondence of David Ricardo*, vol. I, Cambridge: University Press for the Royal Economic Society.

Stiglitz, Joseph (2002), *Globalism and Its Discontents*, New York: W.W. Norton & Company.

Whitman, Marina M. (1999), *New World, New Rules: The Changing Role of the American Corporation*, Cambridge, MA: Harvard Business School Press.

Wood, A. (1998), 'Globalization and the rise in labour market inequalities', *Economic Journal*, **108** (450), 1463–821.

8.   Final remarks

The near-equivalence of the ancestral desire for social status with the need for commodities is a distinctive characteristic of modern Western life. The dominant mindset, which is to appraise the efficacy of economic institutions mainly by their service to the consumer, is comprehensible in light of the cultural orientation of what Keynes termed 'needs of the second order' to ritualized consumption. The iron rule of consumerist values is partly to blame for the failure to evolve socially protective responses to the contemporary brand of shareholder-driven, socially disembedded corporatism. A necessary condition for a transition to a more humanized species of economic organization – one in which consumer satisfaction and shareholder rights stand on roughly equal footing with values such as job satisfaction or self-actualization, income security, fairness, leisure and family time, natural resource conservation or environmental cleanliness – is the casting off of a significant component of the social habit structure peculiar to late twentieth- and early twenty-first-century capitalism.

Stanfield and Stanfield (1980, p. 442, italics added) have written that 'although needs for social esteem and even invidious distinction *may* be insatiable, it is not inevitable that they be expressed in an endless spiral of consumption'. Scitovksy has argued that the insatiability of the social instinct is not intrinsic, but is rendered such by the behavioral expression that it most often takes in contemporary life:

> [W]hen people seek status not in other people's recognition of their specific accomplishments, but in a general token, like income, which is supposed to express the value society places on their services, then status becomes a matter of ranking on a one-dimensional scale, and the seeking of status becomes a zero-sum game. (Scitovsky 1992, p. 119)

The 'paradox of affluence' is rooted in the futility of efforts to satisfy status needs through meritorious consumption.[1] A theme developed in this volume has been that, while the institutional selection of consumerist habit structures has proved advantageous in terms of the maintenance of effective demand, the economic, social and psychological costs of consumerism are staggeringly high.

The corporate system has its virtues. By replacing markets with internal hierarchies, corporations limit the scope of opportunism in vertically articulated production systems and, in this way, give impetus to the diffusion of technology.[2] The function of organizational culture as meme – that is, storage unit of knowledge and replicator of complex business routines – is also deserving of great respect.[3] Moreover, that consumer preference has a plasticity that permits its reshaping from above does not remove the fact that modern business organizations are responsible for some real improvements in the average quality of life. The question remains: is a viable corporatism possible without a high-powered, credit-suffused consumerism?

For Keynes, the only permanent solution to the problem of effective demand is a 'somewhat comprehensive socialization of investment' (Keynes 1936, p. 378). Liberating individuals from the tyrannical hold of materialism will require the public sector to assume a larger role in the economy – that is, if capitalism is to survive. The post-World War II record on this front is regrettably tilted to 'military Keynesianism'.

Another argument pursued here is that economic inequality renders the economy more dependent on consumer credit expansion for growth. It stands to reason that a more egalitarian distribution of rewards is capable of diminishing the pace of household debt creation required to achieve every level of consumption expenditure. The argument can be made that inherited distributive mechanisms are obsolescent to the present situation in which the problem of scarcity has been largely solved. Tampering with income distribution is a serious matter because the main body of society's delicate and complex incentive structure resides within the matrix of monetary transactions by which people receive their incomes. Nevertheless, it is possible to design a tax and transfer policy that corrects for extreme or unwarranted income disparities, provides all families with a decent income, and yet preserves the incentives required to facilitate the 'extended order of human cooperation' (Hayek 1988, p. 119).

NOTES

1. The paradox of affluence is 'the deterioration in the quality of life despite or because of sustained growth of consumption' (Stanfield and Stanfield 1980, p. 437).
2. The cardinal virtue of the corporation is that it removes 'the pecuniary element from the interstices of the system as far as may be. The interstitial adjustments of the industrial system at large are in this way withdrawn from the discretion of rival business men' (Veblen 1904, pp. 48–9). Knoedler (1995, p. 387) explains that 'for Veblen, the interstices were pecuniarily important junctures in the orderly flow of the technological aspects of production. Goods and services traveled through these junctures, or interstices, by means of interstitial adjustments, and interstitial adjustments were accomplished by means of transactions – transactions that could also be used to interrupt this orderly flow'.

3. The term meme is defined as a 'unit of cultural transmission, or a unit of imitation' (Dawkins 1976, p. 177). See also Hodgson and Knudsen (2004).

REFERENCES

Dawkins, Richard (1976), *The Selfish Gene*, Oxford: Oxford University Press.

Hayek, Friedrich A. (1988), *The Fatal Conceit*, Chicago, IL: University of Chicago Press.

Hodgson, J. and T. Knudsen (2004), 'The firm as interactor: firms as vehicles for habits and routines', *Journal of Evolutionary Economics*, **14** (3), 281–307.

Keynes, John M. (1936), *The General Theory of Employment, Interest, and Money*, New York: Harcourt Brace Jovanovich.

Knoedler, J. (2005), 'Transactions cost theories of business enterprise from Williamson to Veblen: convergence, divergence, and some evidence', *Journal of Economic Issues*, **29** (2), 385–95.

Scitovksy, Tibor (1992), *The Joyless Economy*, rev. edn, New York: Oxford University Press.

Stanfield, R. and S. Stanfield (1980), 'Consumption in contemporary capitalism: the backward art of living', *Journal of Economic Issues*, **14** (2), 437–51.

Veblen, Thorstein (1904), *Theory of Business Enterprise*, Clifton, NJ: Augustus M. Kelley, 1975.

Index

NEW DIRECTIONS IN MODERN ECONOMICS

Income Distribution in a Corporate Economy
Russell Rimmer

The Economics of the Profit Rate
Competition, Crises and Historical Tendencies in Capitalism
Gérard Duménil and Dominique Lévy

Corporatism and Economic Performance
A Comparative Analysis of Market Economies
Andrew Henley and Euclid Tsakalotos

Competition, Technology and Money
Classical and Post-Keynesian Perspectives
Edited by Mark A. Glick

Investment Cycles in Capitalist Economies
A Kaleckian Behavioural Contribution
Jerry Courvisanos

Does Financial Deregulation Work?
A Critique of Free Market Approaches
Bruce Coggins

Pricing Theory in Post Keynesian Economics
A Realist Approach
Paul Downward

The Economics of Intangible Investment
Elizabeth Webster

Globalization and the Erosion of National Financial Systems
Is Declining Autonomy Inevitable?
Marc Schaberg

Explaining Prices in the Global Economy
A Post-Keynesian Model
Henk-Jan Brinkman

Capitalism, Socialism, and Radical Political Economy
Essays in Honor of Howard J. Sherman
Edited by Robert Pollin

Financial Liberalisation and Intervention
A New Analysis of Credit Rationing
Santonu Basu

Why the Bubble Burst
US Stock Market Performance since 1982
Lawrance Lee Evans, Jr

Sustainable Fiscal Policy and Economic Stability
Theory and Practice
Philippe Burger

The Rise of Unemployment in Europe
A Keynesian Approach
Engelbert Stockhammer

General Equilibrium, Capital, and Macroeconomics
A Key to Recent Controversies in Equilibrium Theory
Fabio Petri

Post-Keynesian Principles of Economic Policy
Claude Gnos and Louis-Philippe Rochon

Innovation, Evolution and Economic Change
New Ideas in the Tradition of Galbraith
Blandine Laperche, James K. Galbraith and Dimitri Uzunidis

The Economics of Keynes
A New Guide to *The General Theory*
Mark Hayes

Money, Distribution and Economic Policy
Alternatives to Orthodox Macroeconomics
Edited by Eckhard Hein and Achim Truger

Modern State Intervention in the Era of Globalisation
Nikolasos Karagiannis and Zagros Madjd-Sadjadi

Financialization and the US Economy
Özgür Orhangazi

Monetary Policy and Financial Stability
A Post-Keynesian Agenda
Edited by Claude Gnos and Louis-Philippe Rochon

Inequality, Consumer Credit and the Saving Puzzle
Christopher Brown